University of London
Institute of Commonwealth Studies

COMMONWEALTH PAPERS

General Editor
Professor W. H. Morris-Jones

20
The Making of Politicians: Studies from
Africa and Asia

The Making of Politicians: Studies from Africa and Asia

edited by
W. H. MORRIS-JONES

*Director of the Institute of Commonwealth Studies
and Professor of Commonwealth Affairs
University of London*

UNIVERSITY OF LONDON
Published for the
Institute of Commonwealth Studies
THE ATHLONE PRESS
1976

Published by
THE ATHLONE PRESS
UNIVERSITY OF LONDON
at 4 *Gower Street, London* WC1
Distributed by Tiptree Book Services Ltd
Tiptree, Essex

U.S.A. *and Canada*
Humanities Press Inc
New Jersey

© *University of London* 1976

ISBN 0 485 17620 3

Printed in Great Britain by
WESTERN PRINTING SERVICES LTD
BRISTOL

PREFACE

A seminar should justify itself as a learning experience for those who participate in it but there is often a case for wider dissemination of the written material presented at its meetings. During recent years the Institute's informal series of Collected Seminar Papers has in some measure fulfilled this aim. On a more selective basis publication of papers in book form has been undertaken in this Commonwealth Papers series when the subject appeared of more general interest.

The papers contained in this volume are selected from a larger number presented during 1972–74 to a seminar on comparative politics at the Institute of Commonwealth Studies. The exploration on a cross-regional basis of the processes of political change is one of the Institute's interests. By bringing together the studies of those working on different areas and by focusing attention on processes and problems common to several parts of the world, area specialists can be encouraged to make comparisons with regions outside their own and thence to address new questions and undertake fresh approaches even to their chosen area.

The Editor wishes to thank participants for their papers and also for their communications and contributions to discussion which helped in the preparation of the Introduction.

W. H. M-J.

CONTRIBUTORS

Judith Brown is Lecturer in History, University of Manchester.

G. W. Choudhury is Professor of Political Science at North Carolina Central University and Adjunct Professor of Political Science at Duke University.

Richard Crook is Research Fellow in Political Science, Centre of West African Studies and a member of the Department of Political Science, University of Birmingham.

John Dunn is Fellow of King's College, Cambridge, and University Lecturer in Political Science.

Hugh Gray is Lecturer in Politics with reference to South Asia at the School of Oriental and African Studies, University of London.

James Jupp is Senior Lecturer in Politics, University of York.

Nelson Kasfir is Assistant Professor of Government at Dartmouth College, New Hampshire.

James Manor is Lecturer in Politics, University of Leicester.

C. J. May is doing research on Kerala politics at the School of Oriental and African Studies, University of London.

John McGuire is Lecturer in Methodology, Western Australian Institute of Technology.

W. H. Morris-Jones is Director of the Institute of Commonwealth Studies and Professor of Commonwealth Affairs, University of London.

Gyanendra Pandey is a Junior Research Fellow at Lincoln College, Oxford.

Thomas Pantham is Reader in Political Science, Maharaja Sayajirao University of Baroda.

Ken Post is Professor of Political Science, Institute of Social Studies, The Hague.

Peter Reeves is Professor of Modern History, University of Western Australia.

Michael Twaddle is Lecturer in Commonwealth Studies, Institute of Commonwealth Studies, University of London.

CONTENTS

INTRODUCTION

W. H. Morris-Jones

An introduction to a set of papers may not be able to secure their full integration into a tidy frame but it should at least seek to place them in a common context of ideas, suggesting ways in which they relate to each other and to common themes.

The initial stimulus to our discussions lay not in any rigorously formulated hypothesis but in the loosest of exploratory hunches. The boy with the chemistry set who loses the instructions may in almost purely haphazard fashion—or 'idly', as we say—wonder what will happen if he adds the white powder to the red liquid. We were a little less idle but we too were asking what results might come from putting together two elements. The first of these was political biography. The effort and art of the political biographer must be to place his chosen actor on the stage of his times and show the audience the roles he performs and how he interacts with his environment. The biographer has to combine in some proportion this cool analysis of his subject in relation to the social context with the different task of re-creating the man's personality and living it to the extent of portraying the environment through his subject's eyes.

Not unnaturally the political biographer is drawn to the leading figures. There is an established public curiosity about such men which creates a demand for the study. Moreover, the outstanding leader appeals as intrinsically challenging and important: the relation between a man and his times seems to presuppose someone who has left his mark on events, who has some claim to be a Colossus astride the world in which he acted. But the merits of such a subject matter become its defects. A tension is set up between the biographer and the historian, between 'the life' and 'the times'. It matters not whether the great man is seen as good or evil, as hero or as villain; it is enough that he should be seen as great, his 'life' then expanding, his 'times' diminished. This, however, is not all, or even the main point. An author may avoid those dangers, producing what for that very reason is acclaimed a good political biography. He may be judged to have got the proportions and the perspectives right. But from at least one point of view, that of those who want to use the political biography as a window on to the institutions and processes of politics, the difficulty lies not in the biographer

who may be carried away by his outstanding subject but in the very
fact of the subject's being outstanding. For he is then by definition
unrepresentative, somewhat set apart from the other political actors.
Where the latter have had largely to accept as facts of life the structures
and procedures they found on 'arrival', the top leaders are men who in
some measure and by some method—not necessarily sudden and violent
—have been able to reshape and remould the rules and frames to suit
their needs and styles. If we wish to look *through* lives to structures,
the lives of the great may not be the ones of greatest value; instead of
viewing through clear windows we may find ourselves staring at
glass which is tinted and patterned.

The second element was the general study of political man, or, more
precisely, particular segments of that study, notably those concerned
with the recruitment of citizens to more active roles in political life
and the career routes followed by those who could be said to have
become politicians. Interest in these matters stemmed largely from a
concern with political elites, perceived as important elements in
determining the character of a political system and shaping the decisions
emerging from the system. More generally, however, political recruitment and careers clearly suggest perception of politics as a profession.
This idea requires cautious handling—not least because in many if not
most political systems the politician is not engaged continuously on a
full-time basis in politics as an occupation, and indeed will frequently
have a different and parallel professional employment. Nevertheless
scholars have in recent years found it quite rewarding to make the kind
of enquiries about politicians that might be made of any professional
group. What qualifications appear necessary? At what age does the
typical recruit enter politics? How is the choice to enter made and what
outside influences are important? At what points or levels is entry
effected? Are there typical career routes, and what factors are favour-
able to advancement? Can branches of the profession be identified and
what are the roles of choice and resources in determining the allocation
of persons to these? These and other similar questions have been addressed both to individual political systems and to different systems,
with a view to making comparisons and drawing out the character of
each. Most such work has been done in the spirit and with the approach
of the sociologist rather than the biographer; the subjects are not
named individuals but sets or samples of persons in defined categories—
town councillors, legislators, party officials—with their anonymity
preserved. Usually the information sought is factually simple, though
attempts may be made to relate career factors to particular political
affiliations and attitudes, perhaps with a view to establishing a typology
of politicians. Only a few political scientists have been so bold as to

probe, as a biographer would, questions of motivation and personality. To have emulated the work of such pioneers along the frontiers of politics and psychology would have been one way of putting together the two elements of political biography and political sociology. That way was not open to our seminar; our lack of qualifications apart, such a venture would have called for the systematic collection of fresh data, while we could only discuss data already to hand and in the process of being worked on by seminar members. Instead, we brought the two elements together by, on the one hand, pulling political biography down from preoccupation with the great to a focus on the less known, on the other hand addressing the questions of the political sociologist not to groups or samples but to available data on specific individual political figures. It may not be claiming too much to say that our intention was to try to show that political biography and political sociology can be located on a methodological continuum rather than on a methodological battlefield. One way of underlining this point was to secure the inclusion of Thomas Pantham's contribution, a 'straight' piece of political sociology but at the same time almost an essay in the collective biography of its universe of 310 party activists, particularly with its close-up personal narratives of a dozen of these. The seminar's theme was given the title 'Career biographies of middle-rank politicians'.

From this point our problems only began. The first puzzle was the scope we should establish for our enquiries. Our institutional setting pointed towards a concentration on Commonwealth countries and towards recent or contemporary periods. We found no need to move outside the Commonwealth; the question that was raised was rather whether it made sense to look at our subject in any Commonwealth country or only in the developing countries. I took the view that in principle comparisons could usefully be made across the board, including Australia or Britain as well as Ghana and Sri Lanka. Several members of the seminar did not share this view, holding that the range would then be too wide. Discussion took place on the opposing research strategies for comparative politics: the 'narrow range' school urged that one should compare only the comparable, that otherwise variables proliferated wildly and no meaningful patterns emerged; the 'wide range' adherents argued that the questions we had in mind were universal in applicability, that insights often came from the sharpest of contrasts, and that in any case one could not beforehand be sure which variables were the most significant—e.g., that size rather than 'development' could be crucial, that therefore India and Canada might prove closer cases than India and Ghana or Canada and Britain. The matter was not resolved—at that level. In the event, most of the papers secured for the seminar and all those which could be conveniently included in the volume deal with South Asia and Africa. (The two papers on Canada and England are omitted, not because their questions and answers were eccentric to the seminar's concerns but because each dealt, as it happened, with a very special situation.) The papers appear here in two African and South Asian 'blocks' but this will not conceal the common historical structure which they share and which cuts across differences of continent and culture. All papers deal with a phase —some with more than one—of the movement from late colonial rule through decolonization to independence and with situations of political expansion, with new parties to be built, new electorates to be won over, and new methods to be learnt.

'Middle rank' also posed difficulties. Every contributor was led to wonder whether his specimens belonged to the category. The preliminary working note (see below, pp. 14–16) had insisted that it was to be used very broadly, not confined to those operating in 'middle' regional arenas between local and central politics but open to big men in small political worlds and backbenchers at the heart of the capital. But 'middle' continued to cause anxiety; the word denotes a layer between a top and a bottom and seems to beg for delimitation. Since we were concerned essentially only to exclude national notables at one end and local nonentities at the other, definition was not easy and 'middle' became a nuisance. Judith Brown, significantly well placed looking down from her own subject, Gandhi, towards his 'lieutenants', threw out a lifebelt labelled 'lesser leaders'; this was seized upon to sanction non-definition.

These were preliminaries, mere clarifications as to what was to be undertaken. It was not to be expected that methodological doubts would disappear when we began to examine our 'cases'. The most radical challenge came in the paper from Ken Post, who, before proceeding to his discussion of Nigerian and Jamaican politicians, formulated a Marxist objection to 'individualist explanations of historical events' or 'social analysis which has individuals as its starting point'. He makes the point that a Marxist must not only 'refuse to see historical change as in any way the product of the initiatives of "great men" ' but also has to distrust sociological enquiry which seeks '*finalist* explanations founded on the *motivations of conduct* of the individual actors'. Richard Crook furnished some valuable comments on this argument as an introduction to his own paper. For our part, we remain unconvinced that the particular exercise represented by the seminar is vulnerable to this attack. Apart from the fact that 'great men' are excluded from consideration—for the reason, it is true, that they might have too great an influence on the political structures within which they operate—we have also disavowed any intention even to enter into the area of motivation assessment, much less to find therein any 'finalist' explanations. Moreover, the attack seems to err in making no distinction between 'individualist explanations of historical events' and 'social analysis which has individuals as its starting point'. The former is no part of our exercise and none of the papers makes claims in that direction; it is, in any case, to be noted that Post himself insists that the Marxist view allows individuals an influence—even a 'very strong' influence—on the 'destinies of society'. The latter is a different matter and most of the papers do begin with individuals—but they do not end there. Precisely where they do end is indeed the question left open to each author. Marxists or not, all participants were agreed in looking at the individual politician not as the ultimate and intrinsic point of interest but as a pointer or tracer element which could show up the context in which he worked. (This would be true even of some biographers, especially some political biographers.) It is with respect to the character of the context that different views can emerge. For some there is no satisfaction short of reaching through to 'social relations', understood as the inescapeable conflict of classes which are defined with reference to, and determined by, economic relations. For others, context may have other meanings and there can be satisfaction if the view provided through the 'window' of 'individual' careers is one of the structure of the political system, seen as a determining, as well as a determined, thing in its own right. Thus the approach through career biographies should be seen as doctrinally fairly open, as implying only that we learn much of what we wish to know about politics by the study of politicians.

A second methodological point, less radical perhaps but of some importance, centred on the question of the 'representativeness' of the individuals included in our study. Evidently what we have here is a collection of studies put together on no rigidly structured system; it may be readily admitted that one of the advantages of the theme was that many scholars had suitable material to offer which was a by-product of work with quite different orientations. As already mentioned, it is true that the cases we present here relate to developing countries which have had experience of British imperial/colonial rule. But some are in South Asia, others in Africa; some are concerned with political activity under British rule, others with post-independence situations. It therefore behoves us—and the reader—to exercise caution in deriving from our studies any very general conclusions. A limited basis for generalization may be safely accepted: each author is thoroughly familiar with the region and period of which he writes; we may follow him without danger when he generalizes from his one or few individuals to his region and period as a whole. Beyond that we are in the realm of suggestion and hypothesis—but interesting suggestions are of more use than wrong or dull conclusions. In principle, an inspection of the papers as a whole might be expected to furnish a set of questions, categories, and propositions whose general value can only be tested by work more systematically organized for the purpose, for example by the construction of carefully matched samples. The latter course would probably draw scorn from those like John Dunn, whose contribution here brilliantly expresses some scepticism as to the value of even this present exercise which is seen as underestimating the role of the purely contingent in these affairs.

Our interest, then, is in the relations between the political actor and the stage on which he plays his roles, the structures within which he operates. If we now review the themes which emerge from our papers we shall find that even if we focus on the cases of individual politicians we find ourselves at the same time looking through them at institutions and structures.

Before turning to the individual actors who appear in these pages, we may underline a couple of points already mentioned. Some authors (Gray, McGuire, and to some extent Kasfir) have focused on one person and treated him in some depth. Others (including Brown, Jupp, and Reeves) have dealt each with a small batch selected as having much in common but also with interesting differences among them. A few papers deal mainly with post-independence politics, some with the imperial/colonial period, most with both. These variations are in no way awkward, for nothing emerges more clearly than the continuities across the transfer of power; independence is seen not as a single, revolutionary change but an instalment of change in a series.

Politics is a competition—in any but the most rigid traditional society. The differences between societies in this respect lie in the size of the area of political activity, in how far the competition is open, and in how far it is public. On a static view, a political system performs in accordance with the wishes and attributes of those who operate it, who are in turn selected for such positions in accordance with rules which form a basic part of each system. Such harmony scarcely exists in the real world, where change enters at some point in the circle, establishing tensions which then result in further changes. It is little wonder that when we look at African and Asian political systems over the past half-century or more we see systems undergoing changes which affect every aspect of the personnel of politics. What are the aspects which emerge from the papers?

Entry into political life entails two distinguishable processes: the establishing of 'qualifications' to be eligible and actual selections for admission to some part of the system. Eligibility has in turn been analysed into three components—legal (who *may*), practical (who *can*), motivational (who *wills*). The first of these has limited importance and our papers deal mainly with the second. As regards the third, we have (as already mentioned) taken it for granted and generally avoided deeper probing; there are always more people—in modernized societies very many more—who possess the formal and practical 'qualifications' for a political career than actually seek it. Some comments on motivation are, however, suggested by the papers. Judith Brown points out what is clear also from other contributions (e.g. Pandey, McGuire), that motivation need not, initially at least, be towards a specifically political career; there may be such a fluidity between 'social work' and 'politics' in situations of limited political institutionalization that men may seek one and discover the other. Again, it may be that occupation of certain social positions—Reeves' landlords seem a case in point—already entails such a degree of political influence that the move towards formal political office is scarcely perceptible and calls for little positive motivation. It is also evident that in other situations the motivation of a socially well-placed aspirant may have to be greater than that of a humbler man; politics may entail risks and even certain sacrifices and thus the man who has more to lose may, in the absence of strong motivation, hesitate the longer—as we see in one of Manor's cases.

'Practical' eligibility for politics is determined by a set of factors which seem remarkably constant over quite different kinds of societies: social position; education; skills of appeal and mobilization, of organization and/or negotiation. However, the precise content of each and the proportions in which they have to be mixed certainly vary greatly with different political systems. During the period of a century over which our papers extend two kinds of changes took place. First, the area 'available' to politics expanded as both imperial/colonial bureaucracy and indigenous traditional ascription systems were eroded and confined. Secondly, in many sectors of this expanding world of politics there were changes towards democratization or, more precisely, some shift in the processes of politician selection from nomination from above to election from below. Both kinds of change had the effect of altering and making more diversified the qualifications for eligibility. The opportunities (or 'demand') for politics grew and the criteria of eligibility (controlling 'supply') were diversified to meet the situation. Broadly, we see one established type of politician joined, or more often challenged, by a new type with a different mix of qualifications. The former rely ideally on their social position to carry over into political influence and, if necessary, political office. The latter are more self-made men; they may or may not be more educated than the former, but whatever education they have was hard won, has set them somewhat apart from their own social groups, and is to be made to serve in lieu of social position as a lever for political elevation; as to the skills of politics, they may or may not be better endowed in this respect than the older type but they are more conscious of the need for their cultivation and more adaptable in their use.

The middle ranks of political life during such a phase of change seem indeed to be occupied by representatives of both types, each with their own strengths and their own limitations. Crook's pair of Ghana politicians exemplify the contrast well. Jupp's five leaders from Sri Lanka, on the other hand, seem to manifest contrast not so much in the differences between them as in the tensions between opposite elements contained within each of them. The Indian papers show with remarkable clarity the various chronological stages and their characteristics. A century ago, the new men have scarcely appeared, a handful in a couple of advanced centres such as Calcutta. There, as McGuire shows, a Kristo Das Pal with unusual abilities can just manage to infiltrate into a specialist role. The landlord politicians of Reeves are men who by the late inter-war years can be seen to be living politically on a diminishing stock of social capital, while with varying degrees of effort and success trying to make the most of their other qualifications. The newer men of the same period discussed by Brown, Pandey, and Manor are combining more modest social qualifications with other bases of eligibility and are finding in Congress mobilization opportunities for their own initially small parts on the stage. The subject of Gray's paper emerges latest and has the most modest equipment—but just as the landlords discovered that their social qualifications now concealed disadvantages which had to be overcome, so the weaver in Gray's paper finds that he can start travelling politically on the strength of his very weakness.

The case of the weaver draws attention to another point: the relevance of a strong particular (e.g. local) base as a resource or qualification for a political entrance. This might well have been included as a separate element in the list of qualifications already given. Alternatively, it may be seen as an extension and special form of 'social position'. Some reference to a person's capacity to secure a core of support in a particular locality is to be found in most of the papers. Oddly enough, perhaps the clearest examples are those at opposite ends of the social scale—the landlords whose support core is on their estates and the weaver whose core is constructed on the basis of caste-occupation particularism. Such a particular base, needless to say, is a resource which has to be supplemented and in a measure transcended if career advancement is to be sustained.

As regards the actual processes whereby general eligibility is translated into successful entry into political life and selection for political office, nothing is more striking on a reading of the papers than that the identification of one particular entry moment is difficult and, further, that for all the competitiveness of politics and the shift from nomination to election, the politicians of our papers entered the profession by essentially informal methods of selection, facing open elections only at a late stage. These features are probably much more marked in our cases than they would be in those of politicians making entry into established democratic systems; the almost imperceptible and often informal mode of entry reflects a situation of limited institutionalization during most of the period with which our papers are concerned. The role often played in Britain, for example, by elections to local bodies is not wholly absent but is relatively unimportant.

It is true, of course, that even in systems which have have well-recognized competitive entrance gates there is ample room for private and informal methods—witness the working of party selection committees, in Britain or elsewhere, on the task of choosing candidates for election contests. This is understandable enough, given both the predominance of political parties as controllers of entrance gates and the fundamentally ambiguous character of party as being stretched tensely between private association, on the one hand, and public institution, on the other. In any event, the leaders in our papers found party a crucial entry point. Even Reeves' landlords had to acknowledge this, though they were big enough at times to be the creators of parties. The same is true of Jupp's prima donnas from Sri Lanka who combined some recognition of the need for party with somewhat cavalier attitudes towards membership of particular parties.

This latter point draws attention to a matter of general significance. There emerges a real, if not wholly distinct, difference between the man who enters a party in the humblest capacity and owes his subsequent position to advancement and achievement within that framework and the other type of person who already possesses resources quite independent of party before he joins it—and in extreme cases is actually wooed by the party. This is the difference between the two men in Crook's account; it is also the contrast between Krishnappa and Nijalingappa in that of Manor. This may affect attitudes towards the party later. Nor need the resources always consist of social status or economic independence; the politician considered by Gray had neither of these, but he had already shown organizing ability to build up weavers' co-operatives before he turned to take party membership. Evidently, however, a resource that can be cashed as a means of livelihood—land ownership or a parallel professional career—has advantages; there are times when a politician wishes, even temporarily, to withdraw from the fray: Akenten's cocoa trees may have been useful for him even in his years of exile.

The papers by Pandey and Brown point to features of interest concerning entrance into politics in India of the inter-war years. The starting point of the political careers of the four men in Pandey's paper is by no means unambiguous. At some point each of them becomes an occupant of party office and a party candidate in election contests. But before that each had been engaged in work sponsored in some degree by the party in social uplift campaigns, labour unions, or peasant associations. Even these activities had been preceded by a spell at a social service training centre which prepared them for such work. Moreover, they had previously attended a nationalist college outside the regular educational framework, early sign of response to the calling of the cause. Evidently here—and perhaps it is not in this respect wholly atypical—there is no single entry gate into a political career; the smoke-filled rooms lie at the end of a series of corridors and ante-rooms. (These gradations of political entry could pose difficulties for more systematic studies of careers.)

The same question—how peculiar or how general?—is prompted by the emphasis in Brown's paper on the role of an established, more senior politician in the recruitment of assistants and successors. The case presented is almost notoriously special: Gandhi's careful personal selection of his lieutenants. Here the initiative comes almost entirely from above, a leader seeking disciples, many being called in varying degrees and some, also in varying degrees, being chosen. The grounds of eligibility are here dictated by the leader and prominently include attributes of personal dedication and loyalty. But the evidence suggests that attention was also paid to candidates' possession of political resources in terms, for example, of local influence and organizational skills. Also, of course, the importance of initiative from the top cannot obscure at least a certain readiness on the part of the candidates, such an attitude containing some element of political aspiration as well as personal and ideological commitment. That this type of entry mechanism is not peculiar to the Gandhians is indicated by references to similar relations of followership in other papers: Lal Bahadur Shastri attaches himself to and is taken up by Tandon (Pandey); Konda Lakshman Bapuji's course was partly shaped by his followership of Raju (Gray). The *guru-chela* relationship is deep-rooted in Hindu culture but that its political form is not confined within that culture is suggested by the importance for the early political years of Mujib and Zahiruddin of their being protégés of Suhrawardy (Choudhury). Outside South Asia it is perhaps less significant; Duncan-Williams' being given accommodation as a poor 'verandah boy' by Akenten seems to have had nothing of this kind about it in intention, certainly not in consequences! Thus, while there may be validity in the comment by Brown that sponsorship of lieutenants points to the relatively unformed nature of party organization at the time, it may also have a specific cultural component. Another variable which has been suggested (Crook, in a private communication) is that of level of operation: the higher reaches of a structure are more likely to contain the patrons who can easily attract a band of lieutenants.

Having established or achieved qualifications for eligibility and having secured admission to a political career, our politicians are launched. But what influences shape their voyages and where do they travel? In particular, and since we are looking at lesser leaders, can we see why they remained lesser in contrast with others of their contemporaries who went to the top? These latter are better known and we may be able to keep them in mind; in any case they are not absent from our pages, for the papers have sometimes dealt not only with lifelong middle-rankers but also with the middle-rank stages of those who went high, such as Mujib, 'Father' and Prime Minister of a new state (Choudhury), Lal Bahadur Shastri, Nehru's successor (Pandey), and Nijalingappa, Congress President (Manor).

It seems that career routes are less patterned than career openings. Some general factors are at work and the dark variable of individual motivation is still operative. In addition, however, the role of fortune appears enhanced. Moreover, the mixture of jobs that most politics must contain gives a certain undifferentiated appearance to many of the careers: manning the party committees, standing as candidate in electoral contests, conducting an agitational campaign on a particular issue, specializing to some extent on given 'fronts' or 'wings' of party activity—these are the regular involvements of all our personnel. The proportions no doubt vary somewhat—our data do not permit comment on this—and such variations would depend partly on differences in the political systems and situations during the career period, partly on the natural wish of any person to do mostly what he is best at. One could venture the further general remark that the politician who aspires to the heights of the profession has at the same time to avoid getting too 'typed' as a specialist in one field, has instead to cultivate precisely the areas in which he is least adept or least experienced: the mob orator needs to become the committee negotiator, the labour union organizer, the 'catch-all' vote-collector. It is after all the exceptional man—Gandhi, Nehru, Nkrumah?—who can impose his personal style on the movement which he enters. The bulk of our lesser leaders are men who either settle for a very modest specialist role, like Krishnappa, or those who without necessarily being natural all-rounders strive to become so while trying to keep intact any special advantage they possess.

We are thus led back from career routes to initial resources which may indeed have a large say in shaping not only entry but subsequent paths. This seems particularly evident with respect to what may be termed nodal points or moments of crucial choice in the course of a career. It is also evident when we address the question as to why our lesser leaders mostly remained such, that is, why there were clear limits to their advancement. Both points may be taken together when inspecting the papers for illustrative evidence. It will be noticed that the nodal points as well as terminal crises are not infrequently occasioned by structural changes in the political system. Such changes have the effect of checking or even eliminating the less adaptable politician. And such a man is one whose weakness can equally be expressed in terms of resources that are limited and too one-sided.

Three different kinds of nodal points can in fact be identified from the material before us. The first is prompted by institutional change affecting levels of democratization and entailing alterations in the methods and style of political appeal. The second arises when the area of political arenas is in question. The third is occasioned by ideological shifts. The purest example of the first is perhaps provided by Reeves' landlord politicians. Confronted with different choices, one adapts with alacrity and even enthusiasm; Reeves hazards the guess that if he had not died early he would have been able to make a success of a career in a new style. Another resists change for a time, gives in by stages, and survives at a modest level. The third prefers to withdraw rather than to adapt. Manor, presenting a period of rapid transformation from the limited politics of a princely state to the advent of party warfare in an arena of adult franchise, shows how it can mean political death for a Krishnappa but renewed life for Nijalingappa. Twaddle's paper, also concerned with a brief period of rapid institutional change through decolonization, discloses the easy transformation of 'worthless agitators' into branch chairmen of the ruling party.

There are also very clear cases of career choices arising out of questions of arena areas. Kasfir's three men from minority tribes have a difficult choice when their demands for a distinct district are turned down. One chooses the extreme course of secession and becomes king of a new small arena, the other two elect for remaining in the larger mainstream but in the event find little scope there. The contrast in Choudhury's paper between Zahiruddin and Mujib is striking; the former, already politically rather crippled by the first partition, is so crushed by the blast of Bengali nationalism that the second partition places him in the Central Jail. Konda Lakshman in Gray's paper is a curious case of one who overcomes his single-region limitations to become a minister, yet then resigns to campaign for some sort of separatism. He seeks to remain in the party and he cannot join the other separatists because of differences of caste and social policy. Trapped, he is politically thrashed by the whole-hearted separatists in his own region and alienated from the main body of his party in the state. Not dissimilarly caught was the colourful entrepreneur Adelabu, of Post's paper. He sought to use his regional base for what he saw as a national party but found himself losing out to the development of single-region parties and loyalties.

Pursuit of ideological commitment in some cases forces politicians into what are, at least in the short run, irrevocably subsidiary minority roles. This holds for Post's Jamaican Marxists as well as for the left and right breakaways from centre Awami League in Choudhury's account. A more mixed situation is that revealed to Crook's paper. Here one politician who is locally rather weak pins his faith to a centralizing party and is able to move steadily up its hierarchy—until it is toppled by a coup (which, however, still permits him to retire to the mansion he has gained!). The other, a substantial local power, resents central interference and breaks with the ruling party to back a regional farmers' party; he pays the severe price of seven years' exile—until, with the coup, he is more than restored.

These remarks by no means exhaust what can be drawn from the papers which follow, but they serve to show something of the richness of this particular vein of enquiry and presentation. Each paper has its intrinsic interest and value, but each also contributes to a general perspective on the less-than-outstanding leaders in politics. Nor is it surprising that these men's political lives should yield so much insight into the political systems in which they were active; after all, these men are the work-horses of any political system. Through them the papers show us some of the significance and meaning in terms of practical political life of constitutional changes in boundaries, franchise, rules, and the like. Through them we see the changing mixture of roles to be performed in relating people to their governments—the voicing of grievance, the mounting of pressure, the adjustments with allies, the uses of power.

We have spoken of our lesser leaders as 'windows' and 'tracer elements'. In the end, however, it is fitting to admit to some fascination with the men themselves, the members of this strange and most valuable profession. There are some dull and sad politicians, but compared with most occupations they contain a high proportion of colourful individuals happy in their 'social' work.

PRELIMINARY WORKING NOTE
FOR THE SEMINAR

W. H. Morris-Jones

The purpose of the seminar is to examine how far fresh understanding of a country's politics can be obtained by the study of the careers of its politicians of middle rank.

Political biography has long been valued as a way of throwing light on aspects of political processes; even autobiographical memoirs may yield insights. Not all political systems spontaneously yield such products (and it could be interesting to note the variations—including minor ones such as the relatively low output of the United States—and try to account for them) but no system would fail to be illuminated by such writing. Even political cultures which encourage biographical approaches to the portrayal of political life tend, however, to concentrate on the leading figures. Though readily understandable, this has disadvantages. The writing focuses on personality and the subject becomes hero or villain—either way, larger than the life about him. Moreover—and this is especially the case with all but the most open and competitive systems—the top figures are in various respects so exceptionally 'gifted' (using this word to include inherited position and chance circumstance) that they are too remarkable to be representative. Thus the political biographies (and autobiographies) we get are not those which would provide the clearest windows on to the political system.

But if these are valid reasons for avoiding the 'peaks' of politics, what should one mean by 'middle-rank politicians'? It is not obvious precisely how our specimens should be fenced off from their fellows; it may be a case of *solvitur ambulando*, with a definition best left to emerge towards the end of our discussions. At this stage it may be sufficient to say that 'middle-rank' must not be taken as merely equivalent to some 'middling arena' between 'centre' and 'local'; we should include in our scope some who work (even as big men) in a local sphere, as well as those who are essentially regional or provincial. 'Politician' is just as difficult a term as 'middle rank'. It tends to happen that the higher a person moves in political life the more exclusively he is a 'politician'; on the lower rungs of that ladder men are usually combining other activities with their politics. We should obviously look at people who for at least a large part of their careers have been more 'politician' than anything else.

There are other questions of scope. As to period, there need surely be no fixed limits. Participants will probably choose to discuss recent rather than more remote history. There may be some who wish to select persons still living (and who may later take themselves out of our category of middle rank!). As regards countries, we should aim at a reasonable spread of different kinds of political system; the Commonwealth should offer sufficient range but its limits may be crossed if this seems useful (e.g. to make a contrast between Commonwealth and francophone politicians in West Africa).

There should not be much difficulty in assembling a good group of papers on this theme. Even if one has not specifically addressed attention to this topic, working on any country's politics frequently entails noting career routes and patterns. It will often be a question of re-examining and re-ordering a set of 'field notes' hitherto used in some different framework. The difficulty is that few people, even after such re-examination, will have enough data on a single individual to furnish a paper dealing with that man alone. No matter, we can have papers constructed by looking at the careers of a (small) number of people— either a set of similar persons or indeed a set in which there are interesting contrasts.

Papers should probably not be steered too firmly to a given pattern. But, taking the given person or persons, it would be good to try to establish answers to some of the following questions:

(a) *the 'entry' into politics*: by what stages, on whose initiative and with whose aid, accompanied by what other (non-'political') activities, for what reasons and with what effects on his own life and on his arena? In sum, is it self-selection or selection by others? and what are the perceived qualifications?

(b) *the career course*: what choices of arena, role, style, etc., present themselves and how are they determined? Are the qualifications for advance different from those for entry? How are 'limits' reached which seem to keep a man in the middle rank? Do the requirements of the system (opportunities for the individual) change in his own political life-span?

(c) *what then does this political life (or set of lives) tell us about the system*: not so much 'who gets what when and where?' as 'who is equipped or equips himself for what roles?'. (Some men make their own roles but not many among our middle-rankers.)

Relevant reading would include:

R. E. Lane, *Political Life* (1959).

A. F. Davies, *Private Politics* (1966).

W. H. Morris-Jones, 'Political Recruitment and Political Development' in C. Leys (ed), *Politics and Change in Developing Countries* (1969).

INDIVIDUALS AND THE DIALECTIC:
A MARXIST VIEW OF POLITICAL
BIOGRAPHIES

Ken Post

Quite by chance, a large part of my own research and writing since 1964 has been concerned with biography and individual political careers. Thus I have recently published a biography of Alhaji Adegoke Adelabu (1915–58), a Nigerian political leader, and the study I am now writing of the Jamaican 'labour rebellion' of 1938 involves considerable discussion of Norman Manley and Alexander Bustamante, distant cousins whose political rivalry dominated Jamaican politics for thirty years.[1] Even more germane to this seminar, I am also currently concerned with the group of Marxists which first coalesced in 1938 and then played a major part in the nationalist and labour movements until broken by Manley in 1952. The role of individual politicians of various ranks has, therefore, been much on my mind, the more particularly since in recent years I have also been steeping myself in Marxist theory, having become convinced that work within that frame is the only possible way in which we will ever get to grips with analysis of the problems of underdevelopment, my general field.

The hostility of Marxism to individualist explanations of historical events is, of course, well known. Marx himself made clear statements on the subject, such as this:

... here individuals are dealt with only in so far as they are the personifications of economic categories, embodiments of particular class-relations and class-interests. My standpoint, from which the evolution of the economic formation of society is viewed as a process of natural history, can less than any other make the individual responsible for relations whose creature he socially remains, however much he may subjectively raise himself above them.[2]

The qualification in the last clause of this quotation is significant. It permits an accommodation of Norman Manley, Jamaica's leading barrister, at the point when he put himself at the head of the rebellious workers and peasants (albeit with the intention of calming them and articulating their demands by legal means), and Alexander Bustamante, a moneylender, who also put himself at the head of the labour movement and one of whose chief weapons was the frequent avowal of his own sacrifice of wealth and health on its behalf. Marx and Engels themselves also wrote about Napoleon and Bismarck in terms of their 'rising above' particular classes.[3]

The Marxist objection to social analysis which has individuals as its starting point may, in summary, be said to take three forms. First, Marxism refuses to see historical change as in any way the product of the initiatives of 'great men', or for that matter of their foibles. As Plekhanov wrote, in an essay which first appeared in 1898 and deserves to be better known, the infatuation of Louis XV for Madame de Pompadour (sometimes used to explain, among other things, the loss of Canada by France) is only made meaningful by the form of the French state at the time:

... if this weakness for women had been the failing not of the king, but of one of his kitchen staff or stablemen, it would not have been of any historical importance. It is clear that it is not the failing in itself which is of concern here, but the social position of the one who is affected by it.[4]

Second, Marxism (I would insist) is not a variant of humanism. It does not see social action as undertaken by individuals in some sort of expression of a human 'essence'. Nor, third, does it even see relations among social groups as in some way reducible to inter-personal relations. As Nicos Poulantzas puts it:

According to this problematic, the agents of a social formation, 'men', are not considered as the 'bearers' of objective instances (as they are for Marx), but as the genetic principle of the levels of the social whole. This is a problematic of *social actors*, of individuals as the origin of *social action*: sociological research thus leads finally, not to the study of the objective coordinates that determine the distribution of agents into social classes and the contradictions between these classes, but to the search for *finalist* explanations founded on the *motivations of conduct* of the individual actors.[5]

Thus, for example, by selecting such analytical categories as 'eligibles, aspirants, and applicants', Professor Morris-Jones, in the essay to which he directed us, derived them from the actual body of men whose position he was seeking to explain, which prevents us from transcending his politicians as 'the genetic principle of the levels of the social whole'.[6]

Lest it be thought, however, that a Marxist approach would sweep Louis Napoleon and Bismarck (despite Marx and Engels), Louis XV, Adelabu, Manley, Bustamante, or for that matter Lenin, into some limbo of non-history, let Plekhanov speak again:

.. individuals, thanks to the particularities of their characters, can influence the destinies of society. Their influence can even be very strong, but the possibility of such an influence, as well as its extent, are determined by the organization of the society, by the relation of social forces. The character of the individual is only a 'factor' of social development at the moment and in the measure permitted it by the social relations.[7]

What was intended in the foregoing discussion, therefore, was not (primarily) to put non-Marxists to some sort of torment. Rather, the simple point was being made that 'career biographies' of politicians of any kind imply consideration of structures of social relations. This is all the more apparent when we remember that we are looking at 'middle-rank' politicians, not even those who—like Louis XV—are leading figures because they are the repositories of some 'traditional' authority, or are great personalities endowed with 'charisma'. (In my own work I am at present trying to show that the position of such 'heroes' as Bustamante and Manley must be seen as the reflection of the level of class consciousness of their followers, rather than primarily of some innate qualities; in fact, the two leaders were the projections of two different levels of class consciousness.)[8]

If the general question which we are raising in speaking of the careers of politicians is in fact that of social relations, the question then is: What social relations? 'Middle rank' carries overtones of formal hierarchies, the most likely to be involved obviously being those of governmental structures and those of parties. This in itself causes problems. What is the determining factor in a federal system like Nigeria, where a regional Premier might presumably be regarded as 'middle-rank', a somewhat mind-boggling concept in the case of the late Sardauna of Sokoto, who used to refer to the Federal Prime Minister as 'my lieutenant'? How do we regard Adegoke Adelabu's last few years, when he was successively displaced from his federal ministry, his chairmanship of the Ibadan District Council, and his First Vice-Presidency of the NCNC, leaving him only Leader of the Opposition in the Western Region? Although his political power had undoubtedly declined, it is difficult to treat him as having been reduced to the middle rank when, for example, he was receiving letters suggesting that he ought to be NCNC President in place of Dr Azikiwe.

The concept of middle-rank has obviously also caused others in the seminar some trouble; indeed, Professor Morris-Jones had already sounded a warning note before it had begun with his invocation of 'solvitur ambulando'. From those papers which I have seen I have gathered that a middle-rank politician may be one with a weak personality, or from a subordinated region, a student leader for a major party, the leader of a small party, an adherent of an unpopular cause, the follower of a big man 'where modern politics are in their infancy', those who are frustrated and do not accomplish their objects, those who are not (Canadian) Prime Ministers or 'occasional' provincial premiers, those who are relegated to such a status by 'a failure of scholarship', not too prominent centre politicians, and agitators against colonial rule. I suppose that the kind of politicians with which we are concerned might indeed display any or all of these characteristics, but it is obvious, on the other hand, that there has been considerable hesitation over the problem of 'precisely where we should cut into a political system in order to assess its character and style', if that is to be at the level of the middle rank.[9]

Merely to invoke the importance of social relations does not, of course, solve that problem either. It must not be supposed, for example, that it is being suggested that we take 'middle-rank' to mean, not a place in a hierarchy, but rather 'middle class' (even though in many political systems a disproportionate number of politicians are recruited from that class—lawyers, for example). Let us retain the assumed implication that middle-rank means a place in some hierarchy. (Another possibility is to take it as the middle point of each particular individual's career, though, as Morris-Jones indirectly indicates in his preliminary note, that means that we can only discuss those who are dead or at least definitely at the end of their political careers.) In talking about a 'middle' level of anything we immediately suggest that there are also upper and lower levels. In turn, that implies that there is some sort of definite and regular relationship among the different levels. Now let us take the Marxist view that this is a dialectical relationship, that is to say each level sustains the other and is a condition for its existence, and at the same time each level also determines the range of activities possible on the one below it; on the individual plane we would say that such relations among levels determine a politician's capacity to move from one to another. This is to introduce a processual element, in fact, into our discussions, and to suggest that, in focusing on middle-rank politicians, we are really asking how and why they moved into that position and what might cause (or permit) them to move beyond it. Our reformulation of the problematic of the seminar, then, is as follows: in looking at career biographies of middle-rank politicians we are examining the main sets of social relations which determine the mobility of individuals within a particular political superstructure. This formulation is not unlike that in part of Morris-Jones' preliminary note, but with the major difference that he again there treats individuals as 'the genetic principle of the levels of the social whole', more especially when he adopts such phraseology as 'who . . . equips himself for what role?'.

Much of my own following treatment will come very close to the questions he posed, with the obvious differences which the previous discussion has hopefully suggested. I will, then, consider first the question of entry into politics and proceed from there to the matter of career patterns, focusing upon that period of Adegoke Adelabu's life when he might be described as a 'middle-rank' politician and upon the group of Jamaican Marxists, all but a couple of whom remained at that level.[10] These discussions will be comparative, not separate, because they are based on two variants of a common historical situation, British decolonization in very underdeveloped 'non-white' possessions.[11]

In that historical situation, what sets of social relations appear to have been most crucial? First, we may suggest the structural relationship between the metropolitan power and the colony, which must be seen at a number of levels, particularly the economic (both Nigeria and Jamaica being producers of raw materials for the British market) and the politico-administrative. In this last respect there were considerable variations, warning us against a crude historical determinism: Nigeria, of course, had the usual apparatus of a Legislative Council and an Executive Council, with a mixture of official and unofficial elements, grafted on to Indirect Rule by administrators through traditional or pseudo-traditional authorities; in Jamaica there was no 'traditional society', and a rural capitalist class descended from the old slave-masters dominated the parishes without a British administrative presence and used the Legislative Council to hamper, and even thwart, the policy of the Governor and his subordinates. A second crucial set of social relations involved was the conjunction of class forces in the periods when decolonization was first set in motion and then took its decisive form (i.e. the phases of entry and career development for our politicians). In Nigeria, the first may be taken as 1948–52 and the second as 1954–57 (the consolidation of regionalism). Jamaica's decolonization was set in train in the period 1938–44, and took its decisive form in 1952–55.[12] The third crucial set of social relations were those institutionalized in the superstructure and determined in form, on the one hand, by party and union structures and, on the other, by politico-administrative institutions. Beyond these three structural-relational factors we must introduce a fourth, the question of the perception by the actors involved of how the other factors operated, what—in so far as it was a structured perception—we may call their ideology. We may consider our politicians, therefore, from these four angles.

Adegoke Adelabu first entered politics at the local level, that of Ibadan, his home town, and one of his basic self-perceptions was always as a 'son of Ibadan'. His strong desire by 1949 was in fact to become Administrative Secretary at the head of a reformed city administration, and this was not opposed to the wishes of the British administrators, who, as part of the institutional change felt necessary to lay the base for ultimate independence, wanted to reform local government. But Adelabu's actual entry was as a hatchetman for the traditional chiefs, who wished to cut down one of their number who, they felt, was more interested in becoming a capitalist entrepreneur than in obeying the dictates of tradition. Adelabu organized the agitation in return for the promise that he would get the new post of Administrative Secretary; no doubt he felt that once in office he could curb the anti-reform sentiments of the chiefs. The agitation failed, but provided an excuse for the British to launch the reorganization of Ibadan's local government; however, no Administrative Secretary was appointed, and Adelabu was left, in his own words, 'an artist and idealist' with 'the brilliant career of a genius' before him, but 'at the very margin of starvation'.[13] Since he had left Yaba Higher College in 1936 he had failed in careers with the United Africa Company (having been their first African manager in Nigeria), the Government Cooperative Department, and as a trader on his own account. As an aspiring Nigerian middle class business executive or civil servant, or, alternatively, an entrepreneur, he ran into the obstacles of social relations—the antipathy of white colleagues and superiors, and the pressure of the traditional system in which he was still rooted to spend lavishly and show himself a 'big man', which impelled him to embezzle money from his employers and so be dismissed.

Two further points should be made. First, in terms of class relations, it should be noted that in the Nigerian case we are dealing very much with classes in the process of formation. Adelabu was always both an aspirant capitalist and firmly rooted in Yoruba traditions of the big man who uses his money to build up a network of clients and whose largesse earns him prestige. From a relatively obscure family himself, however, he was never wedded to the traditional chiefs as such, though he was prepared to use them to further his ambitions. What is important in that respect is that the position of the chiefs, themselves a pre-capitalist class whose position was also heavily determined by kinship relations, was a vital element in the social relations of Ibadan which determined in their turn the way in which Adelabu rose in politics. A second point to note is that that rise took place structurally entirely within the new elective institutions which the British began to establish as a first phase of decolonization. Despite his career experiences, Adelabu was no 'agitator'; in the letter just quoted he referred to his 'pre-destined chain of white patrons'—and not merely because the man from whom he now sought help was British. Although he was to portray himself (quite sincerely) only a couple of years later as a fiery nationalist and to write a tract calling for not one but seven revolutions in all spheres of life, even there he distinguished between the work of individual British administrators and missionaries (he was a Muslim) and the colonial system as such.

Adelabu was recruited into the political middle rank at the end of 1951 by his election to the House of Assembly of the Western Region as one of the six new legislators for Ibadan, and marked himself out by being the only one of them who finally committed himself to the National Council of Nigeria and the Cameroons, the voice of Nigerian nationalism. In Jamaica's early phase of decolonization recruitment contrasted with that in Nigeria in that the institutions sponsored by the British were not the only possible forms for the process. Whereas decolonization was launched in Nigeria by imperial fiat, in Jamaica it followed from a rebellion in May-June 1938 (though unarmed and unorganized) which was officially estimated to involve 100,000 participants at its height, when peasants and workers struck, demonstrated, broke bridges, cut telephone wires, besieged landowners in their houses, and destroyed crops. Driven by what one official called 'that oldest and ablest of agitators—hunger', these men and women forced both the Colonial Office and all other Jamaican classes to take a position in response, and so made their own history—if only briefly.[14] Despite the strike of 1945 and other incidents, the Nigerian workers and peasants were not yet formed enough as classes to take the same initiative. Thus, for example, the massive response of the Gold Coast cocoa farmers to the destruction of diseased trees was not matched in Western Nigeria, though the rural areas round Ibadan were the scene of limited resistance, the leaders of which later became important lieutenants of Adelabu.

Politicians of various kinds emerged and took up positions after the Jamaican rebellion. Some of those who later rose to the middle rank (and beyond sometimes) had already begun to respond to rising discontents even before the rebellion. Three of them had begun a new weekly, *Public Opinion*, in 1937, and this had played its part in forming a nationalist consciousness, though at the middle class and petty bourgeois level. After the rebellion the three split. Two of them were instrumental in bringing Norman Manley into politics and forming the primarily middle class and mildly nationalist PNP in September 1938. But Frank Hill (born 1910), son of a well-known journalist and brought up a Catholic, moved from unease at his church's position in the Spanish civil war via the reviewing of Left Book Club literature for his weekly, and under the pressure of the rebellion, to Marxism and support for the USSR. Another middle class recruit was Richard Hart (born 1917), son of a prominent solicitor, who, returning from an English education in 1936, became a solicitor's clerk himself and took up reading his father's collection of Left Book Club and other literature in his spare time. Already holding himself to be a Marxist by the eve of the rebellion, after it he became, with Hill, the intellectual centre for a group of lower middle class and working class Marxists like W. A. McBean, a street vendor, A. A. Morris, a banana tally clerk, and

Arthur Henry, a seaman and former railway mechanic. At first collecting around *The Jamaica Labour Weekly*, founded by H. C. Buchanan, himself a Marxist since the early 1930s, in immediate response to the action of the workers and peasants, the group decided early in 1939 to work within the PNP. The orthodox Comintern line was taken that a bourgeois democratic nationalist phase under PNP aegis must precede a struggle for socialism.[15]

In the next years the Marxists provided a nucleus (they never exceeded perhaps twenty-five in number) of dedicated organizers for the PNP and the labour movement. What mass base the party had was largely due to them, and their efforts were recognized by the Governor when he ordered the detention for four months under wartime emergency regulations of four of them, Hart, Henry, Frank Hill, and his brother, Ken (born 1909), who had now joined the group. Alexander Bustamante, the hero who had also emerged from the rebellion, and whose semi-worship by workers and peasants is the clearest indication of the limits of what they achieved in 1938, was himself detained for fourteen months, though staunchly anti-Communist and pro-Empire, but retained his control of the largest trade union central, the Bustamante (sic) Industrial Trade Union, and also won an overwhelming majority of seats at the first (decolonizing) election with adult suffrage in 1944. Dedicated work by the Marxists through their Trade Union Congress and in the PNP, however, had begun to erode the base of the BITU and its Jamaica Labour Party by 1949, especially in Kingston, the capital, though Bustamante still dominated the greater part of the peasants, whom the Marxists ignored, and who feared godless Communism. Such efforts also kept the leftists firmly in the middle levels of the PNP, though they preferred to be organizers and propagandists rather than to enter the ranks of the legislators and conform to the rituals of Westminster decolonization. They were, understandably, more powerful in the TUC, and two of them, Ken Hill and Richard Hart, rose to leading positions in the PNP.

In March 1952, however, the show-down came. Manley and his supporters, having built up an alternative power base among small capitalist farmers and rich peasants since 1947, now expelled the Marxists. The desire of Manley and his supporters to conform to what the Colonial Office expected the decolonization process to be, along with their feeling that victory could be theirs in the 1955 election if they dissociated themselves from godless Communism, above all, perhaps, the pressure of the Cold War and growing US interest in Jamaica, made this break inevitable. The significant thing is that the Marxists could put up no real defence. The Hill brothers flirted with democratic socialism and Moral Rearmament, then Frank dropped out of politics and Ken first joined the JLP and then worked his way back to the middle levels of the PNP (where he is now). Richard Hart tried to keep up the struggle, but in 1963 left for British Guiana to work for Cheddi Jagan. The Left became a tiny and isolated minority of the dedicated, which it remains today.

In March 1952 Adelabu, across the sea in Nigeria, was trying to find some way to project himself beyond the middle rank of regional legislative membership and party office as NCNC Western Secretary, a position which he lost a few months later. It is extremely interesting that his instinct should have been to champion the peasant, but it is also very significant in terms of the pattern of Nigeria's decolonization that the only forum which he used for this was the Western House of Assembly. The short book, *Africa in Ebullition*, which he published in mid-1952, repeated the same theme, but few peasants could read English! Nor were they mobilized as a conscious class force—and this is the crucial factor—for which Adelabu could act as a spokesman. Without this real social pressure to provide a wave on whose crest he could ride, the self-proclaimed militant nationalist himself almost recognized the contradiction between his aspirations to capitalism and the radicalism he was propounding. As he wrote in an unpublished essay, 'Environment and Circumstances incline me to Complacent Conservatism, Conviction and Duty compel me to Militant Radicalism. I AM A PARADOX.'[16] It is interesting that the small group of Nigerian Marxists, themselves now largely severed from the labour movement in which they had once been influential, and trying to find a home in the NCNC, should have looked to Adelabu as a fellow radical and then found him wanting (he upset Nduka Eze, for example, by asking for a fee for a lecture given in Lagos).

How then did he break out of the middle rank of his party? Early in April 1953 he founded the Ibadan Tax Payers Association, known in Yoruba as Mabolaje. Significantly, the latter name translates as 'Do not diminish the splendour', and Adelabu's new organization sought above all to mobilize support on the long-standing issue of the decline of traditional authority. Along with this sort of 'pre-class' politics he was able to combine an appeal to such interest groups as street traders, feeling against Lebanese shop-keepers, and, more generally, dislike of the Christian, wealthy oligarchy which had dominated Ibadan for about twenty years. In March 1954 the votes of only 9.5% of total potential electors, in a fragmented and confused electoral struggle, gave him control of the Ibadan District Council. Later in the year he swept the federal election in Ibadan also, and his gift of four seats to the NCNC from the heart of the region hitherto dominated by its bitter enemy, Action Group, brought him a federal ministry in the coalition government of NCNC and Northern People's Congress and the First Vice-Presidency of his party. These were the high points of his career, from which he was soon to begin to descend.

It is usually easier to begin a paper than to end it. Let me therefore try to summarize briefly. I have suggested that by setting up our problematic in terms of individual career patterns we do not come immediately to the crucial factors in political recruitment, which is the process in which we are in fact interested. If we seek, rather, to isolate those sets of social relations which determine the process, we find that in the comparative situation with which I am concerned, that of British decolonization, several were of prime importance. The extent to which the Colonial Office was able to keep control was a crucial element in the recruitment of both Adelabu and the Jamaican Marxists, affecting even their own ideological perceptions of the process. The former saw himself as a radical in the early 1950s, but accepted that his political career was to be conducted within the institutions felt to be appropriate for Colonial Office-controlled decolonization. The Jamaicans were also very conscious of themselves as radicals, but their decisions to collaborate with middle-class nationalists also resulted in an acceptance of institutions and patterns of decolonization dictated by the Colonial Office. This similarity is particularly significant in that Nigeria and Jamaica experienced very different balances of class forces at the time when decolonization was set in motion and our subjects' careers began, with the degree of their ideological radicalism set by the respective strength of peasant and worker upsurge. In the Nigerian situation, where middle class, petty bourgeois, and even capitalist nationalists completely dominated the party levels of political recruitment which affected Adelabu, his radicalism remained limited and, conversely, he rose beyond the middle rank, falling again when he failed to meet colonial requirements. In Jamaica, where the same class elements had to share influence in the PNP with organized labour, the Marxists remained radicals (within the institutional limits already suggested) and were less concerned to rise in the party hierarchy provided they could control its base. That desire, however, had by 1952 prompted the middle class leadership to agree with its Colonial Office debating opponents that the real enemies to be eliminated were the 'subversives'. The careers of all our subjects (at least as radicals) in fact ended in failure. The various sets of social relations which determined their political recruitment contained important contradictions, between decolonization as a principle and Colonial Office control, between nationalist demands and the desire of middle class leaders to ensure they kept power, above all between such forms of class domination and national independence as a means of liberation for peasants and workers.

These contradictions expressed themselves in the relations among the different levels of political recruitment in such a way as to prevent the permanent attainment of upper-level positions by self-declared radicals.

4

POLITICAL CENTRALIZATION AND LOCAL POLITICS IN GHANA: THE CAREERS OF NANA WIAFE AKENTEN II AND E. K. DUNCAN-WILLIAMS OF OFFINSO (ASHANTI)

Richard Crook

The two men whose careers are examined in this analysis are both local politicians who achieved a middle-ranking significance in national affairs, although one retained his essentially local role while the other moved out of local politics into regional and later national roles. The careers will be considered initially within the context of Offinso local politics, that is, by looking at the tactics adopted and the alternatives open to them throughout a series of specific historical events. Inevitably, Ashanti and Ghana-wide issues and circumstances prove to be of equal explanatory importance at various points; indeed it is a major assumption of this analysis that 'local' and 'national' politics in Ghana are, by the end of the period in question, closely integrated both structurally and ideologically. Nevertheless the subject-matter raises in itself an important preliminary question; in what sense can a study, not just of local politics but of the individual careers of locally-based politicians, support conclusions of general sociological or historical validity?

The study of individual careers does not in itself imply the adoption of an 'individualistic' interpretation of history or society. It is self-evident that any failure to relate the careers to the social structure and historical environment within which they are operating turns those careers into meaningless abstractions; 'Mr A. is born, becomes X, then Y, then Z and dies'; this is clearly of little interest, to either Marxist or non-Marxist. It is a unique pattern, like an individual's fingerprints. The focus of the problem is rather to establish the exact nature of this interaction between the individual and his social environment over time. No good Marxist who has read the *German Ideology* would deny that 'man makes himself' through interacting with society (other men) and nature, and that this relationship is both historical and reciprocal. The Marxist critique in Chapter 3 is therefore somewhat misplaced insofar as it implies that the problem is solved by establishing the philosophical point that social relations or the class structure are, for an individual, 'given', fortuitous, analytically a prior category, and must therefore always be taken as one's starting point, rather than the individual. It is true that, according to this theory, any attempt to build a model of social structure by starting with individual interactions may simply be perpetuating the 'false consciousness' of individuals; for what the individual feels, and what happens to him, is interpreted through an ideology about his place in society, and is coupled with the 'illusion' of free choice. Hence the statement that the individual can only 'subjectively raise himself above his class'. To follow an individual career is to pursue some accidentals of the social structure, subjectively meaningful to the individual, but objectively irrelevant to the 'social whole'. In much the same way it is argued—although from a different perspective[1]—that, from the point of view of the strictly rational individual voter, it does not matter whether or not he votes. Sociological explanation is in a quite separate category from the analysis of individual behaviour.

Nevertheless, Marx himself was not content with the circularity of a position which saw the relationship of the individual to his environment as purely subjective, or confined to the realm of 'consciousness'. Rather, he saw that men interact with their environment in a physical or 'real' sense, through their work and their social intercourse: 'The social structure and the state are continually evolving out of the life-process of definite individuals, but of individuals not as they may appear in their own or other people's imagination, but as they *really* are, i.e. as they operate, produce materially. . . .' Moreover, men are not the passive objects of history, for 'men, developing their material production and their material intercourse, *alter* [my italics], along with their real existence, their thinking and the products of their thinking . . .'[2]

It is clear, therefore, that even if we take the social structure as given, to investigate the manner in which individuals 'make their own history', especially through reacting to developing tensions between their given social and economic roles and the forces of social change, is a perfectly valid procedure. It is not necessary to become caught up in the subjectivity of individual perceptions—although these are themselves an interesting part of the dialectic of change—provided one can grasp the social meaning of the objective behaviour. Methodologically there is no reason why one should not commence one's empirical investigation by 'cutting into' the political system at this point.

The position we take, then, is that a study of the individual career should not be simply an illustration, a glimpse into the 'smoke-filled rooms' of politics, but should involve the selection of individuals who have played social roles which have interacted in some crucial or important way with an historical process of social change. The skill lies first in selecting roles which are paradigmatic, since whatever generalizations can be made are not based on any quantitatively significant social sample, but rather on the extent to which the study does provide a paradigm which is heuristic. This can be tested only by asking others with equal knowledge of the society in question whether the pattern established does construe successfully, that is, whether previously fragmented pieces of knowledge about different areas and levels of the society at once spring to mind as being more generally and yet more parsimoniously explainable, in the light of the sets of relationships put forward as paradigmatic. Secondly, although one sacrifices the principle of a quantitative generality, one gains by grappling with the 'real' relationships of certain individuals, since one is forced to analyse, in examining the progress of a career, the way in which the individual both determines and is determined by his social role. Some elements of his behaviour may be purely accidental, others may come from a consciousness which is part of a more generally developing phenomenon; and, through experiencing contradictions between his 'objective' position, his ideological perceptions and new socio-economic forces or historical circumstances pressing upon the definition of his role, he may try to maintain the role in its old form or, in redefining it, contribute to a process of structural change. Through this detailed study one can at least develop a soundly-based assessment of the process of social change as it affects the 'life-process of definite individuals' engaged in a set of social relations which are not in themselves confined to those particular individuals.

To return, then, to the problem of generalization, it is important to select individuals engaged in roles which are especially salient to the historical changes which one wishes to illuminate; the 'career' is, after all, the longitudinal study *par excellence*. There is no scientific guide to this problem of selection; it is, one may conclude, a matter of the observer's 'inside knowledge', a hunch dependent on his long and close acquaintance with the society in question. The idea of the 'middle-rank politician', in so far as it is specified *a priori* and then applied to a wide variety of societies, does direct our attention to a crucial but fairly general area, that of social mobility and its relationship to changes in the political system. Its ability to produce studies of salient roles, capable of generating paradigmatic generalizations, depends very much on how it is handled in each context. In some societies middle-rank national politicians may be of marginal interest; in others the indentification of middle-rank with local or sub-national levels of political action may be equally lacking in relevance to the problems of mobility and political change to which the study of middle-rankers should be directing our attention.

In the Ghanaian context, however, it may be argued with some justification that local politics and politicians have played an especially salient role in the socio-political changes of the last twenty-five years. The interest lies, not in a simple correlation between 'local' and 'middle-rank', but rather in the fact that, with increasing centralization, local politics have been a pivotal point for the emergence of representatives of opposing social groups, who have been forced to achieve at least middle-ranking importance in the national political system in order to pursue their various interests in the fate of the local political systems. The general role that interests us, therefore, is that of the local politician who moves into nationally-organized political activity and achieves at least a middle-ranking position of influence in that wider sphere. The 'middle-rankness' of these politicians is not a residual category, but rather serves to define the structural meaning of the type of centralization which has occurred in Ghana. For the study of who has achieved these roles and under what historical circumstances, indicates, first, the degree and type of mobility achieved by competing social groups; the specification of this first factor then illuminates a point of more general significance about changes in the Ghanaian political structure—namely, why local politics, while being integrated into a centralized political system, have still retained their vitality, both locally and as a source of issues at the centre and an integral part of the national political elite's networks.

The selection and analysis of the careers which are studied below was thus not made in a conceptual vacuum. Certain known, general features of the Ghanaian political system were taken as given. Since the formal inclusion of Ashanti and the Northern Territories into the Gold Coast political system after the Second World War, there has been a general although uneven trend towards centralization of political and economic power in Accra. Ghana's political elite is also small and well-integrated. However, because of the extent of rural development in Ghana during the colonial period, this elite is not purely a product of the capital city. The wealth generated by cash crops expressed itself in the numerous small towns and regional centres characteristic of modern Ghana, especially in the southern half of the country. The political elite continues to be linked through dense networks of economic, kinship, and social ties, to the hinterland; except perhaps for parts of the North, there are few areas of the country which are as isolated socially as they might appear geographically.

There exists, therefore, a constant tension between the emergence and survival of localized centres of economic and social development and the logic of institutional centralization. The normal dichotomy implicit in the distinction between 'elite' and 'local' politics does not, however, present a wholly accurate picture of the Ghanaian situation. On the one hand is what we have termed 'institutional centralization'. An important feature of Ghanaian politics over the past twenty-five years has been the development of formal institutions which, contrary to what is often asserted about the 'underdeveloped' countries, have been the effective 'carriers' of political and social change and real battlegrounds for the competition for power and status.[2a] The sheer multiplicity and overlap of institutional development can indeed be analysed in terms of the institutionalization of political conflict. In one sense, therefore, this process has been integrative and, in the case of institutions such as the Convention People's Party (CPP) and the administrative system, deliberately intended to promote a unitary state with weak local or sub-national mediating structures. On the other hand, because the elite is not entirely a capital city elite, potential sources of local and regional autonomy continue to survive. The interlocking of these two major structural features of Ghanaian politics can be seen, first, in the fact that centralization has been incorporative rather than destructive of local politics. Although local *autonomy* has decreased, issues of local power and status, or even of the very shape and existence of local political institutions, have not disappeared but continue to be fought out at higher levels of decision-making. Members of the more widely incorporated elite form a new national network within which they act interchangeably in local or national affairs. (Even the military elite cultivated local power bases and involved themselves in issues which would formerly have been confined to the local context).[3] Secondly, the interpenetration of the formally incorporative institutions by personal elite networks has meant that Ghanaian politics has retained many of the features of a 'face-to-face' society, being personalistic and factional, and perceived as being so, at all levels. This forms another type of identity between 'local' and 'national' politics, and has important implications for the study of the careers of people moving between these levels.

Nevertheless, in spite of these movements of structural and institutional integration, some unresolved tensions remain, and give rise to further questions. Since there has been such a centralization of allocative power, why have 'local politics' survived at all, insofar as there still exist more or less autonomous systems of political status and resources, generating their own conflicts and issues? It is not sufficient to attribute it simply to a cultural preference on the part of the Ghanaian elite. Further, why have the socio-economic changes which produce new, cross-cutting social strata and their attendant political forces not reinforced the effects of institutional centralization and worked against the 'elite networks' model? It is in studying the interaction of all these factors that one selects a paradigmatic career pattern, that is, a pattern which will focus our attention on the changing relationship between a local political system and national politics, as mediated through institutional and socio-economic development.

Offinso, the locality chosen, is an *oman* (state) of the Ashanti Confederacy, a large rural district lying to the north-west of Kumasi. Its history and traditions, as a 'pure Ashanti' border state straddling the Ashanti expansion northwestwards, are still of importance today, both economically and politically. The term 'rural' should not be understood to mean backward or traditional; the area is a centre of highly commercialized cocoa, timber, and food-crop production, and there is a large migrant population, mainly from the north of Ghana. Although the chieftaincy remains the main institutional focus of its political identity, the area has, in the last twenty years, formed the core of a local and district council, a parliamentary constituency, and, since 1959, an administrative district. Its relationship to the centre is formally mediated through the Ashanti Region, the latter being a powerful focus of political consciousness with its own political institutions and elite groups.

The career of Nana Wiafe Akenten, *omanhene*[4] of Offinso, provides an insight into the way in which local and regional elites have responded to two waves of social and economic change in post-war Ghana: first, the post-war boom in cocoa and timber which lasted through the 1950s and turned Ashanti into the centre of a highly commercialized and capitalized agricultural economy; and, secondly, the social revolution which brought the CPP to power, and gave positions of influence to underprivileged groups hitherto excluded from the patronage networks of the old Native Authority elites. These changes were potentially destructive of Offinso social relations and political institutions, and they were manifested in two apparently contradictory developments. From outside Offinso, the growth of Kumasi (capital of Ashanti) and of socio-economic strata common to the wider population of southern Ghana caused an objective discontinuity to develop between formal political structures at the local level, and the integration of the rural and urban areas through social, economic, and transportation networks. The CPP, preaching a Ghanaian nationalism, attempted to link this development to the institutional centralization discussed above. From inside Offinso, however, the same socio-economic developments spawned a contradictory growth—a more intensive local consciousness focused on individual towns and villages. The hierarchical organization of the state, based on the paramountcy of Offinso town, was distorted by the growth of new centres of economic development and urbanization. The local chiefs, leading farmers, and traders of these centres threatened

the fragmentation of the Offinso state, insofar as they began to differ-
entiate their own local interests from those of Offinso conceived as a
'locality' and represented by the old Native Authority elite. The communal leaders wanted their own symbols of political status, their own
markets, lorry-parks, development committees, cooperative associations, and 'storey' buildings. Similarly, centres such as the old Offinso
town, relatively decaying, were willing to fight back to preserve a
dominance which was a mixture of political power, prestige, and
economic influence—particularly over the now-valuable cocoa lands.

Communal politics,[5] therefore, was an expression of the developing
political identities of nodal points of growth and settlement in the
rural economy; but insofar as it involved conflict with representatives
of the Offinso community such as Wiafe Akenten, committed to
maintaining the integrity of the Offinso state and the dominance of its
'capital' town elite, then it was expressed in a neo-traditional form.
Factional conflict in the state was structured according to the political
and familial relationships of community leaders to the *omanhene*. The
CPP became involved with this local factionalism as the party grew.
Paradoxically, then, it was modern socio-economic development
which boosted a more intensely 'localistic' style of politics that was
both 'traditional' and destructive of traditional relationships. It is true,
of course, that such local conflict appears to be at least as old as the
colonial period itself, but the particular strength and form that it took
in the Offinso of the 1940–50s is undoubtedly connected to the northwestern movement of the cocoa industry in those years. In his role as
omanhene of Offinso, Wiafe Akenten had, therefore, to face a dual
challenge from these simultaneous developments both within and
outside the local arena; as these were developments which could also be
utilized by both internal and external political enemies, his choice of
tactics and alliances was made extremely hazardous.

Duncan-Williams' career, on the other hand, presents a story of
accelerated social mobility typical of the successful CPP 'organization'
man. A person of great ambition, little education, and aggressive
rather than subtle political talents, he chose the correct path in the
mid-1950s—or, rather, failure in the local sphere provided him with
an opportunity to move away from being a local councillor and
'agitator' against Wiafe Akenten to a career in the party hierarchy.
Here he participated in the manipulation and centralization of the local
politics in which he himself had been, and continued to be, involved.
After becoming a CPP District Commissioner in 1959, he was made
Regional Secretary of the Ashanti CPP, finally reaching the CPP
national headquarters just before the coup.

Another factor underlying the choice of these two men is that, as local politicians from the same area, their careers have progressed in a dialectical relationship. A substantial part of the story, in fact, involves their long struggle as enemies. This adds another dimension to the analysis, in that the 'relationship of their relationship' to the general environment also illuminates important social conflicts and bears particularly on the ultimate policies of the CPP towards the chieftaincy. The social conflict in Offinso during the 1950s was not in itself 'anti-chief', and there was no inevitability in the transformation of the CPP's fundamentally ambivalent attitude to the chieftaincy into the more deliberately destructive policy of the 1960s. It was rather that men like Duncan-Williams, who had been involved in a particular kind of struggle with local elites in the 1950s, came to dominate the CPP hierarchy in the 1960s.

If we therefore take Offinso local politics and politicians as the 'catchment area',[6] the particular recruitment process to be looked at is that which led—or forced—these local politicians to move outside local politics, with varying degrees of success. Examination of those factors which influenced their relative success or failure in turn illustrates general movements of centralization and of developing class interest.

Nana Wiafe Akenten succeeded to the Offinso stool in 1946, when he was 34; the measure of his political astuteness is that he is still on the stool, having reigned continuously bar his years of enforced exile, 1959–66. This is a rare achievement for an Ashanti chief. He was, in 1946, the model colonial chief—young, literate, and 'development-minded'. His uncle, Nana Kwabena Poku, *omanhene* of Offinso 1921–29, had sent him to Achimota College, from where he graduated as a teacher a few years after Nkrumah, Gbedemah, and the other big men of Ghanaian politics; he was thus a 'school-mate' of Nkrumah.[7] Before becoming chief, he had taught in Kumasi, and acted as secretary of an organization of Offinso literates called the Offinso Unity Club. No doubt his activities with this Club were influenced by the knowledge that he was a potential heir to the stool. His enstoolment presented him with the opportunity to implement the various plans with which the Club had bombarded the colonial administration in the 1940s, and also, in accordance with colonial reforms of the Native Authority system, to appoint Club stalwarts to positions on the new 'democratized' Native Authority committees.

This small coterie of literates displayed an attitude of hostility, not to say contempt, for communal leaders in the state (mainly illiterate but wealthy farmers or traders) who thwarted, so they felt, the Club's development plans. Their major scheme was for a new town, to be built on a site which would encompass a conglomeration of villages near the main road, 2 miles from 'old' Offinso. They claimed that the new town would 'divert people's energies from quarrels into more useful channels', and accused the populace of refusing to forget 'the petty contentions of the past, often based on ignorance and lack of foresight'.[8] The new town was not, of course, a non-controversial or altruistic piece of 'development'; it was a significant centre of investment opportunity and a source of prestige which was bound to provoke communal rivalry. Wiafe Akenten, then, was initially associated with these 'Offinso patriots' but he soon discovered that his role required a more subtle balancing of interests than would result from a rigid adoption of the Club line—although his ultimate policy was the same, that is, the preservation of Offinso 'unity' and prestige.

Communal hostility towards the Native Authority elite did not, however, come solely from villages affected by the new town scheme. Towns in the northern part of the district, which had developed into agricultural-trading centres with populations larger than Offinso itself, had long been chafing at the bit of Offinso rule, and represented strong centrifugal forces threatening the integrity of the Offinso state structure. The most important of these towns was Akomadan, the community from which Duncan-Williams came, on his mother's side. (His father was a Cape Coast trader.)

These were some of the immediate local problems which faced Wiafe Akenten when he came to the stool. But they were not the most serious: cooperation with the Offinso Unity Club and 'democratization' of Native Authority committees were not sufficient to deal with the social upheavals of the 1946–49 period. This was the time of the post-war inflation, the national boycott of expatriate goods, and the famous ex-servicemen's march in Accra which resulted in nation-wide riots.[9] The cocoa-farmers were also in a state of revolt over the compulsory cutting-out of cocoa trees stricken in the 'swollen-shoot' epidemic. These general problems became merged with local communal issues in a very complex way.

The social unrest of 1948–49 contained a strong 'anti-Native Authority chief' element, partly because of long-standing and continuing socio-economic conflicts between colonial chiefs and farmers, partly because of the chiefs' ambivalent position as representatives of the government and hence of government policy. This was a testing time in Wiafe Akenten's career—a young, inexperienced chief, faced with violent attacks, road-blocks set up by groups of boycotters and angry farmers, and communal fragmentation of his state. Although he publicly stated in the Asanteman Council that he was opposed to compulsory 'cutting out' of cocoa trees, and visited the northern towns to placate communal grievances, he could not escape the general opprobrium which the Ashanti chiefs brought upon themselves when, under government pressure, they recanted their support of the boycotters and farmers. The Ashanti chiefs thereafter supported the reintroduction of cutting-out.

The initial stages of CPP agitation in Offinso were therefore relatively easy, as the support of both communal leaders and cocoa farmers could be obtained for an anti-chief, anti-government stand. The early CPP leadership in Offinso consisted of a group of big farmers in the central Offinso area, small traders and cocoa brokers who moved between Kumasi and Offinso, and Akomadan activists, including Duncan-Williams.

Williams, a typical 'Standard VII boy',[10] was then drifting between Akomadan and Kumasi, intermittently working as a petty trader and cocoa buyer. Wiafe Akenten had given him a room in the Offinso Stool House in Kumasi, taking pity on this Offinso 'verandah boy', as he called him.[11] Although educated, Williams was not one of the inner circle of the Offinso Unity Club elite, neither could he be classed as a communal leader or 'patron' cocoa farmer. But he was prepared to take the aggressive stand demanded by the farmers, and to voice crude communal hostilities to the Native Authority. He was also, in fact, involved in a destoolment dispute between the Akomadan people and Wiafe Akenten.

In the lead-up to the CPP's victory in 1951, local groups such as the Offinso Unity Club were completely outflanked by CPP leaders. This not only caused the eventual break-up of the Club, with some of its leaders jumping on to the CPP bandwagon, but also led Wiafe Akenten to a reappraisal of his tactics. He had been unable to do more than ride the storm of the 1948–49 troubles, given his position as a new chief in the colonial set-up. But his basic instincts were 'patriotic'. He was proud of Offinso's militant anti-colonial tradition[12] and determined to build up Offinso into an independent rival to Kumasi. At the same time, as a big cocoa farmer in a wholly rural, cocoa boom area, his sympathies were very much with the cocoa farmers' grievances against the colonial marketing system.[13] Of course, he had close contacts with the 'financier' farmers, transport owners, and landlords of the area. He was willing, therefore, to support the CPP in so far as *at the time* it appeared to represent most effectively the anti-colonial demands of which he approved. The CPP had, moreover, been adopted into the central government, and although Wiafe Akenten well realized the limitations of its power in 1951–52 he decided to cooperate with the CPP and in this way to try to outflank militant local opposition. He could not be blamed, as a chief, for strengthening his ties with the central government, and he justified to himself his flirtation with the CPP by citing his Achimota links with Nkrumah. Thus, while remaining respectable, he could also appear moderately anti-colonial. The true test of his policy was the introduction of the CPP's new local government system in 1951–52. The revolutionary effects of this measure, which set up Councils with elected majorities, have been much overemphasized, especially for Ashanti.[14] The way was in fact left open for a clever chief to continue to exercise his local influence and economic patronage. Wiafe Akenten went on record in the press as welcoming the new system which would, he said, leave him more time to pursue his interests in Ashanti history and culture! He did not, in fact, retire to his study.

Duncan-Williams was elected the first chairman of the local council, mainly through the votes of the two-thirds elected representatives.[15] But as a formal government body elected on a territorial basis there was no guarantee that the particular clique who made up the CPP leadership could mobilize a solid anti-Wiafe Akenten front. Many of them had not even been elected to the council. And the problems which confronted the council as a governmental body almost immediately created splits, not only between councillors but also between councillors and their rural electorates. Two such issues were local taxation and the implementation of the new town scheme. The result was that Williams was ousted as chairman after only five months in office. This was partly due to a facet of Williams' personality which was to recur constantly in his career. Although he was a good, aggressive speaker, he tended to be excessively overbearing and pompous in the exercise of his authority. In addition, he had offended other councillors by his illicit championship of an Akomadan 'secession' movement and by supporting popular resistance to taxation. Yet he had been hostile to other communal grievances in central Offinso connected with resistance to the planned centralization of local markets.[16]

Wiafe Akenten therefore secured a victory in the election of his own favoured candidate as chairman—a 'moderate literate' CPP-ite. By a clever manoeuvre, personal jealousies amongst the CPP militants had been exploited to gain a vote against Duncan-Williams; the moderates had then reunited with the traditional representatives to exclude the CPP militants from promised committee positions. The council was henceforth to be moderate, and 'development minded' (in the colonial sense), to Wiafe Akenten's liking. One immediate reward was an agreement for the stool to have a two-third share of the stool land revenue. The other reward was the reduction of the CPP militants to a small group who relied on personal enmities and communal grievances to wage a largely unsuccessful campaign against Wiafe Akenten between 1951 and 1954.

It is interesting that Duncan-Williams and his allies, the illiterate core-group of CPP leaders who had never been elected to the council, formed themselves into a separate organization, called the Offinso Ratepayers' Association, for the purpose of fighting these local battles. Williams later made a clear distinction between 'Party affairs' and 'local affairs', as did other local CPP leaders.[17] This is perhaps an indication of the ideological strength of the CPP, although more probably a hindsight from the position of the CPP in the 1960s. It is also a reflection of Williams' own career pattern. The Ratepayers' Association often claimed to represent 20,000 ratepayers, but Duncan-Williams' rival, the chairman of the council, was not sympathetic to their claims. In one enquiry all the Ratepayer petitioners were found not to have paid their rates.[18]

Wiafe Akenten survived the period 1951-54 through a combination of manipulation of local factions and institutions, the backing of the still important Ashanti administration, and the neutral benevolence of the central government. On one issue, for instance, the stool lands question, Wiafe Akenten had been accused of setting up an illegal court to try 'trespassers' on Offinso land. This was a result of his zeal to protect Offinso lands, and his distrust of the local council's efficiency. But both the administration and the chairman of the council had been willing and anxious to reach a reasonable compromise, and prevent the Offinso Ratepayers' Association from pushing the issue too far. At this date, it must be remembered, the local CPP could not so easily call in the central government, for the colonial administration still provided considerable 'insulation' between ministers and local affairs.

The 1954 election, however, was a turning point in the careers of both men, marking the stage at which they both moved into middle-rank political activity. This election was the so-called 'rebel candidates' election, when the CPP was quite unable to control the selection of candidates from the thousands of hopeful MPs.[19] Wiafe Akenten hoped that his tacit alliance with the local council and his good offices with Nkrumah would enable him to influence the nomination of the CPP candidate for Offinso. He therefore put his weight behind the candidature of the council chairman, and made a personal trip to Accra to ensure that the latter was given the official party endorsement. But the local CPP militants, with the cooperation of some elements of the Ashanti Regional CPP, put up a man from Akomadan, a former Kumasi Court Clerk, who had been on one of the Offinso Unity Club-sponsored Native Authority committees in 1949, but had joined the CPP in 1951-52. The rebel candidate's connection with Akomadan was another factor in Wiafe Akenten's support of the official candidate.

Duncan-Williams himself had hoped, and tried, for the nomination, but claims that he stood down in order to support the rebel candidate. Williams was not, in fact, popular enough, nor influential enough compared with the two other candidates, to square up to local expectations of what an MP should be. This influenced his move away from local politics after the election, when the party offered him a new avenue of activity. It is also odd that Williams claims to have supported the *rebel* candidate out of 'respect for the Party's decision'. It is significant that at this time there were serious conflicts between the Ashanti CPP and Accra, which were resolved only after the election. Offinso was atypical in this respect, in that its rebel candidate won and was immediately accepted back into the party. This meant that the rebel candidate's faction was also reintegrated via the regional elements who had supported him but who remained loyal to the CPP during the formation of the Ashanti opposition movement in 1954–55.

The election result was a defeat for Wiafe Akenten. He had lost his chance to develop, through the creation of political debts, a stronger alliance with the central government. Instead, his personal enemies now possessed a potentially more powerful out-flanking alliance, which itself was the result of the growth of the CPP as an autonomous, economically powerful organization. It was obvious that Wiafe Akenten could no longer rely on neutral 'cooperation' with the government and elite personal networks—even though his command of local institutions was still strong, as was evidenced by the immediate re-election of the defeated official candidate to the chairmanship of the local council. Wiafe Akenten had to develop new tactics, and it was then that an entirely new range of alternatives presented themselves. From his personal point of view, they were historically fortuitous, although he soon played an active part in shaping these circumstances. The new alternatives arose out of the disintegration of the Ashanti CPP and the formation of the Ashanti National Liberation Movement (NLM).[20]

Had it not been for the NLM, Wiafe Akenten might have moved closer to the CPP government in an attempt to draw the sting of local CPP militants. But in order to challenge these elements he needed to broaden his political base and move into the sphere of mass politics. This in itself was a new departure for a chief. The NLM was, at its inception, a movement of peasant farmers against the conditions of the colonial cocoa marketing system, which had been reinforced rather than remedied by CPP policies. These policies struck particularly at the big successful cocoa farmer, and at efforts to form cooperatives, private African buying companies or an independent 'association of producers'. However, not only was it radically anti-colonial and anti-government, it was also a nationalist movement, utilizing the concepts of Ashanti rather than Ghanaian nationalism. The movement seemed initially to herald the complete disintegration of the Ashanti CPP, and at the time, therefore, offered an alternative to Wiafe Akenten which was both more appealing personally and seemed a stronger long-term bet compared with the crumbling CPP forces. In Offinso, since the 'rebel' CPP had quickly become 'official' again, there was no immediate alliance between discontented farmers and rebel CPP elements as in other areas. This reduced the temptation for the chief to adopt an orthodox pro-government line as a means of defeating his enemies. The greater part of the mass farmer support lay outside the areas of CPP control—which were predominantly in the northern towns—and was thus available for mobilization by Wiafe Akenten, at the cost of challenging the government.

The NLM, of course, attracted the Ashanti chieftaincy as a whole, some of whom appeared very strange 'conservative fellow-travellers' in such a violent and radical mass movement. But others were in the forefront of the 'secessionist' wing of the NLM, among whom Wiafe Akenten included himself, and he was in fact a leading organizer and campaigner. There were both personal and ideological reasons for this. In the first place, NLM policies on cocoa represented his own interests. Secondly, its nationalism was of the type he could strongly identify with. He and the other militant NLM chiefs regarded themselves as the purist defenders of Ashanti nationhood, in contrast to the 'corrupted' Kumasi hierarchy. Wiafe Akenten was extremely contemptuous of the pusillanimity of the then *Asantehene*. There were also purely local Offinso interests connected with the Ashanti-Brong-Ahafo dispute.[21] A final decisive factor was another historical coincidence—the fact that after 1954 the colonial administration in Ashanti was no longer prepared to stop what it would never have allowed to happen before, that is, an alliance between Ashanti chiefs and a movement of popular protest. Wiafe Akenten indeed felt vindicated by the support he had from the Chief Regional Officer of Ashanti against the Governor and Nkrumah.

Wiafe Akenten's decision, then, was to challenge the government with the backing of a new mass movement which enabled him to con-solidate control of local institutions, gather popular support and attack the Duncan-Williams faction. Wiafe Akenten took a personal role in the setting up of the Offinso NLM, toured the state making speeches, donated funds, and organized the big landlords and patrons for the same purpose. His own *Twafuorhene*[22] was made chairman of the Offinso NLM. The struggle with the CPP was a violent one, and Offinso was no exception. In becoming involved in such a movement, Wiafe Akenten generalized his local problems on to an Ashanti-wide basis; his struggle against local CPP elements became a struggle of cocoa farmers and the Ashanti nation—particularly the Ashanti elite—for survival. In this sense he ceased to be a local politician, but moved in the inner circles of the NLM leadership. These personal links were to stand him in good stead after the 1966 coup.

Duncan-Williams had left the small Offinso Ratepayers Association faction to fight their unsuccessful local battles between 1954 and 1956, although he remained a local councillor. He became heavily involved in his new job as district manager of the Cocoa Purchasing Company in Sunyani, an extremely influential position which involved giving loans to CPP 'farmers'. This post was a sop for his failure to gain the nomination for MP, and it was here that he really won his party spurs. In particular he was active in the famous Atwima-Nwabiagya by-election, the first electoral contest in Ashanti between the newly formed NLM and the CPP.[23] By being involved in the Cocoa Purchasing Company he was at the core of one of the elements of CPP success—and, of course, one of the causes of the violent opposition to the CPP. His absence on Company business resulted in his official expulsion from the local council, on grounds of non-attendance at meetings.

By 1957 Wiafe Akenten was at the height of his power. The NLM had won the 1956 election with a candidate especially selected by Wiafe Akenten—a weak, unpopular man, a long-standing Offinso Unity Club member and client of the chieftaincy who had failed miserably in every electoral contest he had entered since 1951. Wiafe Akenten's involvement in a mass political party was also part of a significant social change in Ashanti. The chieftaincy and the Ashanti elite had at last made use of the new socio-economic forces which had inter-penetrated the rural-urban sectors. By helping to create a political party, utilizing the most dynamic groups in the economy (the entre-preneurial farmers), the chieftaincy had attempted to transcend communal fragmentation and social groupings which subverted the very existence of political structures such as Offinso. Ashanti nationalism provided the ideological and organizational means for reintegrating these destructive forces at a new level, a wider unity more consonant with the objective movement of society. At the same time the old local structures, instead of representing a discontinuity between institutions and new socio-economic forces, now appeared as integral parts of the new whole. Offinso patriotism could be identified with Ashanti patriot-ism, insofar as the local elite was acting out its new role as aggregator and defender of the wider interest. The reinvigoration of the old structures was, of course, necessary for the revival and preservation of the chiefly elites, led by the regional elite in Kumasi.

This movement, however, had involved breaking the regional elite's ties with the central government. By failing to gain national control, the NLM doomed its supporters and the social interests it represented to defeat, so long as the CPP government lasted.[24] Wiafe Akenten's victory was, therefore, short-lived. By November 1958 he had been destooled, as part of a systematic government campaign to eliminate all Ashanti NLM chiefs. But Wiafe Akenten was not easily removed. It took a year and a half of legal and customary wrangles, special Acts, the 'abolition' of Offinso state, bribes, threats, and, finally, a platoon of police to evict Wiafe Akenten forcibly from his palace. It took another special Act[25] to send him and his friend, the *Wenchihene* (Busia's brother) into exile in Nigeria. Duncan-Williams had, of course, been active, re-entering local politics with a revived local CPP organization (most of the leaders had fled to Brong-Ahafo) and becoming, very briefly, chairman of the local council again. But it must be said that the destoolment of Wiafe Akenten was an affair almost entirely dependent on central government intervention. An extraordinary feature of the destoolment was that the whole State Council (elders and sub-chiefs) remained loyal to Wiafe Akenten, with one exception, and continued to resist the enstoolment of his successor after his departure, until they themselves were all destooled. The unprecedented loyalty of the sub-chiefs may well have been connected to the wider sense of solidarity which Wiafe Akenten's activities in the NLM had created. Offinso represented a last outpost of NLM resistance, after the crumbling of the NLM leadership in Kumasi, and it was thus something of a struggle of political principle.

The remainder of the CPP period is concerned with Duncan-Williams' rise through the CPP hierarchy.[26] Consequent on his role in the Cocoa Purchasing Company, he had been 'elected' chairman of the 'Young Farmers Club', which gave him some standing in Accra in 1956–57. After reintroducing himself into local politics in 1958–59, he achieved his first ambition. With Wiafe Akenten, his old enemy, out of the way, he became the undisputed 'boss' of the new Offinso district, the first CPP-appointed District Commissioner.

In taking up this position he displayed attitudes which are very reminiscent of those found in the 'self-made man' in England. He was snobbish and ambivalent about his background, on the one hand pointing to his meagre education with pride, and even claiming a relationship to the Akomadan royal family, and, on the other, being equally proud of the fact that he, a 'verandah boy', had succeeded the last white district commissioner as controller of Offinso.[27] Indeed, as District Commissioner he had the full weight of the central government behind him, and he was not slow to make people aware of exactly what this meant. One of his first, rather petty, actions was to remove all the furniture from the office of the local council chairman, and transfer it to his own. The chairman was informed that this was the District Commissioner's prerogative as personal representative of the government and Kwame Nkrumah.[28]

Duncan-Williams' immediate task was the 'Cipification' of the district, and this he undertook with great vigour. The Seventh Day Adventist Church was informed that neutrality on religious grounds would not be tolerated, and a process of intimidation began which was to transform village politics. The CPP was no phantom institution, for its influence became so pervasive that even the normal petty, drunken quarrels and back-bitings of village life became affairs of state.

As District Commissioner Duncan-Williams not only extorted opposition elements or anybody against whom a report had been lodged but also exercised wide political and economic patronage, through control of nominations for party posts, the local council, and the local United Ghana Farmers' Council and Ghana National Trading Corporation branches.[29] But this brought him into several conflicts with the Regional Commissioner, usually over the sharing of bribes, or cases of rival bribing. He also became too closely involved in Offinso local politics—as was natural, given his history—in particular an infamous and intractable stool dispute. Duncan-Williams experienced almost exactly the same difficulties as previous rulers of Offinso. Communal issues cropped up again, but he took the same hostile view of village resistance to centralization of markets—still unresolved in 1960—as had Wiafe Akenten.[30] The village market problem had finally to be settled by the Regional Commissioner himself in 1961. Williams' personality, moreover, did nothing to help the smooth administration of the district, even though his qualities were useful in other ways.

In 1960, therefore, six months after becoming District Commissioner in Offinso, he was transferred to Kumasi. This was a promotion, but also put him out of harm's way and under the eye of the Regional Commissioner. It is here that the 'bureaucratic' stage of Duncan-Williams' career begins. After 1960 his advancement depended very much on his personal relationships with the officials of the CPP regional hierarchy, on his participation in committees, and his ability to demonstrate his loyalty and dynamism to officials of the national headquarters who came into contact with the party in Ashanti. This included Nkrumah. Even after the coup Williams did, in fact, display considerable emotive loyalty to Nkrumah. It is at this level of politics, it may be noted, that the concept of a 'charismatic' leader and his lieutenants may have considerable analytical relevance, even within an ostensibly bureaucratic system. Until he reaches the magic 'inner circles', a politician tends to keep his options open; once inside, classic patron-client relationships begin to operate.

Between 1960 and 1962 Williams' time was spent mainly in Kumasi, apart from a brief spell as District Commissioner in Teppa. In Kumasi he was on important party committees, including finance and organization, but he continued to take an interest in Offinso affairs, an interest which was acknowledged by the hierarchy when he was called in to help settle a deadlocked dispute over the Offinso council chairmanship 'election'. The bureaucratization of the party had gained momentum by 1961, involving a vast proliferation of offices, and regimentation of complex lines of authority and precedence.[31] Relatively unknown figures from headquarters became the dominant men in the party, with resounding titles such as Deputy Chief Administrative Officer (North). Williams toed the correct line, appeared at party 'seminars' to give talks on party organization and ideology, and was very active on the Regional building fund committee.[32]

The high point of his career was his appointment as Regional Party Secretary in March 1963. This was a reward for his years of party service, his personal loyalty during the faction-ridden days of the Kumasi hierarchy between 1960 and 1963 and also an acknowledgement of his considerable organizing ability. His task was to 'revive the party spirit', especially by tightening up on the creeping saturation of high party positions by ex-opposition converts. It is doubtful whether this could have been effective, given the morass of self-seeking, corruption, factionalism, and opportunism which now riddled the party. His great achievement as Regional Secretary was the master-minding of the 1964 'Referendum on the One-Party State' in Ashanti. This was a triumph of logistics and population movement, if nothing else. His dynamic campaign produced the desired result: 425,022 for, 0 against.[33]

Williams was overshadowed, however, even in this position, by the appointment of the former deputy chief administrative officer (North), from party headquarters, as 'Regional Education Secretary'. One of the latter's functions was, no doubt, to keep an eye on the Ashanti party. At the end of 1964 Duncan-Williams was transferred to a comfortable job at the national headquarters in Accra, connected with the Young Pioneers. The regional secretaryship did in fact seem to be the natural limit of his career, given his personality and capabilities.

Although he was investigated after the coup, Duncan-Williams now lives comfortably in a large mansion in the residential Airport area of Accra. Wiafe Akenten returned after the coup, and was reinstated as chief of Offinso by the National Liberation Council. It is since 1966 that he has really reaped the benefits of his earlier middle-level political activity. Until the fall of the Progress Party in 1972, he was for the first time in his career living under a government which he fully supported and with which he had intimate personal links. Although, out of personal choice, he concentrated his efforts on the rebuilding of Offinso, and his own local position in it, he was neither a 'local' nor a 'national' politician but simply a member of the Ghanaian political elite, well known nationally and moving easily in all spheres according to his convenience. He has, for instance, devoted much effort to the work of the National House of Chiefs and achieved a prominent position in it; he also accepted, for the first time, a formal position at the national level—membership of the influential National Capital Investments Board. His old score against the late *Asantehene* was paid off after the coup, when he refused to take the oath of allegiance to the *Asantehene* on his reinstatement as *Offinsohene*. He claimed that, as he had never been properly destooled, he had no need to take another oath. As every other chief took the oath, this was a bold insult which won him fame in Ashanti; he was able to get away with it because Victor Owusu, an old NLM associate, was Attorney-General under the NLC military government and was prepared to indulge Wiafe Akenten's principles.

With the setting up of the Progress Party under Busia, Wiafe Akenten really came to the forefront again in local political activity. The Offinso Progress Party was very much dominated by old NLM cronies, big patron farmers and businessmen—not the modern managerial types from Kumasi but illiterate Offinso meat-traders, saw-mill owners, transport-owners, and landlords. Wiafe Akenten, as in old times, secured the nomination of his young protégé as Progress Party candidate in the 1969 elections. This man, a graduate lawyer and nephew of one of Wiafe Akenten's oldest sub-chiefs, won a resounding victory but he was not of the calibre to progress very far at the national level. Wiafe Akenten does not like local competition.

Finally, in the sphere of local government, Wiafe Akenten succeeded in turning the clock back to 1949 by being appointed, under the Busia government, chairman of the Offinso local council management committee. He has, therefore, reintegrated the chieftaincy and local government, still two separate institutions, under his own personal control. One of his main ambitions is to regain control of the land, especially the granting of timber concessions, farming permits, collection of revenue, and so on. This is both a personal and a patriotic interest. Wiafe Akenten is no less the cunning politician now than he always was. He constantly seeks ways to reinforce his popularity— letting it be made known publicly, for instance, when he, as State Councillor, has granted money to the local council for development; or, when the lorry drivers complained about the state of a road leading to the lorry-park, immediately taking action to have it tarred. He is still, of course, faced with the age-old communal problems of the northern towns. But there is no doubt that he will survive and prosper for many years to come.

In conclusion, we may note that Duncan-Williams, who was something of a failure in local politics, nevertheless achieved a limited success with an 'organizational' career in the CPP hierarchy. The CPP offered him a mobility which he would never otherwise have experienced. The condition of his success was that he moved out of local politics, once the CPP had lost a considerable part of its rural, mass support to the NLM. Men like Duncan-Williams, who could not wholly identify themselves with communal politics, were reduced either to the attempt to manipulate factional hostilities to the local elite—in which game the latter had all the advantages—or to jumping on the centralization bandwagon. Once involved in this channel of mobility, they were anti-farmer, anti-chief, anti-local; forces which the CPP attempted to incorporate, then suppress, but without enduring success. The enduring strength of the 'Standard VII boy' legend, as an indigenous model of the politics of these years, is rooted in the anger of local elites that local 'good-for-nothings', even illiterates, were able to challenge deeply entrenched structures of economic and political power.

Wiafe Akenten, although he has never moved far out of local politics, has been much more the successful politician and achieved a wider influence. His struggles have been representative of the interaction between class interest and Ghanaian political structures. If we return to the question initially posed—the problem of how to account for the survival of local politics within a centralizing political system—it is clear that the decision of men such as Wiafe Akenten to move into a wider sphere of political activity to achieve at least 'middle-rank', particluarly within the context of the modern political party, provides a large part of the answer to that question. The political process set in motion was not simply the action of a few atavistic 'traditional' chiefs, but the reaction of a widely-spread group with a clearly defined position in the colonial social structure—the chiefs, lawyers, businessmen, and their clients who composed the old Native Authority elites. They utilized modern socio-economic developments to preserve the structures upon which their survival depended. 'Local patriotism' was thus an ideology facing two ways, being at the root of local communal conflict, and expressing a wider class interest within the Ghanaian political system.[34] Three major factors, the rise of communal politics, the campaign of the local elites for survival, and the forces of modern political parties and the bureaucracy, interacted to produce that organic link between local and national politics which is characteristic of modern Ghanaian politics. It is also clear that any attempt to analyse Ghanaian politics in terms of a 'dual society', or 'tradition-modernity', model is quite misplaced. There is no such distinction to be made between the local and national, or rural and urban arenas, as is normally implicit in such a model. Finally, Wiafe Akenten's final position under the Busia government shows that the process is continuing, and that the 'circulation of elites' at the top should not be considered in isolation from the total social structure.

5

THE ELIGIBLE AND THE ELECT: ARMINIAN THOUGHTS ON THE SOCIAL PREDESTINATION OF AHAFO LEADERS

John Dunn

To approach the study of political structures by considering the biographies of politicians affords a number of important advantages. It provides a subject matter which is sufficiently obstinately ideographic to resist the simpler stereotypes of social causation. But if it is adopted in at all a systematic fashion, it also makes very clear how little the political life resembles the free flow of individual fantasy—how painfully much with them all politicians are apt to find the causal universe to be. It is convenient to begin with Goffman's distinction between the 'natural history' conception of a social career, an institutional approach to the study of the self, and the rather inflected sense of the word in colloquial English in which the careers of politicians are perhaps peculiarly subject to being judged as 'brilliant or disappointing', successes or failures.[1] It is plain that the careers of politicians have more in common with the careers of opera singers or pop stars than they do with the careers of postmen, though it would be agreeable to feel confident that their social function was often as substantial as that of the latter. To study the careers of major politicians—politicians of the front rank—without attending largely to the brilliance or disappointment which they display would be likely to appear capricious. But with village Hampdens and Cromwells guilty at most of the blood of the neighbouring village, a less mesmerized type of attention can more readily be maintained. The reason for this may be merely historiographical tradition, but its convenience scarcely requires any more profound conceptual justification. The virtues and vices exhibited by village politicians are not likely to differ greatly in moral depth from those of their political superiors down country, and the conditions of political action, in village as in metropolis, are likely to mean that the career of a politician will consist more in learning how to like what he can get than it will in learning how to get what he already likes.

All politicians are leaders. Their trade, however part-time, is securing the cooperation of large numbers of other men. The extent to which they succeed in securing such cooperation and the terms on which they are able to secure it are the measure of their power within a single arena, though they may also constitute a necessary foothold for (or a barrier to) their ascent into another arena in which the terms of political trade are startlingly different. The politics of Nkrumah's court, for example, with their extreme ambiguity as to who was really included within that charmed circle,[2] were beyond the reach of all Ahafo politicians. But it would be difficult to argue that it was their social and geographical derivation or their scanty local political re-sources—and not simply more individually contingent aspects of their political abilities—which precluded their access even to these vertiginous heights. At least two men who were politically associated with Ahafo in the period since 1951 did cut a figure of some sort in Ghanaian national politics.[3] But whatever might be learnt about the conditions for political success and the risks of political debacle in the national arena by studying their careers in national politics, a concentration on their Ahafo base would add only the crudest of insights. The prospects for learning something of interest about political recruitment and political leadership *within* the Ahafo arena seem, by contrast, appre-ciably brighter. The institutions of Ahafo are institutions as partial as one could well expect to come upon, and the moral careers of Ahafo politicians thus naturally lack the clarity of outline of the moral careers of Goffman's mental patients or of other sharply stigmatized person-nel. Fragmentary and disconnected institutions generate scruffy career lines, offering as they do wide opportunities for innovative manoeuvre but also ample chance for agents to become hopelessly confused. Ideally, an analyst might hope to be able to employ the scruffiness of the career lines to trace out the fragmentariness and disconnection of the institutions. Every society in some measure gets the leaders it deserves, and thus, soberingly, may be held in part to deserve the leaders which it gets. To examine the leaders which Ahafo incurred is to begin to understand how Ahafo *could* have experienced what it in fact had coming to it. It is not necessarily, however, to assent whole-heartedly to the view that minor genetic or indeed traffic contin-gencies might not have brought it something rather different. We can infer that the leaders of Ahafo were eligible from the fact of their becoming leaders at all, but we do not have to see them, with an excess of veneration for the historical process, as any sort of an elect.

The analysis of leadership is at the centre of the understanding of politics and it poses some very fundamental dilemmas, dilemmas which have been noticed at intervals ever since the writings of Plato. Leaders have power and they have responsibilities. The analysis of leadership tends to be cast in one or other of two superficially incom-patible idioms. If power is seen as the metaphysically primary aspect of social relations, leaders are seen as its possessors (or on occasion as the instruments of its possessors) and the relationship between themselves

and their followers is seen as one of manipulation and passivity, power
and subjection. Such a picture can be sophisticated in a purely mechani-
cal fashion and set out as an elaborately calibrated study of inequalities
of exchange. The study of political elites has been conducted predominantly in this idiom. Although it has often resulted in ludicrous
projections of the scope of power of elite members,[4] there is no
conceptual reason why it could not incorporate causal understanding of
the terms of power trading between leaders and led of the most exquisite
precision. The second idiom is inherently more moralistic. Leaders are
conceived of as the instruments, defective or otherwise, of social
purposes, or, more broadly, moral purposes. They serve (or fail to
serve) those whom they lead, represent their interests, respond at best
sensitively to their effective demands. In this perspective Napoleon
appears not as an over-promoted and licentious Corsican adventurer
but as the World Soul on horseback[5]—and Hitler not as a lunatic and
ranting postcard painter, or even a contingency of the economic
organization of German society, but as, perhaps, the World Soul in
the charnel house. The disparity between the two idioms does not lie,
as is often supposed, in their estimate of the motivation of politicians
but in their judgment of what constitutes an adequate understanding of
the significance of political power. It has frequently been noticed that
the two idioms stand in a somewhat paradoxical relation to one
another. Hume, for example, points this out with his customary
deftness: 'It is, therefore, a just *political* maxim, *that every man must be
supposed a knave*; though, at the same time, it appears somewhat
strange that a maxim should be true in *politics* which is false in *fact*.'[6]
But his resolution of the dilemma in the confidence that men charac-
teristically behave better within their families than they do in the
Cabinet has a rather pre-Freudian ring to it. It seems preferable instead
to resist any *a priori* identification of individuals, organizations, or
societies as solidly morally wholesome or unwholesome. What
requires to be mapped out is the substantial element of manipulation in
the conduct of all leaders and all followers and the full range of moral
characterizations, expressed and implicit, of the context of political
leadership to which participants, observers, and analysts are led. It is
essential to retain the opportunity to take analytical account of the
extent to which all political leaders are, to adapt Sir Henry Wotton,
more or less good men kept at home to lie on behalf of their country.
The complexity and ambiguity of political values cannot be tamed
intellectually by the pretence to rise analytically above them into the
purer air of value-free natural science, but only by the fullest commitment to explore their ramifications. The most pervasive temptation for
the analyst of political leadership is the adoption of a persisting moral

favouritism towards either leaders or led. All resulting historical accounts of good peoples betrayed by bad leaders or good leaders betrayed by bad peoples are in the end not merely analytically jejune. They are also politically corrupting.

To study the moral careers of politicians is certainly, then, following Professor Morris-Jones,[7] to shift one's attention from institutions to actions, but it is also to attend with some energy to the point that it is the culture of a society as well as the individual consciousness of an agent which determines what an action is. The social and economic structures of Ahafo (a cheque to avoid cashing) no doubt largely determined what persons in Ahafo could have been eligible for entry into political roles at different points in time. But what it was about them which made them eligible, which constituted their eligibility, was determined by the function for which they were perceived to be offering themselves. There are usually more eligible persons in politics than there are persons who are actually elected. In Ahafo the process of selecting among them has at times been assisted by short-term cash flows. It would be silly to ignore the causal efficacy of such transactions. But it shows a footling level of political understanding to be so mesmerized by the passage of the money that one cannot take in any other causal features of the selection processes. Cash may help to decide the selection from among the eligibles. Cash in substantial amounts disbursed with skill over time may indeed suffice to establish eligibility. But (as the qualifications indicate) eligibility is not a simple or immediate function of cash. There are rich men in Ahafo (perhaps richer men than any who have become members of parliament from the district) of whom it would simply not be true to say that they, in the words of Marlon Brando, 'could have been a contender'.

One last preliminary point which requires to be made about the career lines of Ahafo politicians is more a caveat than an analytical argument. To talk of entry into political roles as 'political recruitment' sounds, as has been pointed out,[8] comfortingly definite. One is recruited, for example, into armies, highly organized institutions with clear boundaries and criteria of inclusion and exclusion. To Whips and commissars political parties may be thought of fondly as institutions of a similar character. But Whips and commissars do not really at present evoke much resonance among the inhabitants of rural Africa, or indeed India. It would be a very nice point who, if anyone, today in Ahafo is a politician. If one had been asking the same question once a year since 1951 one would have found the most striking concertina effects in the composition of the cast list. Since the role of politician in 1976 is known to be subject to such a high level of structural underemployment, it is perhaps by now less likely than it would have been ten or fifteen years ago that many would allow themselves to become defined to any great extent by these particular institutions. The moral career of an Ahafo politician in the near future (in so far as it is licensed at all) is likely to be closer to the moral career of an asset stripper than to the solid investor in that grander and less pest-prone surrogate for farming or broking cocoa which it appeared perhaps in 1953, or even in 1961. Politicians are not the only persons in Ahafo who exercise political power, or even who take part in national politics—chiefs and business-men, for instance, have both been known to do so.[9] Perhaps no one in Ahafo has been a politician continuously since 1951, while even for those who have taken prominent parts in politics at different times it has not always been the case that their participation in politics has been their most important social role, either in their own eyes or in those of other members of their community.[10] The blurred nature of these boundaries is extremely important. But, despite its importance, an arbitrary distinction must be made for present purposes between those who are plainly politicians and whose careers thus need to be considered as a whole and those, on the other hand, who are politicians very much on occasion and whose careers may be referred to largely for purposes of contrast.[11]

All Ahafo politicians in this understanding are politicians in practice in virtue of their membership of one of the two political parties which, under a variety of names, have contested the political primacy of Ahafo (when permitted to do so) during virtually the last quarter of a century. Before 1951 no one in Ahafo was permitted to be a politician in this sense, and it is still the case that the role of politician operates (or is prevented from operating) under licence from those who control the central apparatus of the state (the colonial power, the CPP govern-ments, etc.). In terms of the social structure of modern Ghana, it is clearly correct, for these reasons, to see the position of MP, even in an opposition party, as a form of public office in one of the less stable but more lucrative sectors of public employment. Incumbent chiefs or members of the permanently established public services (administrators, policemen, or soldiers) are not normally entitled to enter such a competition without resigning their offices, nor do they normally—in Ahafo at least—have any very adequate motive for doing so.[12] Ex-chiefs, however, are not in any way precluded from competing for these prizes, and aspirants to chiefly office in the future would also not be precluded from doing so.[13] If one were attempting to explain entry into the ranks of competitors in terms of perceptions of purely egoistic advantages, it might be most helpful to think of political office as a choice among a multiplicity of possible investment forms and to attempt to understand the flows into and out of the ranks of those competing for it in terms of differential access to market information (and perhaps, ideally, of differential rationality: commercial skill varies). One might note, for example, that all competitors to represent Ahafo in the legislature before 1965 who got as far as being nominated (no very lofty hurdle) had extensive social experience outside Ahafo. But, even at this level, such a perspective is tendentious. Several of these competitors, for instance, had displayed some measure of active commitment to political life before 1951—before, in fact, it was clear that the role of politician was to become a fully licensed role—and hence long before it was clear that it was a form of *investment* at all. (A similar methodological error would be to explain the occurrence of ghetto riots by the fact that looting sometimes takes place in the course of them.) Furthermore, to think of access to political office solely as an opportunity for individual upward social mobility is in itself to distract attention from the issue of what criteria determine whether an individual is indeed eligible for moving upward by this particular channel. Individuals dispose of varying quantities of political capital when they attempt to enter political office, and much of the capital of many well placed competitors does not take the form of private wealth at all. Candidates for nomination by prospectively victorious political parties, and candidates, again, for legislative seats, face expenses for entry into the political market; but the expenses which they face are in part determined by their own qualities as candidates—by how much they have to offer to their parties and how much their party is simply in effect 'donating' to them. The perceived capacity to serve effectively what are identified as public purposes is a form of political capital, even at times a criterion of eligibility, fully as much as are individual economic resources. Whether it is closer to being a sum of wealth held in a different form or to being a criterion, a precondition for being permitted to enter the auction for candidature at all, depends largely on the extent to which the competition is genuinely open between parties.[14] Parties which know that they cannot lose the election can, if they choose, dispense with all but the most modest of abilities in their candidates. Parties which know that they are certain to lose an election also have no great need to exhaust their imaginations on selecting the candidate with the most vivid and diverse appeals. But parties which are genuinely competing in elections where the overall outcome is in doubt *need* candidates who (in their own fallible judgement) can enhance their corporate appeal.

What attributes, then, rendered candidates eligible to represent Ahafo at different points in time? The first attribute is genuinely a criterion, a necessary condition: to be eligible at all each prospective candidate had to be capable of expressing himself in English and to be in some measure literate. Since debates in the legislature (when there is such a body) are conducted in English, this is not an unreasonable requirement. It does, however, of course sharply restrict the ranks of the eligible since most Ghanaians over the age of about twenty do not satisfy it. Indeed, persons who possess great power in national politics may still fail to satisfy it. Another attribute which is close to being indispensable for a candidate in Ahafo is the capacity to express oneself fluently in Asante Twi, the language of the majority of local residents. Carpetbaggers face major disabilities in most Ghanaian constituencies and, even in such a culturally provincial and incoherent area as Ahafo, it would be politically imprudent to go to the electors in a foreign accent. Some measure of continuing local residence is also an advantage to a candidate, perhaps even more so today now that constituencies are so much smaller than they were in 1951 and now that politics are more obviously an exacting and communally important zero-sum game and no longer a rather ill-differentiated exercise in the universally bene-ficient pursuit of 'Free-dom'. In the 1951 election it was no particular disadvantage for B. F. Kusi, even among the Ahafo voters, to come from a town some way from Ahafo and to work in Kumasi. By 1969 it may well have been a crucial handicap for the young engineer from Tema, Yaw Podiee, with his British MSc in engineering, to have returned so seldom to his home town of Mim until the contest for the Progress Party nomination had actually begun. A Legon BA (Third Class) in History who had actually come home looked a more reliable instrument of local purposes than the somewhat obviously déraciné young man standing a little uneasily besides his newish Mercedes.[15] Not that Ahafo voters would have had anything against the newest of Mercedes as such; but they did like to know who its owner was and, preferably, who he had been for some time. The political marketing of a blatantly eligible candidate could manage his ingratiation with the electoral consumers by establishing his possession of a highly consoli-dated local identity. Parties and their leaders, being essentially unlocal (or perhaps super-local)[16] phenomena, had perforce to be vouched for by those with local identities. It was a considerable help when it came to vindicating the merits of a party's local candidate if he himself did not impose any additional strain on the audience's credulity—if he could in effect vouch for himself. An abundance of well cultivated local friends was a more substantial means for influencing people than a healthier bank balance and a set of rather neglected relatives.

Already eligibility has begun to shift from a precondition for being permitted to compete at all towards a series of attributes more likely to favour the chances of competitors. The genuinely eligible comprise a far smaller group than the totality of those who are not formally ineligible. The two most important dimensions of eligibility in this more demanding sense have so far been corporate political fidelity and educational attainment (the latter seen as a rough index of modernist political expertise and thus of the prospective efficacy of a representative, if only he were trustworthy). The significance of party loyalty was established by the attitudes of party stalwarts, not by any undue party bigotry among the electorate at large. Indeed, the fact that it was important at all in Ahafo might be thought to be simply a result of the exceptionally bitter and all-encompassing struggle there during the NLM/CPP conflict.[17] There were certainly many other areas of Ghana in 1969 in which a continuing real commitment to political parties as such was very much weaker, if in fact it can plausibly be claimed to have existed at all.[18] The importance of education as a criterion of eligibility must, on the other hand, have risen in virtually every Ghanaian constituency except perhaps the one in which Mr Joe Appiah was competing. None of those who represented Ahafo before 1966 had enjoyed more than a bare secondary education before beginning to do so, though one of the earlier MPs, Mr B. K. Senkyire, contrived to augment this handsomely during an electorally imposed furlough between his two spells in the legislature. By 1969, though, it was a real disability for a candidate who wished to contest the nomination for the party expected to win (the Progress Party) not to have attended a place of higher education. Adequate candidates for Ahafo elections have thus recently been far more local and far better educated than they were over twenty years ago, a result of the subdivision of the initial constituency, of the rapid expansion in opportunities for higher education (particularly for those from the more prosperous cocoa zones like Ahafo), and of a sharpening sense of the increasingly competitively exacting and socially important character of the politics of governmental resource allocation.

If one were, however, to consider the definition of eligibility in this way solely in terms of the careers of MPs, one would miss a number of points. Ahafo may appear to have been slow in grasping the promise of the new investment form which the political career represented and perhaps also to have been initially rather underendowed with citizens educationally qualified to take it up. Now, too, that it is apparent that the most portly of these argosies may miscarry so drastically, those whose assets equip them for entry into less risky markets may prefer in future to enter these rather than take up the servitudes and grandeurs of political life. But even to the backwoods of Ahafo modern politics came before the prospect of drawing an individual salary from it had become apparent. The institution through which it came and which has reappeared on every subsequent occasion when a government has permitted the recrudescence of local political activity uncontrolled by the centre was the local scholars' union—the Ahafo Youth Society, to give it its longest lasting title. Initially an agency of mild protest at the constrictions of the post-war phase of 'indirect rule', it soon became the basis for much local development effort and the core of the local CPP branch. Later, with the NLM/CPP split, its utility disappeared for a period. But with the coup of February 1966 and the end of CPP rule it again became an independent organization within which all the most articulate local residents could unite to press for the interests of the area as a whole. Just as the leading members of both CPP and NLM (United Party) in the constituency had learnt many of their political skills and acquired much of their political reputation in this body before the split of 1954–55, so the PP and NAL candidates and leading organizers had for the most part done the same in its lineal descendant between 1966 and 1969. In such an institution it is never easy to distinguish clearly between the elements of social recreation, endeavour to serve a public, and exploitation of a private channel of social mobility. But it would be fanciful to suppose that the motivation for participating in it was much less or more single-minded than, for example, for participation in a university Labour club in this country. It is a matter of pressing concern for politicians who try to ride the roller-coaster of Ghanaian public life that the moral nuances of success or failure are not too obtrusive. One enters politics in the hope of striking a handsome bargain of mutual benefit between self and community. If the bargain goes somewhat astray for one or for both, it is reassuring to be able to continue to define one's self by the indulgent milieu of social recreation and public service, despite the blockage of the mobility channels. Hopes can sometimes be high in Ahafo, both individually and communally; but no Ghanaian ever *expects* that any man will do his duty. There is much human tolerance and a fair amount of consensus on the moral desirability of furthering communal ends, as well as a certain complicity among scholars, in the Ahafo Youth Society. The moral career of an Ahafo politician dodges with greater or less agility between these supports. If open careers are ideally the due reward of talent, talent also sees itself—and is seen by others—as having its obligations. Indeed, as the moral respect for formal competition between political parties as a means of acquiring governments has waned, with the passing years (and governments), the definition of politician as local public servant and instrument of local development has, if anything, sharpened. When the two most active constituency organizers of the Progress Party were released from custody by the new military regime early in 1972, the Regional Commissioner who had ordered their release specifically urged them to

continue with their organizational efforts to promote local development, an encouragement which they have been happy to follow. It
would be hard to provide more unequivocal testimony from the
possessors of state power itself of the recognition of how far the local
politician's career was made up of what they liked to call 'voluntary
work' and not merely of private appropriation. Private appropriation,
where it had been possible, had always depended upon a lien on state
power. Once the lien on state power had been conclusively sundered,
the residual 'voluntary work' (which was in fact virtually all that the
PP's local leaders' role had ever amounted to, even while the party held
power), was uncontentiously a form of public service. By defining
local development as service and aspiration to national power as subver-
sion, the holders of post-colonial state power have moved with increasing determination *à la recherche du temps perdu*. It is a nice point
whether they should be seen as having rejected the legitimacy of the
politician's career *in toto* or merely delimited the arena within which it
can for the moment expect to operate under state licence. But to ask
such a question is to adopt a metropolitan perspective. Within Ahafo
itself the more important point is that the locally resident political
leadership of both the CPP and the UP have joined forces in the
Ahafo Youth Society to fight for the development of local education
and to preserve local control of Ahafo's land revenues.

It may be helpful to raise some more general issues in relation to
this Ahafo experience. The careers of politicians plainly require analysis
from at least two different points of view: firstly, what the role of
politician can do for a social actor (or looks to him as though it might
be able to do), and, secondly, what a social actor appears to those who
support him to be able to do for them (i.e. what makes it seem rational
to an agent to undertake—and then again to persist in—the career of a
politician and what makes it rational for those who in various ways
enable him to undertake it to choose him against other possible
candidates for their adherence). In the case of the second, the attributes
considered important will vary very much with the roles of the considerers but, as long as there is some real element of electoral competition, all considerers, including the most assertive of party bosses, will
have to keep in mind attributes perceived to count with electors.
About the rationality of entry and persistence for politicians themselves,
there is little general to be added on the basis of the Ahafo experience—
except perhaps a renewed emphasis on the importance of the highly
indeterminate and insecure context of all Ghanaian entrepreneurial
activity. The rationality of social selection, however, deserves some
further consideration.

Politicians hold roles which are specified in terms of political parties (in the context discussed here: not, of course, in all possible contexts). Parties are more or less formal organizations, sustained by the commitment of individuals, supplemented by their corporate capacities to provide individuals with extrinsic incentives. The simplest way in which to consider leadership in Ahafo is thus to look at politicians as members of organizations who show a greater or less distance in self-definition from the organization's definition of their roles and who are tied to their roles by a combination of normative allegiance (however incurred), rational incentive, and what Goffman calls 'secondary adjustments of a contained or disruptive kind'.[19] It is substantially less easy in the case of political parties than it is with mental hospitals (despite the central role of cant in both) to separate the normative definition of roles, primary adjustments, from the content of secondary adjustments. Where did the CPP end and Ahafo begin? In Nkrumah's head and in some of its printed handouts the CPP had one—perhaps more than one—rather strong normative definition. But as a social fact it could without undue cynicism be said to have been largely constituted by secondary adjustments and this crude consideration was plainly one which played a fairly salient role even inside Nkrumah's head for most of the time. Nkrumah may have pretended not to understand—on paper and in conversation with impressionable English visitors—but he was in fact relentlessly aware that he was in Ghana and not in Camden Town. If his left hand had often to appear unaware of what his right hand was doing in practice, it would be rash to suppose that both may not have been at some level governed by the same tough rationality. (Possibly this judgement reflects simply academic sentimentality. Is the rationality of 'needs must when the devil drives' really so tough?) In any case, Nkrumah may not have liked some of what he had to do very much, but he was extremely clear that he *had* to lump it.

There is no doubt that the CPP as a real organization did have what might be called an operating ideology (if hardly an operational code), and it is possible that this may have shown a fair measure of homogeneity throughout the land area of Ghana. But we simply do not know as yet (if indeed we ever shall) how far this was so. There have been some attractive attempts to sketch out the outlines of such an ideology for particular areas, notably Richard Crook's treatment of Offinso,[20] but it would be wholly premature as yet to totalize them to Ghana as a whole. Yet, if the party as an institution does not provide a neat conceptual niche in terms of which to specify the activity of Ahafo leadership, neither, unfortunately, does the nature of Ahafo as a place assist us to do so. Joan Vincent could study leadership in the immigrant community of Gondo parish, Uganda, nicely enough in terms of the ecological, economic, and normative integration of the community because Gondo really is a community and leadership is a painfully achieved status within it.[21] But Ahafo is emphatically *not* in any continuing sense a community and it is hard to see individual stools or towns of Ahafo as the sites of a community as morally self-subsistent as Gondo. Incorporation into the Ahafo periphery is probably still not much more demanding (unless you happen to be a citizen of a foreign African state) than incorporation into the society of Gondo. But Ahafo is much too rich and has too many substantial concentrations of wealth for incorporation into its periphery to be at all close to incorporation into its centres. Leadership is certainly an achieved status in Ahafo, as in Gondo, but it is achieved by ventures more speculative, less central to community functioning, and more heavily dependent on initial private advantage. Something like a free market in leadership can be seen as operating in Gondo parish, if one looks at it over the whole of a man's life-span. The Ahafo leadership market in contrast, though it is not uncompetitive, is pronouncedly oligopolistic and entry into it is effectively restricted to those with substantial initial capital of one kind or another.

One further point is aptly made in a recent discussion on comparative grassroots politics in Africa[22]—despite a certain botanical innocence over the range of diversity among grasses. Communities with a high degree of internal political faction, non-solidary communities, are more likely to appear where their external integration into state and market is seen by their members as facilities, while solidary communities with an integrative community leadership are more likely to appear where the mode of external integration of the community is seen as highly coercive. It is thus important that the mode of integration of Ahafo into both the world market and the colonial state was seen much more continuously as an extension of facilities than as an imposition of coercion: a cocoa farmers' view, though not one which even in Ahafo they have maintained consistently and one which could become sharply inverted in the fullness of time.[23]

A final point concerns the implications of the conceptual gap between the Eligible (whom sociology can aspire to describe analytically) and the Elect (whom it must be left to history to record). It is a point which Goffman makes, for rather different purposes, about mental hospital admissions: 'Separating those offences which could have been used as grounds for hospitalizing the offender from those that are so used, one finds a vast number of . . . career contingencies.' (Examples are: socio-economic status, visibility of the offence, proximity to a mental hospital, amount of treatment facilities available, community regard for the type of treatment given in available hospitals and, above all, the degree of familial intolerance towards individual behaviour.)

'The society's official view is that inmates of mental hospitals are there primarily because they are suffering from mental illness. However, in the degree that the "mentally ill" outside hospitals numerically approach or surpass those inside hospitals, one could say that mental patients distinctively suffer not from mental illness, but from contingencies.'[24] In the degree that the eligible (those who satisfy the minimal descriptive conditions for being chosen) outnumber the elect (those who are in fact chosen), political leaders succeed not in virtue of possessing a distinctive range of socially identifiable individual attributes but essentially because of a variety of social contingencies. To say this is not in itself to say much. What student of politics, let alone practitioner of politics, has ever doubted that politics is quite largely a matter of luck? But if it is so obviously and trivially true, it has perhaps some implications which are less obvious. A deterministic social science operating with 'objective' social categories and an *explanandum* which it is confident that it has identified adequately can look down on the rather vague and perhaps bland functionalist perspective adopted here. It can observe at a glance that this is blatantly incapable of being transformed into a taut explanatory scheme, whereas a 'who-pays-what-to-whom' model of economic exchange nicely combines a less superstitious and moralistic view of social process with an exemplary explanatory rigour.

But this is fundamentally mistaken. It is mistaken, firstly, because the *explanandum* (how the societies which we study are in fact led at different levels) is so weakly identified that nothing can be gained by relating external chunks of behaviour to it. (Compare the 'official' conception of mental hospital admissions in Goffman's argument.) It is also mistaken because it is grasping at a will-of-the-wisp, a picture of demonstrative logical linkage between actual social events and universal social theory which we *indisputably* have no good reason to believe subsists in reality and which it may well be thought we have by now fairly good reason to believe does *not* subsist in reality.[25] It seems more fruitful, at least provisionally, to use the frank recognition of contingency as a ground for attempting to map social processes over a much broader field, deserting the accumulation of naively identified behaviour for something which is obviously more speculative, impressionistic, and interpretative, the search for a more adequate understanding of what really happens. If one is not in a position to *describe* adequately what is happening, there is little prospect of being able either to understand or to explain it, however much 'behavioural' data one is able to accumulate in relation to it.

To look at the ways in which societies incur their leaders as a process of social integration, although it is plainly a functionalist perspective, is not either naive nor in a pejorative sense conservative.[26] It is, in fact, a necessary condition for the causal understanding (such as it can in principle be) of the political structures of the real world. The processes by which leaders are incurred from inside societies (conquests pose different problems) do not either excuse or indict the actions which the leaders proceed to perform. Looking at the consequences of the leaders' actions in many countries—not least our own—we may well feel little moral sympathy for those who sit in the seats of the mighty. But that does not mean that it is possible to grasp how they came to sit in those seats without understanding that trajectory as part of a process of social integration. Societies are integrated by violence and deceit (among other things) and politicians hold power often by the judicious exercise of violence and deceit. But even Machiavelli, who knew this and *felt* the knowledge as deeply as anyone has done, knew that social integration and political success are a product of opinion; and that deceit and violence are merely instruments—and at best occasional instruments—for controlling opinion. (As Hobbes put it in Behemoth: '. . . if men know not their duty, what is there that can force them to obey the laws? An army, you will say. But what shall force the army?')[27]

One further point about career biographies as such and what can be learnt from them may be worth making in conclusion. Any sequence of human behaviour can be 'explained' retrospectively as a set of actions by the device of imputing rationality, without being seen to flout the evidence (the dirty secret at the heart of the historian's trade). But rationality cohabits very uneasily with causal explanation because of the role of error—to say nothing of misinformation—in the performance of real actors. Rationality as an interpretative canon can provide powerful explanations of actions. It is much less clear that it frequently provides true explanations of actions. It is a matter of *choice* (and of explanatory ambition) what the superimposition of a very large number of career biographies of politicians can teach one. What is suggested here is that it should at least teach one something about the range of the ways in which different societies can be led and something about the variation in meaning in the role of politician between different cultures and political environments (what it is to be a politician). There is perhaps some danger that, if the concept of a career is made too behavioural and the careers are all compiled by persons who inhabit a single culture, what the accumulation will in fact demonstrate is largely what sort of rationality is apt to be imputed within that culture.

DRAMATIS PERSONAE

For a systematic account of the background of modern politics in Ahafo, see John Dunn and A. F. Robertson, *Dependence and Opportunity: Political Change in Ahafo* (Cambridge, 1973).

Chronology

1951   First Legislative Election. Constituency Kumasi West Rural (= Ahafo
       + Ahafo Ano + Atwima Nwabiagya)
1954   Second Legislative Election. Constituency Ahafo (includes Ahafo Ano)
1956   Third Legislative Election. Constituency unchanged
1957   Independence of Ghana
1965   Fourth Legislative Election (under one-party constitution.) 3 Ahafo seats
1966   CPP government removed by military
1969   Fifth Legislative Election. Constituencies Asunafo + Asutifi
1972   PP government removed by military coup

Major Parties   CPP = NAL   NLM = UP = PP

1951 Election

B. F. Kusi (CPP), born 1922, educated to middle school (Kumasi), Kumasi
   trader, founder member CPP; home town Bisease (outside Ahafo proper)
G. K. Owusu (UGCC). Kumasi trader; home town Goaso
Kusi wins effortlessly—no effective opposition to CPP. During this legislative
term Kusi quarrelled with Nkrumah and left the CPP. He competed unsuccessfully as an independent in the Atwima Nwabiagya constituency in the 1954
election and in 1955 won the first NLM by-election in the same constituency.
Served in Parliament as an opposition member until 1965. Became timber
contractor while an MP and has remained one ever since. Campaigned on
behalf of PP in Ahafo constituency in 1969 election.

1954 Election

B. K. Senkyire (CPP), born 1928, educated to secondary school (Cape Coast);
   first clerk of Ahafo Local Council, CPP member from secondary school
   days, secretary and founder member Ahafo Youth Association; home
   town Kenyase (brother of last two chiefs)
A. W. Osei (Independent), born 1912, educated to middle school (Kumasi),
   retired state nurse and owner of nursing home in Goaso; member of CPP
   up to election; home town Goaso
B. D. Addai (GCP), former member Legislative Council; cocoa entrepreneur;
   home area Ahafo Ano
Osei contested the CPP nomination with Senkyire and believed that he was
deprived of it as a result of bribery. Senkyire obtained roughly three times as
many votes as Osei, who in turn obtained about three times as many as Addai.
Addai was an older and much more distinguished man. There was still no
effective party opposition to the CPP.

1956 Election

A. W. Osei (UP) (=NLM)
B. K. Senkyire (CPP)
Senkyire's vote was halved and Osei's quadrupled. UP electoral dominance of
Ahafo established. Osei served as an Opposition MP until 1965 and became a
(very small-scale) timber contractor during this period. He has continued to

reside largely in Goaso and Kumasi up to the present day. Senkyire in the meantime went to England to study cooperatives on a scholarship and then received a CPP-controlled Ahafo scholarship to continue his studies on law. While in Britain he became chairman of the CPP party organization in the United Kingdom. After being called to the bar and getting a law degree, he returned to Ghana and practised first in Sunyani (the capital of the region within which Ahafo was now situated) and then in Accra.

1965 Election

No Opposition candidates permitted.
3 Ahafo seats: B. K. SENKYIRE, A. E. TWIMASI, S. K. OPOKU.
Senkyire became Minister of Cooperatives until the 1966 coup. Since the 1972 coup he has been able to supplement the business enterprises to which he was reduced after 1966 by occupying the role of secretary general of the Ghana Cooperative Alliance.

S. K. Opoku, born 1931, educated at Mim to middle school and subsequently at intervals at teacher training colleges. Elementary and middle school teacher who kept his position in the teaching service while an MP and acted as a supply teacher while Parliament was not sitting. He was an organizer of the NAL campaign in 1969 and is now cooperating with the former PP organizers, A. W. Osei, Boame, and Benson Anane, in the Ahafo Youth Society's efforts to develop the area. Twimasi was a clerk who subsequently attended the University of Ghana.

1969 Election

Asunafo constituency:

A. BADU-NKANSAH (PP), born 1935, Legon BA (Hons) in History, Deputy Headmaster, Acherensua Secondary School (in Ahafo); home town Akrodie; chosen as Ahfo representative to the Constituent Assembly before the 1969 election in preference to Osei; the selection was made by the government-appointed Local Management Committee, the majority of which consisted of government officials

J. K. OSEI (NAL), educated to secondary school; teacher in teacher training college (situated close to Ahafo); home town Mim; Active member (like Badu Nkansah) of Ahafo Youth Society
    Unsuccessful candidate for PP nomination in Asunafo:

MATTHEW YAW PODIEE, MSc in Engineering from British university; worked in Tema; virtually unknown in constituency before election campaign; home town Mim

Asutifi constituency:

I. K. OSEI-DUAH (PP), secondary school teacher, also active member of Ahafo Youth Society; home town Mim

NANA KOJO BONSU (NAL), businessman; brother of Senkyire; chief of Kenyase under CPP

KWAME ANANE OBINIM (UPP): less than 150 votes; home town Kenyase.

PP wins both seats overwhelmingly (every polling station in Asutifi, 79 out of 81 polling stations in Asunafo). Senkyire himself was prohibited from contesting the election by the terms of the military government's proscriptions. He played a major (though necessarily covert) part in the attempt to organize a CPP party to contest the election under the leadership of Imoru Egala, eventually suppressed by the military government. Badu Nkansah and Osei-Duah both became ministerial secretaries in the PP government. After his release from custody by the second military regime Badu Nkansah went into business on a small scale in Accra.

From the point of view of individual ambition it is no doubt still broadly true that the finest sight an Ahafo politician ever sees is the high road leading to Accra (see Senkyire career line). But the less turbulent career of politician as esteemed public servant naturally rewards, and perhaps even demands, a more sustained localism (cf. A. W. Osei, S. K. Opoku career lines).

6

SEIZING HALF A LOAF: ISAYA MUKIRANE AND SELF-RECRUITMENT FOR SECESSION

Nelson Kasfir

The question of secession poses several difficulties for the use of career routes to shed light upon political systems.[1] We are confronted immediately with questions of *which* system(s) and *which* politicians deserve scrutiny. Isaya Mukirane must be pigeon-holed rather low on the scale of 'middle-rank' politicians, if Uganda forms the political system. He is far more significant, though still of 'middle-rank', if Toro, a kingdom within Uganda at the pertinent time, is taken to be the polity. However, within the Rwenzururu movement in which he was one of several competing leaders, or in the Rwenzururu government of which he was undisputed head, Mukirane must be accounted a politician of top rank.

The notion of 'middle-rank', then, tends toward reification of one political system when others may also be relevant, and lacks specification of the limits within which it is useful to select actors for sustained examination. While some sort of distinction can be drawn between leaders at the top and those of lesser rank—supposing the political system to have been specified—virtually no lower limit can be suggested. All politicians are members of at least the middle ranks, since by definition they are assumed to have some influence over others.

I. ARENAS, RESOURCES, PRIZES AND PENALTIES

The use of career routes to understand politics better is sufficiently important, however, to stimulate us to alter the form in which this problem is stated. A political system may be likened to a three-dimensional billiards table, though one of expanding and contracting edges, replete with hills and valleys, dangerous cliffs, and *culs-de-sac*. The balls are to some extent self-propelled, but derive much of their energy from strategic position and combination with others. As the game progresses, shifts in position may alter the combinations sought by the players. The number of players is never stable. An exceptionally well placed shot may send a ball from one table on to a larger one. A poor one may drive the ball out of the game. The subject for enquiry, then, is to trace the path of the ball and to understand why it comes to rest at a particular point.

The metaphor suggests that we need to be concerned with arenas, resources, prizes, and penalties in order profitably to analyze political careers. The important point is not to take any of these as fixed and unvarying. A politician may be acting predominantly in one arena at one time and in another some time later. To a greater or lesser extent he may make an impact on several arenas simultaneously. The resources at his command often determine the arena in which he operates, but the strategic necessities of some other actor in another, perhaps larger, arena may suddenly endow him with the capability of escaping a local stage for a district or national system. A prime minister concerned with building his own political coalition may alter the position of many lesser actors. Understanding as much as possible of the *situation* in which the actors are currently involved is critical to explaining the arenas in which they choose to act, the resources they are able to amass and (quite a different question) to expend, as well as the prizes they seek and the penalties they evade.

Carrying out this exercise is an enormously complex research task. Being aware, though, of the fluidity with which one sort of political situation can abruptly shift or indistinguishably melt into one quite different helps to prevent the researcher from overlooking important causal factors. In this context, one might broaden the notion of 'middle-rank politician', asking what the constraints are that prevent given politicians from achieving greater influence or higher position in larger arenas than they actually do. Implicit in this revision is the examination of the reasons for the twists and turns their careers take in reaching this final point. In other words, one also needs to be concerned with explaining how they achieved the positions they managed to reach. The task is no different from that called for in considering top leaders. However, there is great advantage in calling attention to the less successful who occupy the 'catchment areas'. 'Who else', asks Morris-Jones, 'entered the race?'[2] The purpose of the question is to learn more about the course.

II. THE RELATIVE WEAKNESS OF INSTITUTIONALIZED PROCEDURES IN UGANDAN POLITICS

The complexity of post-independence politics in Uganda underscores all these considerations. As in many African and Asian countries the degree of acceptance of both formal and informal political procedures was narrow at independence and has steadily diminished since. Ugandan politicians possessing an aptitude for political survival had to take into their calculations at least the following considerations: an extraordinarily late start on Africanization of the higher public service, and poorly disciplined parties jostling one another in a hastily contrived electoral system that granted special privileges for the richest, largest, and most numerous unit. Since that unit (Buganda) was perceived in ethnic terms, particularly after the formation of a Baganda political movement called *Kabaka Yekka* (KY), others strove to mobilize viable ethnic coalitions. These were most plausible when formed at the district level, owing to indirect rule policies that equated 'tribe' and district or county. Consequently, achieving power at the centre depended on the formation of a coalition of support at the district level.

At the same time vigorous competition occurred within districts, in part owing to perceptions of the Democratic Party (DP) as the representative of Catholics and of the Uganda Peoples Congress (UPC) to a somewhat lesser degree as the representative of Protestants. Even as the UPC—the most skilfully directed of the three parties—began to gain ascendancy both in the districts and at the centre, it became painfully apparent not only that it clothed bitterly opposed factions within district branch organizations but that its leaders were becoming more and more closely allied with competing groupings of these factions. For all his many political abilities, Milton Obote proved incapable of peacefully containing these fragmented rival forces and turned to the prisons and the army in 1966 to cut the Gordian knot. This, of course, introduced (or rather reinforced) another complicating political factor, but one into which we need not inquire since Mukirane, with whose career we are concerned, died (by coincidence) in the same year.

A vicious circle became characteristic of Uganda in the half decade following 1962. Starting with new and relatively untried rules, political forces continually fragmented and recombined as politicians searched for adequate resources to achieve their goals and in the process bent the rules out of recognition. This meant that the boundaries between arenas became highly permeable—at least vertically, and occasionally horizontally—to the intervention of other actors seeking support.

To take an example from the present case, the seemingly senseless rigidity with which the Toro Kingdom government repelled the original, rather mild demands of political representation of the minority ethnic units, the Konzo and the Amba, led to a situation in which secession seemed to many the only way out (literally!). It occurred because the Toro government was simultaneously fighting a battle to improve its constitutional position in the national arena, for which it needed to claim (at least fictitiously) that all inhabitants of Toro were 'Toro', while it was also competing for prizes with the newly emergent social forces—the Konzo and the Amba—in the local arena. At the same time, the UPC leaders in Kampala were sending out contradictory signals of encouragement to both sides in an effort to defeat the DP in the 1962 election and subordinate it thereafter.[3] Through this thicket Ugandan politicians had to pick their way, attempting to discover paths toward prizes without benefit of precedent or stable procedures. We must be careful not to carry this point too far. There was a fund of idealism and goodwill that accompanied the UPC into independence. For the first five years heavy emphasis was placed by most officials on the letter of the constitution—political manoeuvring could be halted temporarily through judicial decisions. The political procedures prescribed by the constitution did function (until transformed or abolished). Consequently, there were identifiable structures in which 'encounters' between actors followed particular patterns. These created boundaries demarcating arenas.[4] All was not fluidity, then, though calculations necessarily had to take into account a variety of shifting factors, including repercussions in other arenas.

III. THE CAREER ROUTE OF ISAYA MUKIRANE

Mukirane was a Konzo, and that ethnic designation became quite early in his life the most salient form of identification for him personally and politically, as was also the case for many of his compatriots. Like all other social characteristics, ethnicity is significant in politics only when people decide it is and also decide to act on that perception. For both Konzo and Amba this became increasingly the case as the years of Protectorate rule drew to a close.

Konzo and Amba live on both sides of the border between Uganda and Zaire, with Konzo living in the Ruwenzori mountains but moving down to the plains in increasing numbers, and the Amba living on the plains to the north-west of the mountain range. The area is over two hundred miles from Kampala, in addition to being relatively inaccessible. So it comes as no surprise that education, medicine, and cash crops came later to the Konzo and Amba than to most people in Uganda. In particular, most members of both ethnic units were universally perceived as far behind the Toro (who outnumber the Konzo and Amba approximately 6:3:1). One contributing factor was the alliance the British made with the Toro aristocracy in order to reduce the military potential of Bunyoro when Protectorate rule was established. British officials supported the claims of the Toro Omukama (King) to a realm including those areas in which the Ugandan Amba and Konzo lived.

The contempt that the Toro felt for the Konzo and Amba increased as the gap in possession of western benefits widened. It was further secured by a virtual monopoly of political control up to independence. However, the Konzo and Amba began to make rapid economic strides during the 1950s, with the introduction of coffee, cotton, cocoa, and jobs in the Kilembe copper mines. Soon the counties in which they lived became the wealthiest in Toro Kingdom. The lowland areas began to attract many Toro looking for more fertile farms. The asymmetry between wealth and political control, the increasing competition for land, the discrimination in provision of schools, dispensaries, roads, government loans, and jobs, but above all the contempt in which the Toro held all Konzo and Amba, were the grievances that led to the Rwenzururu movement.[5]

When the British withdrawal became certain, the fears of what independence might bring crystallized the political demands growing out of these grievances and led to intense mobilization of members of both subordinate ethnic units. The Amba and Konzo, traditionally suspicious of each other, achieved a semblance of inter-ethnic unity, primarily at the level of their representatives in the *Rukurato* (Toro Kingdom parliament), which was lost shortly thereafter. The revival of memories of an earlier tax revolt led by three Konzo strengthened the growing movement against Toro control.

Mukirane was born about 1924 and brought up in a lowland area of Bwamba County in Toro. He was the eldest surviving son of his father's favourite wife. Both of his parents followed traditional Konzo religious beliefs. His father was a minor official of one of the few Konzo *gombolola* (sub-county) chiefs, whose daughter Mukirane later married in a Christian ceremony. Mukirane's relations with his father and his brothers were marked by disputes, particularly over land. Several of these reached the local courts.

He was educated at the local primary school and then at Nyakasura Secondary School near Fort Portal. He appears to have become a *mulokole* (a 'saved one'—a member of a fundamentalist Protestant fellowship professing belief in private sin and public confession). He passed his junior secondary leaving examination after three years, too poorly to enter senior secondary but well enough to go on to Mukono Teacher Training College in Buganda. He then returned to Toro to begin his primary school teaching career. The acquisition of a western education ultimately became a valuable political resource, since so few other Konzo had been to school.

He was transferred rapidly from one teaching position to another as he was constantly involved in disputes with his colleagues and headmasters. In several of these positions he lasted no more than a day or two. Most of the disputes concerned trivial matters and revolved around Mukirane's sense of dignity and rightful authority. Many of his antagonists were Toro, but some were Konzo, and his later disputes with Konzo and Amba Rwenzururu partisans follow the same pattern, so the hostility does not appear to have been entirely inter-ethnic, though it must have been partly that. These incidents became a useful resource when Mukirane began actively to oppose the Toro Government.

During one of his periods of unemployment as a teacher (in 1954), he met Tom Stacey, a British journalist, and acted as the latter's guide and interpreter on a two month trip through the mountains. Stacey was collecting material on Konzo customs for a novel, and seems to have provided an example and perhaps a technique that stimulated Mukirane to recover the history and customs of his 'people'. In conjunction with Samwire Bukombi, his father-in-law, who may have begun independently his own researches into the history of the Konzo, and a few other acquaintances, Mukirane set up the Bakonjo Life History Research Society (BLHRS). He became its most active worker and organizer, later assuming the title of President. He obtained permission from the District Commissioner to travel throughout the mountains in pursuit of this 'research'.

His close identification with the revival of Konzo customs, language, and therefore pride, at a time when political uncertainties were growing, later became an extraordinarily valuable resource. More mundane, but of no less political importance, was the growing organization he was building with representatives in each county in which Konzo could be found. These personal contacts with Konzo all over the mountains played a role in the later electoral campaign and proved crucial when the secession occurred.

The Toro government's struggle to gain a kingdom equivalent in privilege to that of Buganda had meant that no direct elections to the *Rukurato* occurred before 1961, which left government totally in the hands of the Toro. The election held in that year resulted in a major shift in political representation. One-third of the representatives elected were Amba or Konzo. They included Mukirane and two Amba who were also recognized as leaders, Yerimiya Kawamara and Petero Mupalya. In an effort to retain political control the Toro leadership failed to select any of the Amba or Konzo representatives for the legislative committee instructed to negotiate the final constitutional relationship between Toro and Uganda. As one of their first political actions Amba and Konzo leaders demanded to be included.

Mukirane was placed on this committee and proposed that the Toro constitution make reference to the Toro, Konzo, and Amba as the three 'tribes' of Toro and that local government positions be divided among them. These proposals were rejected and Mukirane was deliberately left behind when the committee members went to Entebbe to discuss constitutional arrangements with the Governor. (The District Commissioner arranged separate transport for him.) At Entebbe, much to the discomfiture of the Toro members, Mukirane demanded the creation of a separate district within Uganda for the Amba and the Konzo. This escalation of the original proposals was underlined by seventeen of the twenty-one Amba and Konzo representatives walking out of a special session of the *Rukurato*, called to consider this new threat. At this time the seventeen toured their constituencies to build support.

The Toro government struck back by arresting the three leaders, Mukirane, Kawamara, and Mupalya, at one such meeting, on a charge of insulting the *Omukama*. They were placed in prison for six weeks (on remand), convicted, and released on bail pending appeal to the High Court in Kampala. The prison warden confiscated money belonging to Kawamara, intended to be his deposit as UPC candidate for Bwamba County in the April 1962 elections for the National Assembly. As a result Kawamara was unable to run and Rwenzururu was denied the possibility of a spokesman with an official position in the national arena.

After the UPC/KY coalition took office, Obote appointed a Commission of Inquiry under Dr F. Ssembeguya to investigate the problems presented by this conflict. Obote's intervention was at least in part a response to the widespread disorder and refusal to pay poll taxes and licence fees fomented by Konzo and Amba in the areas around the mountains in August 1962, as well as by a steady stream of petitions and newspaper letters composed by the three leaders who were in Kampala awaiting their trial. The leaders urged calm in the Ruwenzoris, confident that the report of the Commission would recommend a separate district. In the event the Commission took a sympathetic view, but advised against carving a new district out of Toro. Of greater significance, the Commissioners produced their report the day after independence, by which time the new Ugandan constitution prevented the government from easily changing district boundaries.[6]

Shortly before the report was released, however, and about three weeks before his trial, Mukirane left Kampala for the Ruwenzori mountains, in violation of his restriction order, and proclaimed Rwenzururu a state separate from Uganda. The original demand for equality had now reached its extreme expression in full fledged secession. This step also marked Mukirane's final break with Kawamara and Mupalya, who insisted—with some later regrets—on a political solution within Uganda. Since the previous March relations between them had deteriorated on a personal level as well, particularly over Mukirane's penchant for issuing documents under his own name as 'President' not only of their organization but also of the Konzo and Amba. Many of the better educated Konzo, including those who had been officials of the BLHRS, were equally dismayed by Mukirane's decision to press for secession.

The last turning point in stiffening his resolve to make Rwenzururu an independent state may have been his rejection of an offer by Obote to negotiate a settlement in February 1963. This offer was carried up the mountains by Stacey, and may have been the only serious attempt by the Ugandan government to bargain directly with Mukirane.[7] After some hesitation Mukirane refused to participate (the proposed site was under the control of the Uganda Rifles), and retreated to the Zaire side of the mountains, leaving Stacey to return empty-handed. From this time onwards the Ugandan central administration followed a complex and not always consistent strategy to give the Konzo and Amba much of the substance of separation from Toro (by directly administering the 'disturbed areas') without attempting the task—made virtually impossible by the exacting provisions of the constitution—of creating a new district. The policy was accompanied by sporadic military and police incursions and, ultimately, the stationing of troops in the lower reaches of the mountains.[8]

Whatever resources Mukirane may have lost by his bid to move from the national to the international arena, he probably gained in the short run. He was able to recapture the most extreme elements in the movement—who had got well in front of him through uncoordinated upheaval. He had a better bargaining position with the government at Entebbe. And he may have believed that, with international assistance, the new state could go it alone—like the hopes of so many other politicians in Africa during the early 1960s.

His first acts were to train both a security force and typists who could publicize his directives and thus make credible the existence of his 'government'. He established an administrative system and collected taxes, using the framework of the BLHRS branches. Plans were laid to close all Ugandan schools in the mountains and re-open them as Rwenzururu schools, using the Konzo language for instruction. Systematic attacks were made on all Toro who remained in the area near or on the mountains, and all Toro in Ugandan or Toro government service. These attacks later shifted to Konzo and Amba supporters of the Ugandan government and those who failed to pay their poll tax and serve the new state.

Mukirane was finally in his element. His leadership was undisputed, though not all his directives were acceptable to his supporters in the mountains. Shortly after he set up the government, he declared himself an *Omukama* and his government became known as the Rwenzururu Kingdom Government (RKG). For the remainder of his life he was the main source of ideas and policies for the RKG structure. Whether or not his goals were desirable, there can be no denying that he was most effective in devising techniques to create a government and make it run smoothly. His followers remained united behind him—prepared to pay their taxes and to follow orders. Perhaps his greatest triumph lay in the continuation of the RKG after his death in September 1966. His son was proclaimed king under the guardianship of a regent, in accordance with his wish. His prime minister took over active direction of the government, though that move led to instability and the ejection of a faction opposing the new leadership a few months later.

IV. CAREER DECISIONS AND POLITICAL SYSTEMS

What does Mukirane's career tell us about the relationship between resources and arenas available in Uganda? In suggesting an answer it may be useful to contrast the route he took with that of the two Amba leaders he left behind in Kampala. All three had been primary school teachers in Bwamba, and their pre-political careers had brought them into close contact. They were elected to the Toro *Rukurato* at the same time. They forged the political alliance between Amba and Konzo, and they were accepted as the major leaders of what was perceived to be a united movement during its early political stages. But their facade of unity was broken by Mukirane's flight to the mountains.

The two Amba leaders stood trial and were sent to prison. After completing their sentences they continued to spend much of their time in Kampala in the belief that their task consisted of influencing national Ugandan leaders to create a district separate from Toro. They chose to act primarily in the national arena, while Mukirane entered a new and smaller one. Aside from an occasional meeting and expressions of sympathy, the Ugandan government tended to by-pass them. By 1964 Mupalya shifted his allegiance to the Ugandan government and accepted the argument that no new district would be forthcoming. He was rewarded, following the reorganization of district administration in 1967, with the political post of Assistant Secretary-General of Toro, and penalized by the loss of most of his former supporters, who regarded him as a turncoat and an opportunist. Kawamara remained outside the government entirely, following the loss of his opportunity to stand for the National Assembly, and never deviated from his conviction that a separate district within Uganda was the only solution. By the late 1960s, however, he was a frustrated and bitter man, unsure that his decision had been correct. He toyed with the idea of entering the elections of 1971 under Obote's unique one-party scheme, but these were cancelled of course as a consequence of the Amin coup.

Any comparison of the three leaders must take into account that the Amba amount to only one-third of the numbers of the Konzo. The plains in which they live are far harder territory for a guerilla band to hold against conventional forces. With the Amba leaders counselling against violent opposition, disruptive incidents in Bwamba tended to be the work of uncoordinated small bands (each employing the name 'Rwenzururu'), and gradually faded away. With the possible resources at their command greatly reduced—partly as a result of their insistence upon operating primarily in the national (and for Mupalya later also the Toro) arena, both leaders ceased to possess much influence on subsequent events.

Mukirane also narrowed his range of options after independence. However, his choice of the small secessionist arena meant that he continued to make a serious impact on the calculations of the Ugandan Cabinet, and more directly on those of the Toro leadership. The resources he could command were beyond the reach of his former Amba compatriots. Like them, he had acquired the western education that gave him deference among his fellows, and like them he had worked in various associations. However, he had been engaged in this process for seven years prior to independence, and had begun building a network of supporters when no one in Uganda (himself included) anticipated that independence would arrive as early as 1962. Support for him had been demonstrated in the 1961 *Rukurato* elections, and his followers were delighted by the accusation that he 'sat on the Toro Omukama's chair'—one of the events that led to the arrest of the three leaders for insulting the Omukama, and to that potent political resource—imprisonment by one's oppressors.

Like the other two, his position as a leader was consolidated by spending time in Kampala close to the national government. His declaration of an independent state was widely accepted by the Konzo and perhaps, at first, by some Amba, until it was realized that he intended more than a bargaining tactic. While losing the support of the few educated Konzo in lowland areas, Mukirane greatly increased his available resources by taking firm hold on the partisans of violence. Through their support, his own organizational dexterity, and the inaccessible terrain of his mountain sanctuary, Mukirane ended up with control over formidable political resources for limited purposes. Central to this achievement was the audacity of his unswerving belief in what he could create were he permitted undisputed command. Having brought him no end of trouble in the earlier stages of his career, his insistence on his primacy, symbolized by his assumption of kingship, ultimately gave coherence to the influence he had accumulated.

We would be wrong to assume that these resources can simply be added one on top of another in order to assess the political distance

Mukirane travelled. A closer look makes clear that his resources were specific to particular situations and particular arenas. For example, Mukirane's personality made him a rather unlikely leader (as distinct from agitator) until the grievances of the Konzo reached flash-point. His educational attainments were useful in one arena, but not in another. They were meaningful to the Konzo, but were not particularly impressive to the Ugandan political elite. His activities in Kampala just prior to independence had the effect of building his resources in two distinct (though obviously inter-related) arenas simultaneously. On the one hand, they reinforced the image among Konzo of the centrality of his leadership (with Kawamara and Mupalya) by his separation from them in the national capital (at the cost of almost losing touch with the situation at home), while these activities also increased the degree to which high officials of the Ugandan government were prepared to meet him, since his proximity and publicity gave him the appearance of speaking for others possessing his ethnic characteristics.

In an effort to reconstruct his decision to secede, it may be useful to conceive of him as following several careers in different arenas, each having an impact on his calculations of future steps in the others. His flight to the mountains, for example, may have been fuelled by the necessity of regaining a leadership that events appear rapidly to have outdistanced in order to strengthen his hand for bargaining with Ugandan officials. Or his flight may have been a decision to change arenas in order to assert personal domination. More likely, he decided to hold on to both options until forced by Stacey's mission to choose between them.

What can be learned about the political systems in which Mukirane participated by examining the path he took to secession rather than recruitment into a relatively unimportant political position in Toro Kingdom? To state the question in this form is to leave out his own perception (at least in 1962 and perhaps earlier) of the third and most promising career—head of a new Rwenzururu district. The Ugandan political system was changing so rapidly at this point, with constitutional conferences permitting questions to be raised about so many prior arrangements, that it would have been politically irrational for Mukirane not to calculate the possibility. Popular support lay there, and the DP government had created a new district in Sebei the year before. Even closer to home, one solution formally proposed for the 'Lost Counties' claimed by both Buganda and Bunyoro (and which lay on the borders of Toro) was a separate district. His advocacy of this course neatly combined popular policy and personal advancement.

By the same token, Toro politicians took a rigid and uncompromising stance towards all suggestions regarding political inclusion of the Konzo and Amba. They saw very well that the absence of established rules might cause the contraction of the arena which they controlled which could have a disastrous impact on their own stock of resources. So a career route through Toro politics could not have appeared particularly promising to Mukirane.

Was it the Ugandan government's refusal to agree to a new district that caused him to opt for and persist in secession, or the personality factors that gave him enormous satisfaction in no longer having to be submissive to any authority? An answer has to take into account both the sympathy of Ugandan national leaders for the plight of the Konzo and Amba and their decision to solve the problem at least temporarily by taking over direct administration of the mountain areas.

Like many other fluid situations, however, this one hardened as Ugandan leaders attempted in the first years of independence to follow constitutional procedures while Mukirane became increasingly wedded to his kingship and his kingdom. Ugandan leaders could increase their power by stabilizing procedures and rules over which they could exert a fair degree of control. Mukirane's limited resources could be maximized and expended flexibly to the degree that politics remained uninstitutionalized. Fluidity of political structures multiplies the number of possible career routes, while institutionalization reduces them. Mukirane's decision to secede was a response to unsettled political possibilities. The Ugandan government's uncertain attempts to reduce these to more orderly channels ultimately failed, though for reasons not involving Mukirane. In the long run, however, the political requirements of each made *rapprochement* impossible, since neither would act in the other's arena.

7

THE POLITICIAN AS AGITATOR IN EASTERN UGANDA

Michael Twaddle

Scholars are frequently naive when expressing opinions about politicians. Sometimes they are too utopian, sometimes excessively cynical. In the first years of African independence it was the utopian strain that was most virulent. In East Africa it was to be seen in the debate about the respective importance of nationalist elites and peasant discontent in the emergence of modern politics, a debate which largely took for granted that it was African rather than European political behaviour which required explanation. With the proliferation of one-party states and military regimes in more recent years, utopianism has subsided and cynicism become more prevalent. Currently this strain is detectable in the widespread assumption outside Africa that, if independence from colonial rule was partly gained by African endeavour, over most of middle Africa it was more than half granted by departing Europeans.

In this situation the only people to take responsibility upon themselves were those with literate, administrative and managerial capacities equally necessary to handle a political party or govern a state. For the people there was hardly any alternative but to follow this leadership. Mass political participation was primarily expressed in a choice, at the occasion of elections, between the issues set forth by the parties.[1]

This was originally written about Mali. If political recruitment was as straightforward as that throughout middle Africa, there would be little point in examining further the careers of any middle-rank politicians in eastern Uganda, beyond setting out in greater detail how in district council elections during the early 1960s there were fewer lawyers and teachers and more farmers and local traders as candidates compared with the competitors for seats in the national assembly, where literacy and managerial skills were in greater demand.

That, however, is not the strategy of the present paper.[2] This revolves rather around an attempt to illuminate the complexities of political recruitment and participation in the first (and, as yet, last) Ugandan general elections of 1961 and 1962, by focusing attention on a category of politicians of an intermediate sort (between 'nationalist elites' and 'peasant discontent') which has hitherto received little attention from scholars. This paper seeks to confirm that this is a category worthy of attention rather than disregard.

Immediately before Idi Amin seized power in Uganda, most of these individuals were considered cynically by local Ugandans as spoilsmen. But that had not always been the case, and we should avoid the cynical error of retrospectively imposing that role on men whose initial entry into politics was as moralistic crusaders against arbitrary colonial rule. We should also avoid the opposite utopian trap of playing down the extent to which much of this moralism was actually written into their early political roles by British colonial officials: hence our concern with the model of 'the politician as agitator'. Largely for illustrative convenience, most of the 'agitators' considered come from Bunyole county in the Bukedi district of eastern Uganda, though for comparative purposes something is also said about similar politicians in the immediately adjacent counties of Bugwere and West Budama and, at the very end of the paper, something about a very dissimilar one in Bukedi district, too.

This, some students of Ugandan politics may retort, is geographically unfair. For, as regards the 1962 election, Bukedi is specifically isolated by Rothchild and Rogin in their standard account of the politics of decolonization in Uganda as one of six 'deviant' districts that caused their statistical correlation between voting behaviour and religious affiliation to be much lower throughout the country than it had been during the election of the previous year.[3] This fact itself, however, makes Bukedi district an important one for understanding the religious constraints (if any) upon Ugandan politics in both years, while some of the reasons advanced to explain statistical deviance ('Bukedi and Bugisu have long traditions of active, complicated and violent politics. Tribal and clan voting are important factors, and elections produce many independent candidates'.)[4] suggest that Bukedi should also be important for an appreciation of the tribal constraints (if any) upon political leadership in late colonial Uganda.

Bukedi district is certainly ethnically heterogeneous. Functioning for several centuries as an 'ethnic corridor'[5] between the Kalenjin-speaking peoples of northwestern Kenya and the Bantu-speakers of northern Uganda and west-central Kenya, it is hardly surprising that each county in Bukedi district contains members of at least one separate linguistic group. Moving from north to south, there are Iteso as well as Bagwere in Pallisa county, Bagwere in Bugwere county, Banyole in Bunyole county, Jopadhola in West Budama, Itesyo in East Budama (Tororo), and both Bagwe and Basamia in Samia-Bugwe county. But there are elements of unity here as well as forces for division. Differing in language, these communities are alike in having been united during the pre-colonial period more through ritual mechanisms than by specifically political ones. Specifically political roles are here the consequence of British colonial rule.[6]

First, between sixty and eighty years ago, Baganda chiefs were introduced into Bukedi district to persuade local cultivators to grow cash crops in order to pay colonial taxes (one by-product of this process was that Luganda became the political language of Bukedi district). Then particular lineages with ritual prestige were transformed into providers of successor chiefs. The first process quickened local ethnic consciousness by providing in the persons of imported Baganda chiefs an ostentatious reference group against which lesser leaders locally might compare themselves.[7] This development was further speeded up by the feeling on the part of many British colonial officials that, however distasteful it might appear to modern Europeans, tribal chauvinism was a legitimate form of political activity for poor African farmers. The second process had the contrary effect, fragmenting rather than consolidating ethnic consciousness in Bunyole county, but its force was nullified by (among other things) the additional feeling of many British colonial officials that, unless provoked by understandable religious hatreds, intra-tribal conflict was an illegitimate form of political activity. It was the work of 'worthless agitators', and as such should be severely suppressed.

The suppression of 'worthless agitators' did not, for most of the time, present British colonial officials, as overlords of Bukedi district, with problems of unmanageable proportions. But in 1960 British management of politics in Bukedi went sadly awry. Serious rioting took place and very quickly got out of hand. The trouble started in Bunyole at a meeting organized by Joseph Wasukulu and Nasanairi Hamala, but most damage was done in Bugwere, Pallisa and West Budama counties. The rioting was not primarily anti-British, as the Provincial Commissioner concerned noted with some relief, but was 'directed principally against the African Authority and Councillors'.[8] This opinion was seconded by the special commissioners, who enquired into the disturbances: 'chiefs were one of the two main dislikes which became manifest during the disturbances', the other being the closely related question of how taxes were collected.[9]

Concerning the causes of the riots, the special commissioners noted three peculiarities of Bukedi district: the heterogeneity of the tribal groups ('greater than we have seen in Africa outside what is popularly known as a detribalised area'), the absence of traditional chiefs, and marked rivalry between Catholics and Protestants. They also remarked upon the behaviour of two local politicians: Balaki Kirya, elected member of the Uganda Legislative Council for the whole of Bukedi district since the (first direct) election of 1958, and Joseph Wasukulu, subsequently to be parliamentary candidate for the south-central Bukedi constituency at the 1961 and 1962 elections. Kirya had toured Bukedi shortly before the riots, telling many of his audiences that men who paid colonial taxes were like men who wore women's clothes. When rioting broke out, Kirya was on a visit to India. Wasukulu was in Uganda, but told the special commissioners that he was 'a "lieutenant to Mr Kirya"' and that 'no meeting could be held by Mr Kirya at which he was not present'.[10] Clearly, for our present purposes as well as those of British colonial officials, both politicians were 'agitators'.

That, however, is not how such figures have been customarily categorized by scholars. It therefore behoves us to justify categorizing them thus in this paper.

To start with, the politician as agitator was an actor's model of politics and one espoused in eastern Uganda by a category of actor (British colonial officials) sufficiently influential in real life for their views to have more than merely academic interest. This in itself makes the model worthy of attention rather than disregard. Analytically, to be sure, British colonial officials made the model explain too many things. But analytical extravagance is not an irremediable defect in social science. British colonial officials also made 'inter-religious strife' and 'tribal differences' explain too many things in Bukedi district, but that did not stop 'religious factions' and 'competing ambitions of a multiplicity of small tribes' both becoming generally accepted elements of post-colonial academic comment on politics there.[11] In fact, the model of the politician as agitator stands up to testing as a conceptualization of real life (as opposed to being just an influential actor's model) much better than the stuff about religious and tribal differences which has passed too easily from the conventional wisdom of colonial officialdom into the conventional wisdom of post-colonial scholarship. More serious charges against the model concern its limitation in time (to the earliest stages of political mobilization) and its cultural bias (towards societies espousing basically egalitarian values), and the suggestion that 'the politician as agitator' is too vague a model to be of much explanatory use. The developmental and cultural limitations we must largely accept, but we may also note that in a poor community of African farmers subjected to arbitrary government by appointive chiefs imposed from above, the politician is likely to emerge (if at all) as the random articulator of anti-chiefly resentment and, where politics are random and vague, loose conceptualization is sometimes preferable to taut definition.

Of course, British colonial officials did not put it that way, largely because they considered Bunyole county to be tribally homogeneous.

After all, Banyole spoke a separate language, Lunyole. But closer inspection reveals not one language in Bunyole county but several: Luhadyo in the east, Lusabi with a markedly different tonal system and vocabulary further west, and Luwesa still further away with both pronunciation and vocabulary much closer to Lusamia than to either of the two other dialects.[12] To these linguistic divisions must be added internal political cleavages, some of them persisting from the pre-colonial period (which in this part of Africa was well within living memory), others the creation of successive colonial chiefly spoils systems. There were also several further cultural differences. Indeed, so many were the cleavages within Bunyole county itself that it was difficult for any budding politician to build durable alliances there without outside assistance. Local social structure did not make it easy for such men to build upon and transcend the role written for them by British colonial officials, the politician as agitator, however much they themselves might have preferred to behave otherwise.

To be sure, one must define carefully what is meant by 'politician' here. Eridadi Mutenga was probably thinking of two still earlier categories of lesser leader in Bukedi district when he wrote that Baganda were the first politicians in Bunyole.[13] It was Baganda chiefs who first introduced a specifically political authority (in the Weberian sense) into what would later become Bunyole county during the last years of the nineteenth century and the first decades of the twentieth century: men who came to Bukedi with Semei Kakungulu, that 'very useful pioneer and imperialist, notwithstanding his black face',[14] and whose initiation into politics had taken place mostly in the nearby kingdom of Buganda well before the period of British colonial rule commenced either there or in Bukedi. It was also Baganda traders who established the first branches of the earliest territorial political associations in Bukedi after the First World War: men like Meusera Busagwa, the local chairman of the Young Buganda Association, who so annoyed one District Commissioner by first failing to dismount from his bicycle when passing the DC in the road, then giving the DC's wife a glance which the DC considered 'open to objection';[15] or Erasito Bazonona, the catechist-turned-trader who bombarded subsequent DCs with regular denunciations of the Indian trade and oversaw the foundation of the Bunyole Welfare Association as a local elite pressure group. But after the Second World War, it was to another category of 'agitator' that both Banyole and British increasingly accorded the title 'politician' —the ex-chiefs, ex-teachers, and ex-clerks who became members of the newly formed councils at district, county, and sub-county levels—and it is with this particular category of lesser leader that we are most concerned in this paper.

The theory behind the newly formed councils must be stated briefly. In 1935 Sir Philip Mitchell became governor of the Uganda Protectorate. Hotfoot from the ideological hothouse that even then was Dar-es-Salaam, Mitchell was appalled at the theoretical slackness which he found among his new subordinates in Uganda: they were calling appointive chieftaincy in areas like Bukedi district 'indirect administration'. That, argued Sir Philip in a special pamphlet, was wrong.[16] The higher subordinates in the protectorate administration soon took the hint, none more quickly than the provincial commissioner of the Eastern Province, where most formerly stateless people were (and are still) to be found in Uganda. The powers of appointive chiefs, ordered the provincial commissioner, should be tempered by the establishment of councils reflecting local sentiment. Thereby not only would 'educated agitators' currently excluded from the charmed circles of appointive chiefs be placated by being given a say in running local affairs as well as chances now and then of becoming chiefs themselves, but the ground would be cut away from beneath the feet of 'worthless agitators' such as ex-clerks, ex-chiefs, and ex-teachers.[17] Alas, neither hope materialized.

They did not materialize because the basic political issue was dodged in Bukedi district: how to reduce the arbitrariness of appointive chiefly rule over poor farmers espousing basically egalitarian values. Indeed, the establishment of partially elected councils at the sub-county, county, and district level made the matter worse rather than better. Thinking that they had dealt with the problem of political opposition, British colonial officials now turned to questions of administrative reform. Bunyole county was amalgamated with Bugwere and Pallisa counties to form a single 'division'. Besides thereby enlarging the room for chiefly manoeuvre, the establishment of partially elected councils at each level within the 'division' made appointive chiefly behaviour even more arbitrary. For, while many of the ex-chiefs, ex-clerks, and ex-teachers whom the provincial commissioner had been so concerned to silence were elected council members, chiefs remained chairmen, and the temptation to manipulate attendance as well as decisions at council meetings was therefore considerable. Many irregularities occurred. At the district level, British colonial officials did not behave so very differently. Having set up the Bukedi district council as basically a talking shop, they too got on with running things much as before.

Inevitably, council members were frustrated. But political frustration does not necessarily lead to political action. For that to happen there must be not only frustration but predisposition among political leaders to act, and congruence between political leadership and popular discontent. In Bunyole county predisposition to act was present in the council members who had lost previous paid employment, while local values ensured that popular respect would be accorded to any individual sufficiently stubborn and well known (these are the qualities most frequently mentioned) to protest publicly against arbitrary chiefly overrule. When such men elsewhere in middle Africa are mentioned in the literature it is usually as 'new men' created by western education, but the most important point about them in local terms is that they were mostly yesterday's men.

On 20 April 1951, the provincial commissioner with responsibility for Bunyole met several such individuals in the district commissioner's office at Mbale, and he told them that

> there might be some slight justification for rivalry between tribes: there could be no justification whatever for dissension between groups within a tribe. This dissension was fostered largely by a group of self-seeking individuals who were uninterested in the welfare of the people as a whole. Amongst these individuals were ex-Gombolola [sub-county] Chiefs who had failed in their appointments, traders who failed to make a success of business, and men who had been jailed for dishonesty. These men made it their business, because they had failed themselves, to try to make others fail.

The substance of this harangue was subsequently circulated throughout Bukedi district, where it was also remarked that such men 'retarded progress' and 'sowed the seeds of dissension in Bunyuli, and made the Banyuli a laughing stock among other tribes of Bukedi', and 'The Provincial Commissioner will not be intimidated by such a worthless set of agitators, and has full powers, which he will not hesitate to invoke, for the suppression of any disturbances these people may try to make.'[18]

This was not the first occasion on which the provincial commissioner had been perturbed by 'worthless agitation' in Bunyole. In 1943 councillors from there had boycotted his tour of Bukedi district because of the amalgamation of their county with Bugwere and Pallisa. To start with, the local district commissioner had assumed that this particular 'agitation' had religious roots. At one of his meetings on tour 'an RC favouring amalgamation was hit over the head', while at others he noticed 'two schools regarding the amalgamation, one led by the CMS teachers and aided by the Mohamedans and the other led by the RC teachers'.[19] A special enquiry by six appointive chiefs from elsewhere in eastern Uganda—two Catholic, two Muslim, and two Protestant—failed to substantiate this hypothesis. Instead, they discovered that most Banyole taxpayers had apparently been in favour of the amalgamation until the division chief, who happened to come from Bugwere, drove through Bunyole county with somebody in the back of his motor-car sounding out the drum-beat 'Surrender yourselves that I may rule you.'[20]

This drum-beat annoyed a number of taxpayers in Bunyole. Soon 465 of them (there were about 8,000 altogether) had put their names to a special letter of protest to the district commissioner; a boycott of shoppers had been arranged ('if any person went to his shop to buy salt, cigarettes or any other sort of article such a man should first be asked by the shopkeeper whether he does not like the amalgamation to Bugwere, and if anyone said that he liked the amalgamation he should not be allowed to buy anything'), special tickets were being sold to raise money, and threats of violence were also being made. Under the stress of the ethnic appeal ('My mother came from Bunyuli and my father lives in Bugwere, which of the two shall I spear?') and the difficulty of keeping any anti-chiefly coalition together in Bunyole county for any length of time ('Have you chosen this one too? Only the other day his father surrendered to the Europeans as if he were a female dog'), the anti-amalgamation campaign soon fell apart—but not before the campaign had been taken to protectorate headquarters in Uganda, and the leader of the campaign also threatened to go to London if necessary. That possibility was disturbing to local British officials. In London the objections to amalgamation might well sound reasonable ('They were deprived of their own county chief, the headquarters of the division at Budaka was far away and there was a big swamp in between, also they have received no profit from the amalgamation'), while British reactions to the agitation in Uganda might well appear rather mean in London. For, upon first protesting against the amalgamation, the leading protester had his pension as an ex-sub-county chief stopped, and his response to this piece of spitefulness could prove embarrassing if broadcast around London: 'On constituting councils in each tribe the Government impressed upon us that every tribe might bring forward its difficulties through the councils.' This was precisely what the unfortunate ex-chief had done. The governor of Uganda acted speedily. Bunyole county was unamalgamated. Two sub-county chiefs who had proved least energetic in repressing the campaign against amalgamation were dismissed. The ex-chief who had led the campaign also did not have his pension restored.[21]

His name was Musa Kasakya. In 1936 he had been retired from the sub-county chieftaincy of Kachonga for reasons that are not entirely clear, and little is known about his early life beyond the fact that he was the protégé of a Ganda Muslim chief who came with Kakungulu to Bukedi. Also involved in the anti-amalgamation agitation was Erika Higenyi, a former CMS teacher who had recently lost his job on taking a second wife, and Nasanairi Hamala, a cash clerk in the African local government office at Mbale who had been dismissed from his post when somebody stole some money and somebody else remembered that Hamala had been convicted of corruption in the army during the Second World War.[22] For all three loss of paid employment was a serious blow in a poor farming community. To add to their discomfort the provincial commissioner harangued them about being failures in life; he made no attempt, however, to restore Kasakya's pension. It was therefore hardly surprising that when the next spate of 'agitation' erupted in Bunyole county Kasakya was again its leader.

This concerned the succession to the sub-county chieftaincy of Mazimasa. There was considerable resentment in Bunyole over the way Yakobo Munabi, the new county chief, was building up his patronage network of friends and relatives from the two westerly sub-counties of Budumba and Busaba at the expense of the three easterly ones of Mazimasa, Kachonga, and Butaleja. Fortunately for Munabi, written denunciations tended to be either simply insulting ('His character is the same as that of Hitler') or impossibly allusive ('recently he received a bribe from a sergeant who had stolen a cow at Tororo'). But in March 1951 Munabi rigged the sub-county election at Mazimasa so that it went to another eastern man. Musa Kasakya protested. He collected sufficient signatures for the local district commissioner to be compelled to investigate the matter. While admitting privately that there might have been some small irregularity ('The absence of these four councillors may have upset the balance of power'), he thought the councillors naive in the extreme: 'They apparently look on chieftainships as a source of profit which should be distributed among the more clamorous sections of the community without any regard to the merit of the candidates or the public good.' 'Obviously', he continued without conscious irony, they had 'much to learn concerning the working of councils and democracy in general.'[23] To add injustice to untruth, the charge that Musa Kasakya, Erika Higenyi, and Nasanairi Hamala among others had levelled against the county chief was now levelled against them. As a circular now issued to all local chiefs declared: 'It would be better for such people to work for the good of their country rather than merely for the good of themselves and their immediate relatives.'[24] Not unnaturally, this increased their sense of injury and heightened the normative appeal of the first emissaries of the Uganda National Congress to arrive in Bunyole county.

This was in 1952. UNC had considerable difficulty in arousing initial support in Bunyole, as almost everywhere in eastern Uganda, but in Musa Kasakya, Erika Higenyi, and Nasanairi Hamala it found attentive listeners and energetic allies. All three became early branch chairmen. All three are usually mentioned whenever an elderly Munyole is asked about political parties in Bunyole. The slogans which they shouted ('Drive the European away so that we may eat meat') easily lend themselves to retrospective interpretation as the slogans of spoilsmen, as, too, does their early uprooting of township boundaries as epiphenomena of anti-Asian sentiment. But the very frequency with which politicians like Higenyi say that what first attracted them to the Uganda National Congress was distaste for being repeatedly told that Africans were incapable of organizing anything should not be dismissed as mere rhetoric. It is the cry of men previously condemned by local society as well as by British colonial policy to being 'worthless agitators' now being initiated into a wider political consciousness.

Within four years Congress reached its peak of popularity in Bunyole county. The peak itself was probably the visit to Butaleja by Kabaka Mutesa II of Buganda shortly after his return from unwilling exile in Britain. The visit is popularly remembered for two things: Mutesa's suede shoes, and his appeal for everybody to join UNC. For Banyole, the success of this appeal was symbolized by the playing of *ebasa* drums alongside *ekongo* ones on that occasion, signifying participation by people living throughout Bunyole county and beyond.

For reasons that are well known, things soon fell apart. The faction committed to defending 'our things' triumphed in Buganda, and in 1958 Buganda boycotted the first direct elections to the legislative council in Uganda. UNC suffered several splits. The newly formed Democratic Party spread beyond Buganda with such success that it won the 1961 election, though another electoral boycott in Buganda also helped: the UNC splinter-groups that were now the Uganda Peoples Congress came a close second. In 1962 the tables were turned, largely because this time the *Kabaka Yekka* ('King alone') party contested the election in Buganda in alliance with the UPC, which now only contested seats outside Buganda; the DP contested seats in both parts of Uganda.[25]

To achieve electoral success outside Buganda, however, the Democratic Party had to accommodate itself to local grievances much like its rivals. In Bunyole county it entered, much as the UNC had done almost a decade before, through a politician whom British colonial officials considered a 'worthless agitator' and whom local people respected for his stubbornness and persistence in protesting against chiefly abuses. Sebastian Orach came from outside Bunyole, from West Budama county. He was a Catholic. He attacked 'Protestants who have been ruling us too long' during his electoral campaign for the south-central Bukedi constituency as DP candidate in 1961, as also did his Muslim supporters. Considering that there were many Catholic voters in his constituency and Protestant-Catholic conflict was well known in that half of it lying in West Budama county (Kisoko, Paya, Nagongera, and Kirewa sub-counties), and not wholly unknown to British colonial officials in the other half lying in Bunyole county (Mazimasa, Butaleja, Budumba, and Busaba sub-counties), he should have won hands down. He lost. He was not an unimpressive personality. He did not lose because his opponent, Jospeh Wasukulu, amassed more tribal support: Mwima Hyabene, the third candidate, would have lopped his 1,231 votes off Wasukulu (who got 8,196) rather than from Orach (who got 6,739) if 'tribalism' had been as important a fact in voting patterns as is frequently assumed. Banyole say that he lost because Wasukulu was a better speaker and a better known politician as a result of the Bukedi riots, when together with Nasanairi Hamala and Balaki Kirya he had championed the right of African taxpayers to pay lower taxes; and, in view of the respect with which previous 'worthless agitators' had been held in earlier 'agitations' in Bunyole county, this seems a much more likely explanation.

In 1962, however, the tables were turned locally between DP and UPC. Orach stood down as DP candidate in south-central Bukedi, and in a two-man contest the new DP man, a Muslim trader, got 12,842 votes to the 10,200 obtained by Joseph Wasukulu. Muslim opinion in Bunyole split two ways: in the east mostly voting for Wasukulu, in the west largely supporting Ali Kasakya. In so far as any common factor is mentioned as an explanation by Banyole for voting behaviour during this election, it is personal self-interest. For every voter mobilized because of his religion, there was another mobilized because he was a relative, and a third recruited because he lived in the same area. The chiefly spoils system now coalesced with networks of agitators and non-agitators alike. In north-central Bukedi constituency the former county chief, who had been the principal target of Kirya's populist attacks before the Bukedi riots, now became one of Kirya's main supporters. Statistical correlations between voting figures and tribal or religious affiliations are not very revealing in this situation. Nor are lists of candidates' formal qualifications. Their most useful informal qualification in Bukedi district was to have been branded as 'worthless agitators' by British colonial officials who regarded tribal separatism as inevitable in black Africa, religious conflict as understandable in light of earlier European history, but 'intra-tribal conflict' of the sort engaged in by 'worthless agitators' as politically illegitimate. The nature of Banyole society also largely condemned such men to the role of random agitator until UNC came into existence. Then they acquired new roles as lieutenants to aspiring MPs when they did not become parliamentary candidates themselves, roles that they continued during the era of competitive party politics in Uganda. Towards the close of this period most of the individuals mentioned in this paper were regarded cynically by local Ugandans as spoilsmen. But this is not a development demanding total cynicism about earlier periods in the careers of these particular 'lesser leaders'. For, as was pointed out over fifty years ago, 'After coming to power the following of a crusader usually degenerates very easily into a quite common stratum of spoilsman'.[26]

None the less, we need to distinguish most carefully here the various political thresholds through which any anti-chiefly crusader had to pass in Bukedi district before qualifying for such opprobrium. To start with, there was the threshold of political credibility which had to be passed before any 'worthless agitator' in Bunyole county could become something more. That particular threshold appears to have been passed in most parts of Bukedi when Mutesa II toured the district shortly after his return from British-imposed exile in London, thereby demonstrating to local people not only the possibility of successful African defiance of British colonial authority but more than hinting at the likelihood of other Africans succeeding in this direction too—provided that all Africans united together in a dynamic political party.

Another turning point in the careers of the lesser leaders we have focused attention upon came with the very rapid democratization of politics that took place in Uganda immediately before the two general elections of 1961 and 1962. This second threshold on the road from 'worthless agitation' to independent democracy arrived much more speedily after the first in Uganda than was the case in Ghana or Nigeria, and it had, of course, happened far more quickly there than in British India. But, once the universal franchise arrived, political parties in Uganda made urgent overtures to non-agitators (or 'social leaders') as well as agitators, in order to muster maximum support at the polls during their hastily improvised electoral campaigns. As a result, there were several political surprises.

In many ways the most successful politician to pass through both thresholds came not from Bunyole county but from Bugwere, next door: Balaki Kirya. His early years at Namirembe Church of Uganda school before joining the British army as a signaller during the Second World War mark him out as almost a carbon copy of those archetypal figures in the history of African nationalism, the Standard VII leaver and the ex-serviceman. But, whatever may have been the psychological fallout from these experiences, behind Kirya's claims to being a 'brave man' (*mugumu*), an 'intelligent one' (*wamagezi*), and 'a man who does not fear the European in any way' (*atatya Muzungu nakatono*) in his final election manifestos, lay his long record of opposition to appointive chiefly oppression in Bukedi district since resigning his post-war position in the Welfare Department in order to represent the Iki Iki area on the Bukedi District Council during the 1950s. In 1953 Kirya denounced 'harsh government' (*enfuga ey'okubambula*) in one of the Baganda newspapers,[27] and thereafter the DC's files at Mbale are filled with letters of complaint against Kirya by Israeli Kabazi, the county chief of Bugwere, and intransigent replies from Kirya. In 1958 Kirya was elected to the Ugandan Legislative Council as representative for the whole of Bukedi district on the first direct vote, and shortly after the 1962 election he was appointed Minister of Works in the new UPC-KY government headed by Milton Obote. This was the highest office yet held in Uganda by any politician from Bukedi or Bugisu districts. Just before the 1962 election, however, Kirya's prospects had seemed much less secure and urgent approaches were made to the county chief whom Kirya had attacked so bitterly throughout the 1950s and whose resignation had been forced by riots in 1960 for which Kirya was at least partly responsible. Israeli Kabazi was told personally by Milton Obote that support for the local UPC candidate would not go unrewarded should UPC come to power after the 1962 election. Nor was it. When subsequent ministerial intrigues against Obote's leadership in the resultant UPC-KY coalition led to the imprisonment of Balaki Kirya along with the other principal plotters, the overthrow of the quasi-federal status of Buganda, the inauguration of a republican constitution, and the reintroduction of a system of nominated rather than elected district councillors, Israeli Kabazi was one of the only two lesser leaders mentioned in this paper to retain a seat on the Bukedi district council (the other one was Erika Higenyi, who had been specially elected there in 1964 and had in the meantime developed considerable interests in the South Bukedi Cooperative Union). Kabazi had been brought up in the household of an early Ganda chief in Bukedi, but that did not prevent him from subsequently becoming secretary of the Young Bagwere Association, campaigning for the removal of all expatriate Baganda from administrative positions before British administrators silenced this particular 'educated agitator' by making him a chief, and his colleagues in the Young Bagwere Association by inaugurating the multi-level system of partially elected councils. In earlier times Kabazi's removal from chiefship in 1960 might well have caused him to become yet another 'worthless agitator'. But times had now changed. For reasons that Colin Leys has analysed so well in Acholi,[28] Kabazi not only now became a district councillor but shortly the member of several parastatal bodies too.

Under the Uganda independence constitution, district councillorships were not inconsiderable political consolation prizes for defeated parliamentary candidates, though it would perhaps be a mistake to treat them as much more than that for Joseph Wasukulu or Sebastian

Orach. Wasukulu, to be sure, did rather well as one, becoming constitutional head of Bukedi district in 1964 and remaining as such until Obote introduced his revised republican constitution into parliament three years later. Orach, too, continued to make the Bukedi district council his principal political arena after standing down as parliamentary candidate for south-central Bukedi after the 1961 election, though, as Fred Burke has pointed out, Orach now also campaigned for Bukedi district to be divided into two.[29] Of all the lesser leaders mentioned in this paper, however, Orach retained his popular reputation as a fearless campaigner against arbitrary government, and progressive repression of the Democratic Party by Milton Obote's successive regimes in Uganda seemed merely to stiffen his stubbornness in remaining a member of it. Only when Obote announced his plans for multiple-constituency elections within the framework of a one-party state in 1970 did Orach finally declare himself a member of UPC, but the main force of this declaration was, of course, nullified by the seizure of power in Uganda by Idi Amin on 25 January 1971.

The post-colonial career routes of Kirya, Kabazi, Wasukulu, and Orach therefore underline, if underlining be necessary, the arbitrary course that the wheel of political fortune has followed in Uganda since 1962. Neither Wasukulu nor Orach could have predicted that a largely elective Bukedi district council would only last a few years before a return to the system of nominated councillors with attenuated powers, let alone the subsequent overturn of the whole Ugandan political system by Idi Amin. Analytically, however, the earlier careers of the lesser leaders we have noted in Bunyole, Bugwere, and West Budama counties do define one 'catchment area'[30] from which many members of late colonial councils and parliaments were recruited in Bukedi district. The model of the politician as agitator, which we have taken more seriously than most scholars in this connection, has been seen to define this area of political recruitment more accurately than either religion or tribe. The need to democratize as rapidly as was the case in late colonial Uganda, however, did not enable any effective transition to take place between random articulation and anti-chiefly protest and the establishment of durable channels of parliamentary representation. Instead, networks of agitators and non-agitators coexisted uneasily together in the hastily improvised UPC–KY coalition, and this unhappy friendship did little to stem subsequent disillusionment with democratic politics in Uganda.

Now the political system of Uganda has returned almost to colonial square one. Praetorian guards are located in strategic centres of power in the country alongside a rudimentary system of military governors. Already, however, Idi Amin has denounced 'confusing agents' in

Bukedi district who have been bold enough to criticize military misdemeanours at Tororo, and he has recently publicized plans to increase popular participation in government at village level, if no higher. Is it purely utopian to see in such developments the emergence again in this part of Uganda of the politician as agitator?

8

KRISTO DAS PAL:
POLITICIAN AS INTERMEDIARY

John McGuire

Among the Hindus in Calcutta in the middle of the nineteenth century two political systems were observable: an indigenous and a colonial system. Although these two systems had been modified over time by each other's cultural values, they represented different sets of behavioural interactions through which values were authoritatively allocated.[1] The indigenous system was essentially local, was subject to the demands of a supra-colonial system, and had no formal regime or set of political authorities. As a result of these characteristics, the political roles in this system were diffused among other social roles, and in many cases were scarcely distinguishable from them. On the other hand, the colonial system, which ranged from the municipal to the imperial level, was defined by sets of formal political authority roles that the colonial regime has established, and by institutions such as voluntary associations and the press that the Anglo-Indians had introduced.[2]

Owing to these differences, the requirements for political leadership in the two systems were different. In the indigenous system, the most important political leadership roles were performed by the individual who filled the social role of *dalapati*,[3] a role that was linked to the *dals* or social organizations into which Calcutta society was divided.[4] Generally, within each *dal*, the role of *dalapati* (leader of a *dal*) was assumed by the *karta* (the chief member of a Hindu family) of the leading family in the *dal*, the rank of which was determined by a number of variables, the most important being its wealth, its lineage, and, to a lesser extent, its *jati* (subcaste). In the colonial system, the characteristics of political leadership roles varied according to levels within the system. At the higher levels, of course, such roles were filled exclusively by Anglo-Indians. At lower levels, however, certain political leadership roles were filled by Hindus who were prominent in the indigenous system, and who were therefore able to utilize their positions within this system in order to acquire political influence in the colonial system. While a few Hindus were equipped to function effectively in both indigenous and colonial roles, however, there were a number who were not versed in the skills and ideas of the transferred culture, and who thus filled colonial political leadership roles in name

only. Partly because of this situation, Hindus who were conversant with
the transferred culture were utilized in colonial political leadership roles
even though they were not influential in the indigenous system.

Such men were truly lesser leaders, occupying top rank in neither
system. Indeed it happened quite frequently that this kind of leader
would acquire a relatively modest share of power, influence, and
authority in the indigenous system only after he had risen to some
prominence in the colonial political system. A study of such an individual (or individuals) should demonstrate, among other things, some
of the ways in which the two systems were linked, and how such a
relationship changed over time.

Broadly, an analysis of this question may be approached in two ways.
In the first place, the problem could be examined empirically by means
of a collective biographical approach, in which a set of individuals is
selected according to a number of indicators, and analysed under a
common set of variables. In this way a theory might be developed
about the political behaviour and roles of lesser Hindu politicians in the
middle of the nineteenth century. Alternatively, the problem could be
tackled along more impressionistic lines, and an individual could be
selected according to a few general indicators. Although this approach
is not as precise, it does lend itself to deeper study and, in relation to
other papers in this book, is more appropriate. For these reasons, then,
the latter method has been adopted; an individual has been chosen
partly because he inherited no position of socio-political authority in
the indigenous system and partly because he was very involved in the
British colonial system during his career. Of the Hindus[5] who fit this
description, one of the most interesting is Kristo Das Pal.

Pal was born in Calcutta in 1838, into a family with few material
advantages. His father was poor and his kinfolk were unimportant.[6]
He belonged to the *Tili jati*, a group which, though by no means
unimportant, lacked the economic resources of the *Dakshina Rarhi
Kayasths* (traditionally, members of the writer caste from south-west
Bengal) or the *Saptagram Suvarnavaniks* (traditionally, members of the
gold-merchant caste from Hooghly district in south-west Bengal), and
the high ritual status of the *Rarhi Kulin Brahmans* (traditionally, high-
ranked priests from west Bengal). The *Tili* were traditionally a group
that belonged to the *Teli* (oil-merchant) caste that resided in and
around Calcutta. In short, Pal's family had little influence in the
indigenous system in Calcutta. Moreover, in so far as the few positions
of authority that were given to Hindus by the colonial regime at this
time were assigned to members of important families within the
indigenous system, his family were insignificant within the colonial
system. Yet, when he died in 1884, Kristo Das Pal was the manager and

editor of the most influential Hindu-owned newspaper in Calcutta, secretary of the British Indian Association, a member of the University of Calcutta Senate, a member of the Calcutta Municipal Corporation and ex-member of the Bengal Legislative Council, a member of the Viceregal Council, and was on the committees of at least nine voluntary associations.[7] During a period of forty-five years he achieved a position of political eminence within the colonial system: not a top rank position, but nevertheless one of some importance. Furthermore, as a result of this acquired status, he also advanced his position within the indigenous system. In analysing the political status which he acquired, we can raise two questions. First, given that Pal's family had negligible resources, how did he manage to enter the colonial political leadership sub-system? And, secondly, having entered this system, how did he advance within it?

The geographical location of Pal's family is perhaps the most appropriate starting point for an answer to the first question; for, by virtue of his residence in Calcutta, Pal had access to resources not readily available in other parts of Bengal. Most importantly, he had access to the English education system which provided an Indian with the skills necessary to obtain a well paid job in the British colonial system, which thus enabled him to improve his status in the indigenous system. Despite this geographical accessibility, however, he was prevented by his socioeconomic circumstances from entering either the Hindu College or one of the missionary colleges—the only institutions offering a higher English education. He could not afford the high fees at the Hindu College, and owing to the prevalent fear of conversion to Christianity, he was not allowed to attend the missionary schools where the charges were nominal. Instead, he was enrolled at the Oriental Seminary, one of a number of Anglo-vernacular schools from which a middle-grade English education could be obtained at a low fee. Although he displayed only average ability in most subjects at this school, he seemed to have a particular gift for the English language, in both its oral and written forms—a gift which eventually won him two silver medals for excellence, and which would some years later win him the accolade of being called 'one of the best writers and speakers'[8] to be nominated to the Bengal legislative council.

The English education which Pal received at the Oriental Seminary was inferior to that which could be had at the Hindu College or at one of the missionary institutions and it did not therefore qualify him for one of the highly sought after posts in the uncovenanted civil service. Pal's family were obviously aware of this, for, in spite of the fear of proselytism, he was allowed to continue his studies under the missionaries after he had graduated from the Oriental Seminary. He was withdrawn shortly afterwards, however, when it was discovered that the Bible was being used as a teaching source, and, in normal circumstances, Pal's formal English education would have terminated at this point.[9] As a result of a structural change in the education system, however, his schooling was extended by three years.

In 1853 both the Government of Bengal and the Hindu leaders in Calcutta assumed a greater role in the development of higher English education. The former, who had previously shared the management of the Hindu College with the Hindu leaders, took complete control of that institution and increased its facilities. The latter, on the other hand, attempted to retain their influence within the English education system by establishing a new institution called the Hindu Metropolitan College.[10] These developments provided more scholarships, and thus facilitated entry into the higher English education system for more young Hindus. Pal, who had been unable to enter the higher institutions, won a scholarship to the Hindu Metropolitan College, where he was able to study under Captain Richardson, the doyen of English teachers in Bengal at that time. As a result of this opportunity, Pal, with his natural aptitude for the English language and a capacity for hard work, was able to master the language and the ideas which he found expressed in its literature. During this period he also had his first taste of politics as defined by the British colonial idiom. Along with a number of other students, he joined the Calcutta Free Literary Debating Society, a voluntary association which had been established by a group of Anglo-Indians and Hindus.[11] In this association, he was able to acquire formal organizational skills which were the key to the British colonial political system and to begin to develop valuable friendships with members of some of the more important Hindu families who belonged to this body.

Given that Pal won a number of scholarships, it may still be asked why he was able to remain at school for such a long period. Two reasons suggest themselves, although they cannot be documented. First, as the basic social unit in the Hindu society was the joint family, he was not solely dependent upon his father's income for support; and, secondly, as a result of this system, families were prepared to support those male members who manifested ability in English, for it was recognized as the major avenue for improving the socio-economic status of the family. Success for Kristo Das Pal meant success for a whole network of people, as Pal himself suggested when he wrote some years later to Sambhu Chandra Mukherjee: 'I am, as you know, a poor man, and cannot spare much for others, in fact you do not know how many hangers-on there [are] on me, chiefly poor relations and neighbours.'[12]

The second factor which helped to determine the direction of his political life was that of career choice. Like the majority of English-educated Hindus around this time, Pal's first choice was the uncovenanted civil service—the covenanted civil service being closed to all except the British. In 1857 he was appointed translator to the court of the district judge of the twenty-four pargannas. He was not destined to carve out a career in this particular profession, however, for a short time after he had been appointed he was dismissed for 'incompetency' by Mr Latour, the district judge.[13] Although Pal must have felt that his career prospects were severely damaged by this incident, biographical studies of others suggest that, had he remained in government service, his political life would have been markedly different. Certainly his position would not have been as significant as the one he ultimately achieved, for government service meant not only that an individual spent most of his time in the district areas away from the political centre, but also that he was tied economically to the government. In consequence such an individual could not afford to be as vocal politically as his counterpart who held a non-government job.[14]

Pal's subsequent career choice of journalism was obviously very appropriate to his skills. Although he had contributed articles to the *Morning Chronicle*, the *Citizen*, and the *Hindoo Patriot* while still at college, he had made journalism only a part-time activity because the monetary rewards it offered were so low. Having lost his post with the government, however, he turned, more through necessity than choice, to this work on a full-time basis. Along with Sambhu Chandra Mukherjee, and with the financial assistance of Prosad Das Datta, he started the *Calcutta Monthly Magazine* in 1857. Like of lot of similar magazines which were established around this time, however, it did not have the necessary reading public to support it, and it ceased to exist after six months. Having failed to establish his own journal, Pal continued to eke out a living by writing for other newspapers, such as the *Bengal Hurkaru*, the *Central Star*, and the *Hindoo Patriot*.[15] Although he was unable to improve his financial status during this period, he did acquire a valuable education in the art of political criticism, as well as a reputation for operating effectively in the British colonial idiom.

But Pal had more than the ability to think and write in English; he was also imbued with a strong political instinct—an instinct which he used to full advantage. For instance, after the mutiny had subsided, he organized a petition on behalf of the Calcutta Free Literary Debating Society, congratulating the British Indian Association for the support which it had given the government during the crisis.[16] In so doing, he carefully placed his name before a body which was at that time the only formal Hindu political pressure group operating in the colonial system, an organization which was in fact controlled mainly by Hindus who also held leadership roles in the indigenous system. In the next few years he was more and more noticed by the Association and was befriended by some of its members. In particular, he was patronized by Haris Chandra Ghose, a Hindu who filled both the position of *dalapati* within the indigenous system and, as a committee member of the British Indian Association, that of gatekeeper for political demands of Hindus within the colonial system.[17] In consequence, in late 1861, when the position of assistant secretary to the British Indian Association, and that of editor and manager of the *Hindoo Patriot*, the Association's newspaper, fell vacant, Pal was recruited for both appointments. He was selected by the leaders of the colonial political organization partly because he had the ability to operate effectively in the British idiom, and partly because he had shown himself to be a potentially loyal client. He was, in short, hired to fill roles which the members of this Association could not fill, because they lacked the necessary skills, could not spare the time, or felt that such activities were beneath their social status; as editor and assistant secretary he would act as spokesman for the political demands of this body.

Yet Pal's career was by no means assured. Between the death of Haris Chandra Mukherjee, the previous long-term editor, early in 1861, and the appointment of Pal, the meagre circulation of the *Hindoo Patriot* fell; conceivably, it could have ceased to function altogether in the years that immediately followed. But, more important, the British Indian Association at this stage of its development was not an integrated political organization. On the one hand, the most powerful leaders of the Association, as *dalapatis* within the indigenous system, were in conscious opposition to one another in exerting their authority. On the other hand, as *zamindars* and owners of Calcutta property, they had in common a set of economic values, to protect which they had to operate in the colonial system, using pressure groups such as the British Indian Association and newspapers such as the *Hindoo Patriot* to voice their political demands. To do this effectively they had to combine, form committees, and share authority roles, something for which the indigenous system had not prepared them. That both the British Indian Association and the *Hindoo Patriot* did survive was, in part, the result of the roles which Pal filled; as assistant secretary, he skilfully drew up petitions, drafted memoranda, and articulated the demands of the Association at public meetings, and, as editor and manager, he improved both the quality and the distribution of the *Hindoo Patriot*. Indeed, the course of Pal's career from this time on illustrates how the Association in general and Pal in particular grew more influential within the British colonial system, but it illustrates, at the same time, the limitations of such a pathway.

Between 1861 and the middle of 1884, when he died, Pal wrote the editorials for the *Hindoo Patriot* nearly every week. Although he touched on a variety of subjects, he was essentailly concerned with political questions and accordingly covered a wide spectrum of subjects, ranging through all levels of the colonial system. At the local level, for example, he advocated a greater decision-making role for Bengalis in the Calcutta Municipal Corporation, while at the provincial level he urged the government to remove the racial discrimination which existed within the judicial system, and, at the British Indian level, he exposed the discrepancy between British promises and British action regarding the opening up of the covenanted civil service to Indian candidates. In expressing these views, Pal was a forerunner of the nationalist politician who began to emerge in the late nineteenth and the early twentieth centuries.

But this picture, so popular with nationalist historians, is monolithic and somewhat misleading.[18] A close reading of the *Hindoo Patriot* suggests that Pal supported only those issues which did not run counter to the interests of the members of the British Indian Association. For instance, he opposed all attempts to introduce an income tax, which would have affected only the wealthy. Indeed, he suggested a salt tax as an alternative, knowing full well that the burden would fall on those least able to afford it.[19] He continually urged that more political authority be given to Indians, yet he attacked the concept of limited franchise when it was introduced by the government at the local level, claiming, among other things, that government nomination was less dangerous politically.[20] Similarly, although he had criticized the government for its Press Act in 1878, he supported J. M. Tagore, who was one of his patrons and president of the British Indian Association, when the latter sided with the government authorities in the Viceregal Council in passing the Vernacular Press Act.[21] But he demonstrated the limits of his political orbit most clearly in his indecisive attack on the Ilbert Bill, one of the most controversial issues to emerge in Calcutta in the latter half of the nineteenth century. Although he was in favour of the Bill, which was drawn up to eliminate the racial discrimination that existed in the Bengal judicial system, and although on most occasions he attacked the negative stand taken by the Anglo-Indian community, when this group looked as though it was going to ally itself with the *zamindars* in petitioning the government to drop the proposed land reforms, he characterized the Tenancy Bill as another Ilbert Bill, thus suggesting that the Bills could be equated as equally dangerous.[22] In fact, if Pal's editorials are subjected to content analysis, he will be seen to have devoted a large part of his time to presenting arguments in favour of the legal rights of the *zamindar* as laid down in the Permanent Settlement[23]—'rights' which came increasingly under fire after 1859. He was, in short, limited to operating according to those values held by the leaders of the British Indian Association, a situation which he denied, but which led Anglo-Indians and Hindus to refer to him as the paid servant of that organization.[24]

Yet such an assessment ignores the complexities of the political system in which Pal operated. He was certainly limited by his ties to the British Indian Association, but without those ties his political career would have been even more limited. At the time when he entered the colonial political system, a link with the British Indian Association was one of the few conceivable pathways to a successful career. Pal understood this and was realistic enough to accept it, yet, as his articles and speeches will attest, he was not without ideals.[25] Indeed, he was able to express his views to a wide audience largely because of his connection with the British Indian Association. He was also able to enter positions of authority and influence which would normally have been closed to him. In particular, he was able to enter government circles. He was nominated by the government to the Calcutta Municipal Corporation in 1863, the University of Calcutta Senate in 1872, and the Bengal Legislative Council in 1874. Pal was promoted by the government party because of his ability to operate effectively in the colonial political system, but that was certainly not the sole reason. His links with the British Indian Association were of primary importance, as the editor of the *Englishman* implied when he wrote in 1864 that

One 'native gentleman' [Kristo Das Pal] we are told is merely the paid Assistant Secretary of an Association which is already sufficiently represented in the municipality, with as much title to be on the list of Justices as a writer in any of the Government offices.[26]

Given the propensity of the Anglo-Indian newspapers to exaggerate when they referred to Indians, such a statement might, by itself, be considered misleading. Yet official statements suggest that it was probably a fairly accurate assessment. For example, in 1874, Sir Richard Temple (lieutenant-governor, 1873–77) wrote to Lord Northbrook (governor-general, 1872–76) asking him to appoint Pal to the Bengal Legislative Council. Temple claimed that Pal would provide him with valuable information.[27] He was in fact acting according to the colonial policy of this time, which was to recruit those who had ties with the indigenous leaders. Government authorities, for instance, rarely nominated those English-educated Bengalis who had divorced themselves from the indigenous system, for such individuals could provide little support for the colonial regime.[28]

That Pal cultivated these connections with the government is borne out by a remark some years later that he 'knew every Lieutenant Governor of his time, and stood on friendly terms with all, except probably Sir George Campbell'.[29] Still, in spite of his ability, hard work, and friendly connections with government officials, Pal was not nominated by the government to the Viceregal Council, the most prestigious official legislative body, mainly because he lacked the qualifications which it considered necessary for such a position: he did not belong to a leading family, he was not independently wealthy, and he did not hold a high position within the British Indian Association.[30] Pal was, of course, being judged according to the government's conception of the indigenous system—but this conception was fairly accurate on some points. For example, Pal was periodically reminded by his fellow Hindus that he belonged to a socially inferior lineage group. In 1864 he was criticized by some Hindus for 'presuming' to sit with his 'social superiors' in the Corporation[31] and as late as 1882 he was the focus of a similar attack during a debate within that organization.[32] Indeed, although he was selected for less prestigious government bodies, he was, as has been noted, recruited not because of his social position but rather because of his usefulness as a link between the two systems.

Yet his political role did not remain static. Pal worked hard at improving his position within the various government organizations of which he was a member, and put his ability in the English language to good use. Having spent a large part of his working life drawing up petitions and memoranda for the British Indian Association, he was better equipped than most Indians to work on sub-committees preparing drafts. Again, having spent much of his spare time in voluntary associations, or at public meetings making speeches, he had little difficulty in adjusting to the conventions of the debating chamber. As the result of his work in these organizations, his position as editor of the *Hindoo Patriot*, his activities in voluntary associations, and his appearance at public meetings, he gradually acquired a position of prominence within the indigenous system, an acquired social status which the government recognized in 1877 and 1878 when it conferred titles upon him.[33]

He also became more influential within the British Indian Association itself, partly because he handled its affairs so efficiently and partly because of the changes which were occurring within the political system. When Pal joined the British Indian Association, there had been few other paths open to him. By the middle of the 1870s, however, he was presented with alternatives as the result of changes that had been effected in the colonial political system. In particular, a number of

Hindus who had migrated from Vikrampur in East Bengal, and who had studied at Calcutta University, were dissatisfied with the goals of the British Indian Association and were beginning to establish their own political pressure groups.[34] If he had chosen to, Pal could have assumed a leadership role in one of these new organizations, for he held in common with their founders a number of attributes. Apart from the fact that he had devoted a large part of his life to the causes of the British Indian Association, however, he realized that this organization was more powerful than the new ones, and that his position within it was secure. By this time he had in fact become an indispensable part of the machinery of the British Indian Association. Not only was he able to voice their demands better than anyone else, but he also skilfully countered criticism which was increasingly directed at his organization by the Anglo-Indian community and the new Indian associations. As a result of these changes, he gradually assumed a position of greater authority within that body—a position which was officially acknowledged in 1879 when he was appointed secretary, a role usually reserved for a member of one of the leading families. Four years later, in 1883, his increased influence within this organization was further underlined when he was selected to represent it on the Viceregal Council.[35] If he had not died in the following year, at the relatively young age of forty-five, he might have risen to prominence in the Indian Congress, and have become a nationalist politician, but then that must remain a counter-factual argument.

What, then, does Kristo Das Pal's life tell us about the political systems in Calcutta at the time? Among other things, it illustrates some ways in which the colonial and the indigenous systems were interrelated. More precisely, Pal's career demonstrates how the two behavioural systems interacted through an intermediary, that is an individual who had the necessary attributes to function in the two systems, but who lacked the power to assume leadership roles in either without the patronage of those in authority. It also shows how increased influence and power in one system could lead to similar increases in the other, and how major structural changes in one could alter the environmental conditions in the other. More generally, it underlines the complexities of a colonial system and the subtle adjustments made by the foreign and indigenous authorities to accommodate one another through the medium of a 'middle man', and how such an individual could outgrow this role and assume a more independent role in either system.

9

PATHWAYS TO POLITICAL ADVANCEMENT: PROBLEMS OF CHOICE FOR TALUQDAR POLITICIANS IN LATE BRITISH INDIA

Peter Reeves

This paper discusses the political careers of a number of landlords from the Oudh region of the United Provinces (UP) in the last thirty years of British rule in India. These men all belonged to a particular landlord group, the *taluqdars* of Oudh, and they thus shared certain common landed interests. They reacted in a variety of ways, however, to the demands and opportunities of the political situation in India after 1920, and those varied responses indicate something of the range of political choice open to politicians and the problems they faced in choosing a political 'pathway'.

The period after 1920 was a period of rapid change in the political system of colonial India. This change rested, in the first place, on a series of institutional innovations which were embodied in the constitutions of 1919, 1935, and 1950, and, in the second place, on the growth of parties at both national and provincial level. The effect of the Government of India Acts of 1919 and 1935 was to create, within the provinces of British India, increasingly representative and responsible legislatures. Elections were from territorial constituencies in the main, and on the basis of a limited property franchise. Under the 1919 Act, elected members were chosen as ministers in charge of certain departments of the provincial administration, although overall supervision remained with the governor and his executive councillors; under the 1935 Act, full provincial autonomy was granted subject to the governor's exercise of special, 'safeguard' powers. Overall, these changes—especially when viewed against the background of very limited representation and the almost total lack of any element of responsible government before 1920—marked a series of major extensions of the political arena within which Indian politicians operated. Following the removal of British colonial authority in 1947, the new constitution of the Indian Union completed this extension of the political system by the introduction of fully responsible state governments and elections on adult suffrage.

The build-up of the party system was in part a response to these institutional changes and in part the development of nationalist and anti-colonial movements which both brought pressure for further change and were in turn stimulated by those changes. The electoral basis of the legislatures, the possibilities of local influence inherent in control of provincial ministries, and the desire for protection against the policies of other parties coming to power, all contributed to the extension of the party system. As a result, we have the situation in late British India in which those concerned with action in the political arena were confronted with a number of possible 'pathways' for the satisfaction of their political objectives, 'pathways' which were identifications with particular courses of political action based on judgements about the action of rivals and the potentialities of the political system in both the short term and the long term. Politicians, such as the *taluqdars* whose careers this paper outlines, had to decide, for instance, whether to work to build a grouping for themselves within the legislature; whether they should rely on British patronage for their own and their 'community's' interests; or whether they should move into some wider political grouping (such as Congress or Mahasabha) in the expectation that this would be buying security in the long term. And, as few came into the political arena unencumbered with previous political commitments or identifications with particular social or economic groupings—and this was especially true of the *taluqdars*—this choosing of political connections could be extremely difficult.

The political careers of the several *taluqdars* discussed here will, I hope, illustrate some of this. Before looking at their individual careers, however, it is necessary to say something of the *taluqdari* group in general because the status, interests, and attitudes which they derive from their position as *taluqdars* are important elements in their make-up as politicians.

The *taluqdars* were a group of agricultural landlords who held (i.e. collected the rents from and paid land revenue for, and hence exercised some form of influence in) about two-thirds of the villages of Oudh, which comprised twelve districts within the central part of UP with a population, in 1935, of about 13 millions. The *taluqdars* pre-dated British control of Oudh, which began formally with annexation in 1856, but the *taluqdari* group as such gained its real strength from the situation immediately following the 'mutiny' of 1857. At that time the *taluqdars* were recognized by the British Indian Government as the owners of the lands of the villages to which they laid claim, and they were increasingly looked to as the basis for British control of the region. In 1859 their position was confirmed by the issue to them of hereditable but non-transferable *sanads* (charters) by the government. The possession of a *sanad* henceforth became the essential basis of *taluqdari* status and the *taluqdari* group was limited to those who possessed a *sanad*. In 1869 the Oudh Estates Act listed the *taluqdars'* estates (then numbering 276), and so further clarified their position. From this date on no new *taluqdari* estates were created and the group was, in this way, closed and definitive. It was not quite static, however, for a number of mortgaged estates were sold up and their *taluqdars* disappeared; by 1935 there were 244 estates still operative. At the same time, however, the number of *taluqdars* did increase because not all families practised primogeniture in matters of succession. By 1935, 413 *taluqdars* held the 244 estates between them. None the less, the group was essentially a closed one because there was no external recruitment to *taluqdari* ranks.

Socially the group was not homogeneous: in 1935 Rajputs (*c.* 55%) and Muslims (*c.* 30%) made up the overwhelming majority, with representatives of other Hindu caste groups, some Sikhs, and one European family, in the remainder. In addition, the group was internally divided by the considerable variation in the size of *taluqdari* estates: a few paid more than Rs 100,000 a year in land revenue and some paid less than Rs 1,000, but the great majority paid somewhere between Rs 5,000 and Rs 50,000. The *taluqdari* group thus had a common legal status but relatively little social or economic homogeneity. If it had not been for the fact that an association—the British Indian Association (BIA) of Oudh—acted from 1861 to look after their interests, it is unlikely that the group would have acted in common at all. Membership of the BIA, however, became obligatory for *taluqdars* (their subscriptions were eventually collected by the administration, along with the land revenue), and, as the association was exclusively theirs, it became, for those who were interested, the focus for political action and activity, both as the vehicle for *taluqdar* political contact with other groups and the government and as an arena for political competition between *taluqdars* themselves, so that personal politics based on complicated family, communal, or regional rivalries and connections became an important part of the *taluqdari* life style. The style, based on traditional ideas of the leisured, autocratic, supervisory role of Raja or Nawab Sahib (sometimes mixed with notions about European aristocratic behaviour) and supported by wealth and often quite large establishments of servants and retainers, became the major shared attribute of the *taluqdars*, although, of course, not all were able to maintain themselves in equally splendid fashion. In terms of the period we are discussing, however, this background of an assured political position and the attitudes they had towards political activity and the proper role for the *taluqdar* were of considerable significance.

The three men whose careers we shall look at are fairly typical in terms of the villages they controlled and the amount of revenue they paid. The basic details of their *taluqdari* positions are set out below:[1]

	Jagannath Baksh Singh	Maheshwar Dayal Seth	Guru Narain Seth
Title	Raja (1924)	Rai Bahadur (1934)	Rai Bahadur (1939)
		Raja (1936)	Kunwar
Estate	Rehwan	Kotra	Maurawan
District	Rae Bareli	Sitapur	Unnao
Caste	Bais Rajput	Khattri	Khattri
Dates	c. 1888—	1906–47	c. 1910—
Villages	25 whole	69 whole	51 whole
(1935)	2 shared	10 shared★	23 shared
Land revenue			
(1935)	Rs. 14,676	Rs. 50,135	Rs. 50,947†
Succeeded	c. 1905 as a minor	1922	c. 1930

★ Shared with two other branches of the family.

† This family also owned non-*taluqdari* property in Agra province; the total revenue paid was about Rs. 67,000.

Rajputs were, as has been pointed out, the major social group among the *taluqdars*. Khattris were, however, in terms of estates, quite a minor group within the *taluqdari* community, and the presence of two Khattris calls for some comment. The fact is that in this period, both within the Association and in the more general political sphere, Khattris came to play a much larger political role among the *taluqdars* than their numbers would at first sight suggest. One reason for this increased prominence was related to the fact that these Khattri families were among the most notable of those not practising primogeniture; Guru Narain's family, for instance, had 9 different sections with a total of 36 *taluqdars* by 1935. The growing number of Khattri *taluqdars* gave them an advantage inasmuch as they all participated and voted in the BIA; certainly there was a marked increase in the proportion of Khattris on the executive committee over the period (in 1922 they had 2 out of 28 members; in 1937 they had 10 out of 37 members), and in 1938 Maheshwar Dayal Seth became vice-president, an unprecedented post for a Khattri.[2] The presence of two Khattris in this present context is, therefore, not altogether surprising.

While the political careers of these *taluqdars* will demonstrate something of the range of *taluqdar* reactions to the political situation after 1920, they do not exhaust the possibilities. There were those who opted for participation in Congress quite openly: the Raja of Mankapur, whose career has been discussed at length by Paul Brass;[3] the Kalakankar family from Pratapgarh from which Dinesh Singh, ex-member of

Mrs Gandhi's cabinet, comes; and Rai Bajrang Bahadur of Bhadri, a cousin of Kalakankar, who became lieutenant-governor of Himachal after independence. There were those Muslim *taluqdars* who were very closely caught up in the Muslim League, the Raja of Mahmudabad and the Raja of Pirpur being perhaps among the best known.[4] And there were many others who neglected or rejected any wider participation at all. I recognize these many other possibilities but I have not here attempted to deal with landlord political activity in general nor have I chosen these three men because they are necessarily the most representative—although their careers clearly do touch on a number of important aspects of *taluqdar* political activity. My choice has been guided rather by the fact that, as these men were politically active, they have left some indications of what they were prepared to do politically, which might in turn throw some light on the general themes of this paper.

Raja Jagannath Baksh Singh had an unbroken thirty-year career in the provincial legislature, beginning with the first elections under the 1919 Act which were held in December 1920. By the time he retired from the UP legislative assembly in 1950 he was undoubtedly the most experienced 'parliamentarian' among the *taluqdars*. With such a career behind him he might be considered a very model of a modernizing *taluqdar*, and yet his long parliamentary career was essentially a kind of holding operation. The reason for this lies in the fact that he gained his legislative place from within the *taluqdari* group itself rather than from any adjustment to the wider challenges of the new political system. The BIA had been given four seats especially reserved for itself in the legislative council set up by the 1919 Act: four seats out of a total of 100 elected seats. And these special seats were continued in the legislative assembly set up under the 1935 Act—although, as they still had only four seats in an enlarged assembly of 228 members, the relative strength of *taluqdar* representation had declined. In each of the six elections held for these pre-independence legislatures, Jagannath Baksh Singh was elected for one of these BIA seats; twice (1920 and 1946) he was returned, along with the other three representatives, unopposed. On four other occasions he was returned in second or third place among the four members. Only once did he venture outside the relatively safe circle of the BIA and that was in 1937, the first elections under the 1935 Act, when he contested the general rural seat for North-East Kheri district and was soundly thrashed by the Congress candidate. Why he should have stood in a district in which he had no personal standing is difficult to understand; it may be that he was invited to come there by local interests and it is noteworthy that the original landlord party candidate for this seat, the son of the Raja of Isanagar, a Kheri *taluqdar*, withdrew from the contest. Or Jagannath Baksh Singh may have been worried about the future of his seat within the BIA constituency itself, because in the 1937 elections a landlord party— the National Agriculturist Party of Oudh—had been formed and had nominated four candidates for the BIA seats. This NAPO was formed by Maheshwar Dayal Seth with the support, initially, of many leading *taluqdars* and with the active encouragement of the provincial government. Jagannath Baksh Singh never entertained any hopes for this party and he never participated in it; indeed, he had a personal brush with Maheshwar Dayal Seth over his lack of support and because he had gone so far as to tell the Governor, Sir Harry Haig, that he believed that it had no chance of winning the elections.[5] In the BIA constituency itself, however, he may have felt it a different matter, and it is possible that he was seeking a second chance for himself by contesting in Kheri district. As it was, he was the only non-NAPO candidate returned for the BIA.

Jagannath Baksh Singh stood in 1937, as he did in all his other elections, as an Independent, i.e. a non-party candidate. But during his career in the legislature he was not unaware of the value of party connections and he made several attempts to build for himself a position in larger party groupings. The only occasion on which he moved into a non-landlord grouping, however, came in 1927–28 when he joined the 'Nationalist Party' led by C. Y. Chintamani (a Liberal and the province's leading newspaper editor), along with a number of other Hindu landlords. Apart from these landlords, this Nationalist Party comprised mainly Liberals and Hindu Sabhaites who were concerned to hold to a 'moderate' and strongly 'Hindu' nationalist position outside the Indian Nationalist Congress, although the issue of the 'all-white' Simon Commission did bring them into a working alliance with Congress in the UP legislature during this period. This was, then, very 'political' company for any landlord to keep at that time and it certainly marked a departure for Jagannath Baksh Singh. The association was short-lived, however, because in 1928 he chose to give up his membership of the party in order—at one and the same time—to work off a personal grievance against one of the incumbent ministers (who was also a *taluqdar*)[6] and to achieve a long-standing ambition to take ministerial office himself. The way in which he did this, however, discredited him in the eyes of the Nationalists, who made his ministerial position untenable, and pushed him once again into the ranks of the unattached.

After this, Jagannath Baksh Singh was fairly clearly excluded from consideration for a ministerial appointment and became a frustrated and somewhat bitter man. He gathered around himself a personal clique which he called the Independent Party, but this was only a small and rather shaky grouping within the Council and offered little satisfaction. In the legislative assembly of 1946–49 he was elected leader of a Landholder's Party; but, as this consisted only of the six special landlord representatives (4 from the BIA and 2 from the Agra Province Zamindars' Association), it was also rather poor comfort. It did, however, enable him to gain election to the Indian Constituent Assembly in New Delhi, and he thus finished his career with a few brief moments as the champion of landed property rights in the Assembly. After the passage of the new constitution—though he was under no pressure to do so—he resigned from his seat in the legislative assembly and retired from political life altogether.

Although he took part in the legislatures during these thirty years, Jagannath Baksh Singh maintained a limited view of the political possibilities with which he was faced. He was basically uninterested in considering new methods to advance either his own position or the interests of the *taluqdars* whom he represented. His one real move towards party politics he spoiled by behaviour that was perfectly understandable within the traditional *taluqdar* context. And he took no part in those movements—NAPO and the later UP Zamindars' Union, formed in 1946 to fight against *zamindari* abolition programmes of the new Congress ministry—which were attempts both to revamp the landlords' image and to provide them with new forms of political organization. In both cases he had a personal antipathy towards the leading figure involved in the organization—Maheshwar Dayal Seth in NAPO and Kunwar Sir Jagdish Prasad in the Zamindars' Union. But, additionally, in both cases it can be seen that these new organizations challenged his political understanding by demanding forms of commitment and forms of activity (canvassing and party administration, for example) which he would not find palatable and to which he was, by the mid-1930s, too old to adapt. It was men like Maheshwar Dayal and Guru Narain to whom this sort of activity came more easily, although they too had many problems to solve before finding the most useful pathway for themselves.

Maheshwar Dayal Seth built a careful base for his political career, first in expanding his family estate in Sitapur district[7] and secondly in securing control of the Sitapur district board (on which he served three successive terms as president, 1928–37). His brother, Bisheshwar Dayal Seth, went into the legislative council for the BIA in 1927 and the family was therefore quite well placed in the district and the association. What was more Maheshwar Dayal was clearly eager to get into the politics of the new style. He was the moving spirit behind NAPO and, unlike most of the other landlord politicians who took

some part in NAPO, he actually realized the organizational and publicity effort that the party would require. This is not to say that he was
markedly altruistic in his outlook, or that he did not make mistakes;
he was still a long way from understanding all the implications of the
sort of party activity on which he embarked in 1934. He was, in fact,
very considerably self-interested in his organizational work; he announced in 1935 that the district which had been chosen for intensive
development as a model of NAPO organization was his own district
of Sitapur. And even so, in the middle of all this activity, he saw no
incongruity in going off for the summer on a tour of Europe and
leaving the organization of NAPO—in Sitapur and in Oudh as a
whole—in the hands of his private secretary. He made errors, too, in
dealing with other *taluqdars* and he alienated a number of his initial
supporters among the leading *taluqdars* because they found him too
self-assertive. And he also saw no further than the usual landlord
theories of how to handle the electorate. The villager, he asserted con-
fidently, 'is a willing tool in the hands of any self-seeking, intelligent
man. His political life is a blank. He is completely ignorant of his
rights and privileges. Any man, with a little knowledge or power can
lord it over him.'[8] The corollary of this was, he believed, that it only
needed landlords to ensure that they organized so as to deliver the
votes they controlled for NAPO to win the election. The result was
quite the reverse; it was experience gained the hard way.

Maheshwar Dayal himself did not lose his election in 1937, at least
not initially. He won the Sitapur East general rural seat on scrutiny of
the nomination papers, when he apparently managed to move successfully that the nomination paper of his rival, Jagannath Prasad Agarwal,
the president of the District Congress Committee, be rejected for some
irregularity. As a result he was returned unopposed and was able to
take his place in the interim ministry formed by the Nawab of Chha-
tari which administered the province while Congress was making up
its collective mind about accepting office. By the time Agarwal's
election petition had been upheld and Seth's election declared void,
the interim ministry had retired from office to allow Congress to take
over; Maheshwar Dayal, instead of fighting a by-election for the seat,
went off on another trip to Europe.

When he came back it was still as the champion of uncompromising
landlordism, this time in a direct clash with the Congress ministry.
Seth was a leader of the group within the BIA which stood out for
unabated opposition to the agrarian legislation which the ministry
were putting through the legislature. Some landlords wanted to seek
the intervention of Gandhi and the Congress Parliamentary Sub-
Committee (comprising Patel, Prasad and Azad), who, they felt,

would arbitrate with the provincial Congressmen and get 'better terms' for the landlords. Seth and his supporters, however, rejected this approach out of hand. Arbitration, they insisted, was tantamont to an admission that the landlords were inferiors; only negotiation—the process that would symbolize the equality of the parties—should be agreed to by the landlords. And if the Congress would not negotiate, then the landlords should 'fight', they declared, in what was an effort to throw into the balance their supposed local influence that could cause problems within the districts for Congress administration. The result was a long drawn out internecine feud within the BIA which effectively prevented any arbitration and did not secure any negotiation either; and which let the legislation go through without any major modifications being carried.

Guru Narain Seth was to some extent Maheshwar Dayal's shadow in these efforts of the mid- and late 1930s. His local base he secured not through the District Board initially (although he did later become chairman for a time); he worked instead through a local landlord association, the Unnao Landholders' Association, which he founded and of which he remained throughout the president. The utility of this association was that it included non-*taluqdari* landholders and enabled Guru Narain to articulate both local and 'small landlord' views and to act as an intermediary between the local groups and the BIA— of which he was for a number of years the joint secretary. Like Maheshwar Dayal, he too was clearly interested in involving himself in the political situation and he was prepared to make the effort at campaigning and organizing—although once again he tended to look to his own area.

In the 1937 election Guru Narain stood as one of the four NAPO candidates for the BIA seats rather than, as Maheshwar Dayal did, for a territorial seat. He presumably banked on his work within the BIA standing him in good stead, but, as it happened, he was just squeezed out of the fourth BIA place by Bisheshwar Dayal Seth. He stayed with Maheshwar Dayal through the anti-arbitration agitation, however, and seemed happy enough to follow his lead in landlord politics. The break came during the war, when both of them moved out of landlord politics into the much trickier waters of Hindu communal organization.

This involvement in Hindu political organizations began in December 1939 when Maheshwar Dayal and a group of Maurawan *taluqdars*, including Guru Narain, joined in a new Hindu Sangathan Committee for UP set up by Sir Jwala Prasad Srivastava, a Kanpur businessman who had been closely associated with NAPO. When Srivastava tried to take over the Oudh Hindu Sabha, against the wishes of the All-India Hindu Mahasabha leadership, however, there came a parting of the ways. Maheshwar Dayal stayed in the Mahasabha but Guru Narain followed Srivastava into yet another new organization, the 'All-India Hindu League', which was founded in April 1940 as a means of combating the Muslim League's newly declared policy for the partition of the country. In the ensuing months both Guru Narain and Maheshwar Dayal found themselves in the forefront of their respective organizations. Maheshwar Dayal, in particular, found himself swimming in very deep water: in January 1942 he found himself arrested, along with 1,200 other Mahasabhaites who had joined in a protest against the refusal of the district authorities in Bhagalpur (Bihar) to allow the Hindu Mahasabha to hold its annual session there on dates that coincided with the Muslim festival of Bakr-Id. By March 1942, with something now of the martyr's glory about him, Maheshwar Dayal had become general secretary of the All-India Hindu Mahasabha as well as president of the UP Hindu Mahasabha.

In mid-1942 the Hindu League began to fold up and Guru Narain and the other UP landlords who had joined it started to move back into the UP Mahasabha. And when, in 1943, Maheshwar Dayal came under a cloud in the Mahasabha for being rather too outspoken about the policies of the all-India leadership, Guru Narain began to see possibilities of promoting himself in the Oudh branch of the UP Hindu Sabha. By later 1944, as a result, he and Maheshwar Dayal were open rivals for control of the Oudh Province Hindu Sabha and their canvassing for votes in the presidential election led to a clash which required a court injunction and a ruling from the All-India Hindu Mahasabha working committee to produce an eventual compromise under which Maheshwar Dayal became 'titular president' and Guru Narain became 'working president' of the Sabha. Such a distinction between 'president' and 'working president' was not unusual in some Indian political organizations—landlords often used it as a means of getting 'big landlords' into conferences and organizations without requiring them to be very active, and in the Mahasabha there was a similar division of functions between Savarkar and S. P. Moorkerjee in the mid-1940s; in this particular case, however, the distinction was probably meant to reflect the relative status allotted to the two men. They continued in this uneasy double harness until early 1946, both campaigning for the Hindu Mahasabha during the elections of 1945–46. Then in March came the clearest break of all: Maheshwar Dayal joined Congress.

Maheshwar Dayal's move to join Congress was the most calculated political step he had taken in his career. It clearly represented a reaction to the election campaigns which had just finished and in which Congress had made a clean sweep of the non-Muslim constituencies. It also was a calculation about what he expected to be 'the final showdown with British Imperialism'.[9] He maintained that his move was due solely to the 'promptings' of his conscience: 'I have not joined the Congress for the loaves of office', he insisted, 'but for service through sacrifice and suffering.' He was elected a Congress member of the constituent assembly but he did not live long enough to have any chance to share in the Congress takeover after independence because he died in February 1947. But he had chosen his future political position and was probably well placed to take advantage of it.

Guru Narain moved very differently and it is here that we can see what was clearly a crucial point in landlord adjustment. He stayed with the Mahasabha immediately following the elections, but when, in August 1946, a new landlord organization (UP Zamindars' Union) was formed to combat Congress proposals for *zamindari* abolition, Guru Narain moved with enthusiasm into the post of secretary of the Union and general helper to the founder-leader, Kunwar Sir Jagdish Prasad. Jagdish Prasad, retired member of the ICS and son of a Raja from Moradabad district, was a former UP Home Member and a former member of the Viceroy's executive council. He was probably the most able and imaginative leader the UP landlords had in the whole period after 1920; he saw himself as a landlord and successive governors came to rely on him in the 1920s to act as government whip in the legislative council and as their intermediary with the landlords. Under his leadership the Zamindars' Union developed a more effective organizational and publicity machine than any previous landlord group had ever had and Guru Narain devoted himself to the Union and its successor (for electoral purposes), the UP Praja Party. In the long run these efforts did not prevent *zamindari* abolition, and the Praja Party was routed in the elections of 1952 (with Guru Narain being an unsuccessful contestant from the Purwa central constituency in Unnao district). In the long run, though, the importance of the Zamindar Union episode was less for its specific achievements against the abolition policy than for the experience it gave men like Guru Narain of something closer to full-time political work and more open canvassing than they had had before. And in terms of the development of political ideology it was probably important as an early demonstration of the lack of appeal of a platform based on broadly stated principles of social and economic conservatism.

Guru Narain managed to stay 'alive' politically at this time because, in 1950, he managed to secure at a by-election the BIA seat which Jagannath Baksh Singh vacated. And from this basis he secured the 24th of the 24 nominations from among members of the old legislative assembly to the new upper house, the Vidhan Parishad. In the Vidhan

Parishad he tried to operate an opposition party of the few non-Congress elements that had survived, but the members gradually drifted off and after some four years he joined Congress. 'To survive in the political world you must belong to a party', he commented in discussing this move some years later.[10] And survive he did, in the Vidhan Parishad, on into the mid-1960s.

We can sum up these three political careers perhaps in terms of the 'minimum adjustment' made by Jagannath Baksh Singh, the 'calculated moves' of Maheshwar Dayal Seth, and the 'trial and error' of Guru Narain. Jagannath Baksh Singh stayed very closely within the circle of safe landlord political activity and he was concerned almost wholly with the maintenance and use of a 'landlord' basis for his political activity. Maheshwar Dayal, who is perhaps the least 'middle rank' of the three, passed through four clear stages: local politics; landlord organization; Hindu Mahasabha; and Congress. And his shift from one stage to the next seems to have been fairly well calculated. He was clearly ambitious and at each stage he assumed that he could find, and fill, some leadership role. It is indicative that even his entry into Congress is heralded by a long and fulsome statement to the press. I think that, had he lived, he would not have been so easily classed as middle-rank, for his drive and his awareness of the possibilities of the system would have given him the chance to gain something like a cabinet appointment. It could be argued that he really delayed his shift to Congress too long—that if a man was going to join the nationalist bandwagon it was best to do so as early as possible, as the fortunes of the Kalakankar, Bhadri, or Mankapur families would suggest. Against this, I think we can see that, for Maheshwar Dayal, the acquisition of experience and reputation at each stage was actually essential for the subsequent transfer; as a landlord-politician, Maheshwar Dayal needed the intermediate stage of the Mahasabha to give him familiarity with nationalist modes of action which his landlord position and activity had made it difficult for him to assume directly. Guru Narain, on the other hand, does in many ways wait too long. But, in addition, he seems to have perceived his own position very differently. While he clearly had aspirations towards leadership (and, of course, for landlords it was peculiarly difficult for them not to have such aspirations, given their social background), he accepted for himself a series of subordinate roles in the various phases of his career. Most usually this is a secretary role and is linked to the dynamism of a more forceful character (Maheshwar Dayal in the 1930s, Jagdish Prasad in the 1940s). And the attempts which he made to go beyond that sort of role were unsuccessful: his challenge to Maheshwar Dayal in the Hindu Sabha, for instance, or his attempt to operate in the Vidhan Parishad. He did not have the strength of local base or the independence of judgement of Maheshwar Dayal, perhaps, and this made it necessary for him to link himself to a stronger character. The result was, however, that he allowed himself to be used by others for political activity rather than using that activity to work to his own advantage. He lacked, in essence, Maheshwar Dayal's calculation. In 1945, for instance, the Mahasabha called on its members to renounce their titles granted by the British; Maheshwar Dayal responded quickly and effectively and became 'Mister' Maheshwar Dayal, but Guru Narain refused and, what was more, argued with the Mahasabha leadership, so that he lost credit within the organization without any gain in 'popular' esteem. He salvaged a political position in the 1950s but overall his relative slowness to move at these various stages seems to have ensured that he remained fairly firmly a 'middle rank politician'.

10

THE SHASTRIS OF KASHI AND LAHORE:
THE MAKING OF CONGRESS LEADERS

Gyanendra Pandey

This chapter examines the careers of four men who shared very similar social and educational backgrounds, yet played varied political roles and achieved markedly different success as politicians. It is a commonplace that men with identical backgrounds may follow very different political paths. The reasons for these divergent paths are less often identified. This essay explores such a development in the peculiar conditions of India in the period between the two World Wars. In the process, it makes certain suggestions which could perhaps help in providing a more general answer to this question.

In the remarkable political advance that occurred in India during and immediately after the First World War, the major nationalist party, the Indian National Congress, acquired a broader base and a more permanent organization and existence than before. Among the means that helped to create this permanence were various newly established 'national' institutions for education and public service. Two of these were the Kashi Vidyapith (KV), Benares, and the Lok Sevak Mandal (LSM)—the Servants of the People Society—Lahore. Both were instrumental in moulding the careers of the men we study here, and a word about them is in order.

The KV was established through the munificence of Shiva Prasad Gupta, Benares *rais* ('big man') and Congressman, and inaugurated by Gandhi in February 1921. A Vidyapith started slightly earlier in Ahmedabad and served as a model. From the start the KV was organized and run by well known nationalist leaders. Dr Bhagavan Das, a leading Congressman in the early 1920s, was Chancellor of the Vidyapith from 1921 to 1940. J. B. Kripalani, Narendra Deo, Sampurnanand, Birbal Singh, Yajna Narain Upadhyaya, Ram Sharan, all of whom were later prominent in the UP (United Provinces, now Uttar Pradesh) Congress, were among the earliest teachers.[1]

In 1925 the KV was extended to include a college. Forty-two students passed through this college in the first four years of its existence. The work they then took up was as follows:

National education	10
Newspaper editing	5
Untouchability uplift work	5
Khadi work	2
Unpaid Congress work	7
Other (unpaid) public work	7
Total	36

Of the remaining six, it was claimed, at least three combined some public work with their personal vocation.[2] Five of those involved in 'national education' were teaching at the Vidyapith itself. The others were dispersed at other centres in the UP, Bihar, and Rajputana. But all of them were in a position to guide young men and help shape their views. The five journalists were working with *Aj* (Benares), *Pratap* (Kanpur), *Sainik* (Agra), *Vishal Bharat* (Calcutta), and *The Hindustan Times* (Delhi), and were thus connected with several important and influential nationalist journals in northern India.

Institutions like the KV inculcated a public spirit rarely found among the products of government schools and colleges. 'The Kashi Vidyapith, as its prototype in Ahmedabad, has really always been the seminary where students are trained in extremists' methods of thinking', the government of the United Provinces noted in 1930.[3] A year later, the Congress report on civil disobedience had this to say: ' . . . the response from the national schools and colleges was certainly remarkable. The Gujerat Vidyapith and the Kashi Vidyapith specially threw their entire resources into the struggle and almost all their professors and students took part.'[4] Perhaps the most telling comment, however, came from the deputy commissioner of Rae Bareli, when the UP government considered issuing a communiqué declaring students participating in 'subversive' movements disqualified from future government employment. The nine students then in the Rae Bareli jail were all from the KV, and the deputy commissioner succinctly observed: 'the students of *Kashi Vidyapith* are not likely to seek Government employment . . .'[5]

The LSM had also been inaugurated in 1921, again by Gandhi, only nine months after the Vidyapith. It was modelled on Gokhale's Servants of India Society, but was more openly political. Lala Lajpat Rai, the Punjab Congress leader, was the founder and first President of the society. Purushottam Das Tandon, the Allahabad and UP Congress leader, succeeded him on his death in 1928. The society supported a select band of whole-time public workers. Each member was given an allowance of Rs 60 to Rs 100 per month.[6] Owing to financial difficulties, members accepted a voluntary cut of 10% in their already meagre allowances in January 1933. In June that year the cut was increased to 33⅓%. Paucity of funds was probably partly responsible for the very small size of the society all along. In 1934 it still had only 14 members, with three assistants.[7]

The area of LSM activity was mainly Punjab and the UP, though one or two members came from Orissa and Gujarat. In the UP, Meerut, Allahabad and, later, Kanpur were the chief centres of LSM activity. The work was varied but at least in the early years of the society's existence concentrated on work among the untouchables, the running of libraries and newspapers, and other social services. Yet the government complained that, by 1927, 'members of the Society were engaged in endeavouring to meddle with the administration in the villages. Though some of their activities, such as an endeavour to improve sanitation and education, are apparently not open to reproach, yet the fact that they persuaded villagers not to call upon the police or courts to help them settle their disputes, and that they opened registers of births and deaths, showed that the Society was beginning to put into force what Congress had been advocating—the gradual establishment of parallel government.'[8] The fact was that, in the political conditions of India in the 1920s, the dividing line between social and political work was a thin one. There was an acknowledged political aspect to the work of the LSM; work among factory workers at Kanpur, which was taken up in the late 1920s, could never be wholly nonpolitical. When civil disobedience began in 1930, this political aspect of the society completely swamped the social, and the government reported that all the members of the LSM had been 'lent to the Congress'.[9]

This report is misleading in setting up too clear a distinction between LSM and Congress work. The LSM was, in one sense, no more than an appendage of Congress. All the men discussed here were, for instance, members of Congress before they were members of the LSM. This was true in a chronological sense as well as in the sense that they owed their primary loyalty to Congress.

By the 1920s Congress was easily the most important political organization in the UP. A perspicacious governor, Malcolm Hailey, who went to the UP from the Punjab in August 1928, recalled later that the task in the UP, unlike that in the Punjab, was 'to maintain the position of government in view of the growing influence of the Congress'.[10] Again, George Lambert, deputizing for Hailey, held Congress in sufficient respect to write to a prominent UP Congress leader in December 1928: ' . . . You have . . . undertaken a tall order. We are keeping a close eye on agricultural developments, and *can compete with you* by having our own staff not only in every district but in every tahsil and parganah . . .' (emphasis added).[11] In this province, in such a situation, every nationalist who was involved in full-time public work inevitably looked to Congress for a lead, and for a successful political career. At least up to the time of independence our chosen politicians would themselves have used success or failure in the Congress hierarchy as the yardstick for measuring their political advancement.[12] It is reasonable that we should do likewise.

Our four examples all came to be widely known by the 'surname' Shastri, though, in their cases, this was not a name at all but a recognition of an attained educational standard.[13] Algu Rai (Shastri) was the son of Dwarika Rai, a Bhumihar Brahmin of Amila village in Azamgarh district. They were a rent-receiving family of moderate means. Harihar Nath (Shastri) belonged to a Kayastha family, from another district in the backward region of eastern UP, Ballia. His father, Ram Avatar Lal, was a sub-inspector of police in Bihar and died a few years after Harihar Nath's birth. Lal Bahadur (Shastri) was also a Kayastha, a Srivastava. His father, Sharda Prasad, had been, in turn, a schoolteacher, a clerk in the railways, and a tax-collector. They came from Ramnagar, a small town on the Ganga near Benares, but on Sharda Prasad's death, when Lal Bahadur was only eighteen months old, Lal Bahadur's mother moved to her father's home in Mughalsarai, Benares district. Raja Ram (Shastri) was the only one of these four who did not come from the easternmost divisions of the UP. His father, Ghanaram Dube, a Brahmin, had a small *zamindari* in the comparatively prosperous *doab* district of Etawah. But repeated divisions had led to a disastrous fragmentation of the holding, and the family was heavily in debt when Raja Ram was born.

All four of these Shastris were born in the first five years of this century. All went to local schools initially. During the First World War, Algu Rai and Lal Bahadur came together at the Harishchandra High School, Benares, an institution noted for the numerous nationalist leaders it produced. Later, all four joined the KV, from where they received the 'degree' of Shastri. Finally, all became members of the LSM, apparently in the same year, 1926. The stimulus for this step was evidently provided by Lajpat Rai, who went to Benares in 1926 in a campaign to recruit new members for the society. For all the men discussed here, however, political interest and political activity had begun much earlier.

In their cases, as in those of thousands of other Indians in educational institutions and the professions at the time, the popular agitations of 1919-22 were a time of awakening. Harihar Nath was already a student at the KV when he was arrested for non-cooperation. He returned to the Vidyapith on the suspension of the movement. Algu Rai and Lal Bahadur were also students in Benares, though not at the KV, at this time. They had heard Gandhi speak in the city in 1916 and 1920, and his speeches had left their mark. Both Algu Rai and Lal Bahadur gave up their studies when Gandhi called for non-cooperation with the British, and Lal Bahadur at least was arrested for a day. The two resumed their studies only when the movement ended, studying now at the KV. Raja Ram was at high school in Etawah when he took part in a *hartal* (strike) to express Indian criticism of the Prince of Wales' visit to the country in 1921. A threat from his father that Raja Ram would be thrown out of the house if he persisted in such 'vandalism' led to the youngster's 'respectful' departure from his home, his school, and Etawah.[14] Raja Ram went to Allahabad and joined the Tilak School, small donations and a little errand work bringing him enough money to pass his high school examination. After that, in 1922, he migrated to the KV.

All these young men had been caught up in 'the spirit of the age'.[15] By the time they reached the KV, nationalist thinking was an important part of their outlook. Their years at the Vidyapith strengthened their nationalism. From there to the LSM was a quite logical step.[16] In the 1920s when Congress and all its associate bodies were considered 'subversive' organizations, the number of men who were willing to devote themselves to full-time nationalist work was small. This meant that those who took to political work in this way were very conspicuous and well placed in the Congress organization, especially at the district or local level. Thus in 1926 Algu Rai, Harihar Nath, and Lal Bahadur immediately gained some importance in the districts where they went to work. Raja Ram stayed on in Lahore to work in the LSM library and lagged behind the others in establishing a district base for himself in the UP. But the others, too, went into different spheres of work and had different degrees of success in their advance in Congress and in public life.

Algu Rai, who with Harihar Nath formed the more enterprising couple of our four examples, was assigned the work of *achutodhar* (uplift of untouchables) at the Kumar Ashram, Meerut. Very soon he gathered around him an efficient group of workers and the Ashram came to have an important place in the public life of the district. In 1930, the members of his Ashram played an active part in civil disobedience. By that time Algu Rai's influence was great enough to enlist some of the leading *rais* and barristers of Meerut as associate members of the LSM. He was also able to obtain donations and land for the furtherance of his *achutodhar* work. Not only in Meerut, but also in neighbouring districts as well, he organized Sweepers' Unions and raised funds for his work. In several of these districts, moreover, he helped organize and conduct civil disobedience in 1930–31, that is, when he was not in jail; he was by this time an important member of the Delhi Provincial Congress Committee (PCC), under whose jurisdiction the Meerut district came.

Yet, in spite of Algu Rai's great initiative and hard work, *achutodhar* work attained no great heights. In November 1931 Algu Rai was looking for a means of giving it 'a new fillip' and 'a new direction'. He wrote to Tandon, the President of the LSM, saying that he realized that Tandon was busy with peasant work but wished that a little attention could be paid to *achutodhar* too.[17] The Communal Award of 1932, and Gandhi's fast against seperate electorates for the untouchables, gave the required fillip. For a few years work for the uplift of untouchables (under the name of Harijan welfare), Harijan conferences, and centres such as Algu Rai's Kumar Ashram flourished. But the work did not help Algu Rai strike deep roots in the district. In 1936 he returned to his home district of Azamgarh to contest the elections to the lower house of the new legislature set up under the Government of India Act 1935. The absence of recognized and influential Congress leaders in that district was one reason for his return. But, from the viewpoint of his own prospects in the elections, too, it was a calculated and wise move. In Azamgarh Algu Rai worked in a variety of spheres— above all, in the role of the chief organizer of Congress in the district— thus building himself a powerful base which, together with the knowledge of his part in the anti-British struggle, contributed to his repeated election to the UP legislative assembly and his later elevation to a ministership in the government of the province.

Harihar Nath, too, began his career in the LSM with *achutodhar* activity. His allotted place of work was Benares. There, in 1926, he supported Sri Prakasa against the industrial magnate Ghanshyamdas Birla in the elections to the central legislative assembly. Birla was a candidate of the new Independent Congress Party, established by Lajpat Rai and Madan Mohan Malviya. As it happened, he had also donated several thousands of rupees for *achutodhar*, to these two leaders and to Swami Shraddhanand. He was not prepared to see a member of Lajpat Rai's LSM, supported by his (Birla's) own money, oppose his candidature in the elections. Harihar Nath stayed in the LSM— whether because of Lajpat Rai's large-heartedness or because the organization could ill afford to lose the few workers that it had—but was transferred, at his own request, to labour work. After a period of training with trade union leaders in Bombay, he went to Kanpur, took up residence in the workers' quarter called Gwaltoli, and became a specialist labour worker.

It was a new field for a Congressman in the UP. Kanpur's most influential Congress leader in the late 1920s, Ganesh Shankar Vidyarthi, had earlier tackled the problem of labour and set up a Mazdur Sabha (Workers' Union). But his interests and activities had been varied, and he had not concentrated on labour. For Harihar Nath, after 1927, labour was a primary, at times almost exclusive, concern. It became his central field of activity and his political base. By 1929 he was general secretary of the Kanpur Mazdur Sabha, by 1931 its president. Soon after he was put in charge of the UP branch of the Trade Union Congress (TUC) and in 1933 elected president of the All-India TUC. He was the moving force behind the new branches of the TUC set up in Gorakhpur, Benares and other places in these years.

Such standing among industrial workers could not be ignored by Congress, especially when that body began to adopt a 'socialist' stance. By 1931 Harihar Nath was vice-president of the Kanpur City Congress Committee. After 1934, with the introduction of a new Congress constitution providing for direct labour representation in Congress, he became one of the TUC's two representatives on the UP PCC. In 1935 he was elected to the PCC's executive council. As a labour leader, he had also inclined more and more to 'leftist' views. In 1934, when the Congress Socialist Party was formed, he joined it, became general secretary of the UP branch, and organized the Kanpur branch. As a representative of labour, he was nominated to the UP legislative council in 1937, elected to the provincial legislative assembly in 1946, then made a member of the constituent assembly and finally elected to free India's first Parliament before an air accident caused his death in 1953. It is possible that his death cut short a promising parliamentary career and more. But there are reasons why, even if he had lived, Harihar Nath could not have advanced very swiftly out of the middle rank of Congress leaders.

There were certain advantages in being a labour leader in Congress at a time when Congress posed as the representative of the 'masses' and the downtrodden. But there were disadvantages, too. Congress was heavily dependent on the commercial and industrial bourgeoisie for funds. Its support for labour could, *ipso facto*, never be total. It would organize labour and preach agitation if the government could clearly be shown to be the enemy. It was more than hesitant when such agitation affected the interests of Indian millowners as well. One result was that Harihar Nath quickly became a labour leader who specialized in compromise.[18] Among the repercussions was the growth of more militant demands, and an anti-Congress stand, on the part of trade unionists who were further 'left', such as the Communists. The Indian Trade Union Congress split into two, then three, splinter groups. Its unity was never restored and the cause of labour suffered. So did the cause of labour leaders like Harihar Nath. Representatives of labour would find it difficult to reach the front rank of Congress leadership anyhow. For representatives of only a section of the workers, such an advance became even less likely.

These arguments apply with equal force to Raja Ram, who in 1931 joined Harihar Nath to work among industrial and other labour in Kanpur. He suffered from the additional handicap of arriving in the field after Harihar Nath, and of being a less forceful personality. He started therefore as Harihar Nath's understudy, and remained in that position until the latter's death. Raja Ram spent his first five years in the LSM in Lahore, working in the society's library, reading a good deal of Marxist and other revolutionary literature, and coming to the conclusion that the organization of India's workers and peasants was essential for the attainment of Indian freedom. He was jailed for civil disobedience in Lahore in 1930. On his release in 1931, after the Gandhi-Irwin agreement, he asked to be allotted labour work and was sent to Kanpur.

Under Harihar Nath's guidance, he edited the weekly paper *Mazdur* (Worker) and the monthly *Kranti* (Revolution). In 1933 he was elected President of the UP TUC. Earlier, in 1934, he had followed Harihar Nath into the Congress Socialist Party, and had been elected a TUC representative to the PCC. There was never room on the PCC's Executive Council for more than one labour leader, and Raja Ram never became a member of that body before independence.

He was elected to the UP legislative assembly in 1937 and again in 1946, as a Congress candidate from a labour constituency. After independence, he joined the Socialists in their breakaway from Congress, and was elected, as a Socialist, first to the UP legislative council in 1952 and then, in a by-election caused by Harihar Nath's death, to the central Lok Sabha in 1955. In 1958 he rejoined Congress and, by election or nomination, has remained a member of the UP legislative council ever since. He has also remained a middle-ranker in the Congress hierarchy, but clearly in recent days more on account of helping hands from above than because of support from below.

Lal Bahadur, the last of our examples, had the most illustrious career of the four. He was the only one who could definitely be said to have advanced out of the middle rank of Congress leadership, and his advance was remarkably rapid. In part, at least, this was because he was not labouring in a field that held him down. Like Algu Rai and Harihar Nath, Lal Bahadur began his career in the LSM as an *achutodhar* worker. He was, indeed, initially deputed to work under Algu Rai at Meerut, though he later worked among untouchables at Delhi, Benares, and finally Allahabad. Work at Allahabad proved to be a turning point in his career, first, because it brought him into close association with Tandon and the Nehrus, and, second, because Allahabad paid great attention to the peasant question in the 1930s.

Lal Bahadur called Tandon his first political *guru*. Tandon, who became president of the LSM in 1928, seems early on to have recognized Lal Bahadur's obvious qualities—modesty, simplicity and conscientiousness. Of the three young LSM men in Allahabad at the time, Mohanlal Gautam, Baldeva Chaube and Lal Bahadur, the last named became his closest co-worker.[19] In 1928, at Tandon's suggestion, Lal Bahadur successfully contested an election for membership of the Allahabad Municipal Board. In the years that followed he shared the lot of every Congressman of this period and went through several terms of imprisonment. When out of jail, his work, under Tandon's guidance, was chiefly among the *kisans* (peasants)—investigating, preaching, and organizing. He showed his worth most clearly as an 'organization' man.

His work as an organizer, especially among the *kisans*, was recognized and valued by Congress at a time when, both for mass agitation and for electoral purposes, peasant support was essential, and when the depression had brought the peasant question to the forefront of the political stage. In 1931 Lal Bahadur became secretary of the Allahabad District Congress Committee. By 1935 he had gone one better and become secretary of the UP PCC. In 1937 and again in 1946 he was elected to the UP legislative assembly, and on the second occasion appointed parliamentary secretary in the ministry of the chief minister, Govind Ballabh Pant. A year later he was elevated to a ministership in the UP government. In 1951 he resigned, at Nehru's request, and migrated to the centre. There he became general secretary of the AICC, organized the Congress election campaign in 1952, was himself elected to the Rajya Sabha, appointed a minister, and passed out of the Congress middle rank for ever.

Inferences on the basis of a rather cursory study of the career routes of four politicians must be hesitantly drawn. Yet a few suggestions may be made. The changed political circumstances of India after 1920 made independence of government an essential pre-requisite for nationalist activity. In this situation a major structural innovation was provided by institutions like the KV and the LSM, which gave many men—who would earlier not have had the opportunity—the chance to be full-time political workers, by providing financial support and a group to work with, in addition to a sense of purpose. This meant that Indian political life gained new types of activists, such as the Shastris.

Our study suggests, further, certain major factors in the advance from the middle ranks of politics to its front rank. Individual qualities and personal connections apart, one of the key factors seems to be the degree of flexibility which the politician retains over the kind of work he does. A political worker who over-identifies with a particular field of activity runs the risk of making himself of limited use to the organization, and consequently of having to remain confined to that particular area of activity. This was seen clearly in the case of Harihar Nath. Raja Ram's situation was similar, though he suffered from the added handicap of arriving late in a restricted field. In the Socialist breakaway, Raja Ram may have been trying to escape from this 'double trap' but the attempt had no more than limited success. Algu Rai apparently saw the problem more quickly; his *achutodhar* work in Meerut brought few dividends in terms of support, and he had, in that district, no real base on personal or kin lines. His return to Azamgarh in 1937 gave him the chance to build a wider, more fruitful basis for a political career. The real success story, though, was Lal Bahadur. His flexibility was revealed in his range of activities: *achutodhar*, work among the *kisans*, and unostentatious but solid organizational work. His organizational and managerial skill, a rare and vital political commodity, was particularly instrumental in his advance out of the middle rank.

Finally, this study suggests the crucial importance of the field(s) of a politician's activities. Given the character of Congress, and the nature of its financial support, labour work was of strictly limited value and potential. *Achutodhar* probably brought much respect for the public worker, but little else. In the UP, especially in the 1920s and 1930s, it was work among the *kisans* that was most necessary and most profitable. In a word, it was politically unwise to concentrate on fields of activity which were tangential to the organization's central interests.

11

'GANDHI'S MEN', 1917–22: THE ROLE OF THE MAJOR LEADER IN THE CAREERS OF MIDDLE-RANK POLITICIANS

Judith M. Brown

In 1919 the Lieutenant-Governor of Punjab province in north-west India reported that emissaries from urban centres of agitation, calling themselves 'Gandhi's men', were activating agents in rural unrest.[1] His hint at the informality of political organization sounds a note of warning. The concepts of recruitment and career patterns, though important tools in analysis of different levels of political leadership, should be used with caution in some contexts. 'Recruitment' has organizational overtones which may be inappropriate in traditional societies under the constraints of colonial rule where formal institutions of modern style politics are probably non-existent or very weak, and tend to be limited in their geographical and social catchment areas. Even the word 'political' raises problems. It may obscure the complexities of public life if the modern political arena is only one among many and men perceive other activities as more effective in the pursuit of the concerns most important to them in the community's life. Where a variety of options are open, some recognizably political in the modern sense and some not, where patterns of action in the modern political arena are not standardized and entry mechanisms into it seldom formalized, the boundaries of public action are often blurred. People can and do drop in and out of politics, changing style and arena, perhaps without such a sense of contrast as their counterparts might feel in the West, where the parameters of politics are more clearly defined and its patterns reinforced by longer traditions.

In the more fluid conditions accompanying political modernization the role of the major leader is particularly important in the careers of middle-rank politicians. The constellation round the 'big man',[2] distinguished primarily by personal loyalty to him, is a marked phenomenon in public life. Such a personal grouping has strong attractions. It promises within the orbit of the strong man influence which might not be equalled by participation in a weak and limited institution. It offers the chance to operate in a wide sphere in public life where specifically political institutions may not cater for the interests of potential participants. In periods of rapid change group membership may also provide a sense of personal security and fulfilment for men whose social and psychological landmarks are disappearing.

One basic pattern in the early phase of modern Indian politics was constellations of middle-rankers round dominant individuals between whom shifting alliances were formed with an eye to each other's standing and to the British *raj*. Numerous variations existed. Some, like Tilak's henchmen in western India, found their solidarity partly in the appeal of the regional hero. Others were united by a blend of emotional and religious commitment to the central figure, as well as by political loyalty. Annie Besant built her all-India following in part on membership of the Theosophical Society and the relationship indicated by Jamnadas Dwarkadas who addressed her as 'My dear Mother'.[3] Commitment to the central figure was the distinguishing mark of these groupings. Another characteristic was their wide range of joint activity. They provided for their members solidarity and strength in spheres of public life other than the overtly political. The Tilakites cooperated in Poona politics, but also in education and local religious festivals. Annie Besant's devotees shared Theosophical Society activities and political work. Gokhale's Servants of India Society bound its members together in social work and politics.

It would therefore seem worthwhile to investigate the operation of such constellations, their role in the careers of middle-rankers and, by extension, their function in the political system. This paper takes as a case study the cluster of middle-rankers round M. K. Gandhi at a particular time—the bloc of lieutenants he built up during his passive resistance campaigns, *satyagrahas*, in Bihar and Gujarat in 1917–18. Having isolated them, it asks how they and Gandhi perceived their relationship and then proceeds to investigate the role of Gandhi and his group in their careers. In a sense Gandhi's constellations of lesser leaders were peculiar phenomena because of his unique qualities of personal attraction and patterns of political activity. But the availability of evidence about him helps to counterbalance this drawback. It permits us to analyse with some precision the operations of one major leader and his group, and may thus illuminate the wider problem of the major leader's role in the career of the middle-rankers clustered round him.

Gandhi's lieutenants are easy to isolate, because the police noted them, and he publicized them, insisting that as 'public workers' without axes to grind they should be trusted and assisted by people and government. In Champaran, Bihar, during his 1917 *satyagraha* for indigo cultivators against their planter landlords, Gandhi deliberately avoided the major Patna politicians and used lesser, local men. Nine of them were lawyers. The most influential was Braj Kishore Prasad, a leading

Darbhanga *vakil* (lawyer) and already a local politician, having sat on the Bengal and Bihar and Orissa Legislative Councils. Since he was too busy professionally to accompany Gandhi all the time, he organized as Gandhi's interpreters M. A. Dharnidhar, a Darbhanga pleader friend, and Ramnawami Prasad, who had just started practising in the Muzaffarpur district court and had time to spare. Other lawyer assistants were Gaya Prasad Singh (Muzaffarpur *vakil*), Ram Dayalu Sinha (Muzaffarpur lawyer), Gorakh Prasad (pleader in Motihari *munsif's* court), and three who practised in the Patna High Court—Rajendra Prasad, Sambhu Saran, and Anughrah Narayan Sinha. Apart from B. K. Prasad, only Rajendra Prasad was at all prominent in local politics: he was a member of Congress and had agitated through the Bihar Provincial Conference and Congress over the constitution of the proposed Patna University. Other local men joined the lawyers as Gandhi's henchmen. J. B. Kripalani, who had recently been dismissed after five years as Professor at Muzaffarpur College, became Gandhi's gate-keeper; and Pir Muhammad, a journalist and ex-teacher, liaised between two other groups interested in Gandhi's campaign—the Marwaris and *mukhtars* (agents) of Bettiah, the local town, and the cultivators' spokesmen. The Bettiah men were peripheral to *satyagraha*, but of the five peasant leaders at least the chief one, Raj Kumar Shukul, should be considered a middle-ranker. The son of a Brahmin cultivator, Shukul had also taken to land management and money-lending, and in his campaign for indigo cultivators had spoken at the Bihar Provincial Congress and the 1916 Congress before acquiring Gandhi's assistance.[4]

In 1918 Gandhi turned to Gujarat. He led *satyagraha* for cultivators in Kaira district against the land revenue assessment, and for Ahmedabad millworkers who were demanding a pay increase. Again, he used a small group of lieutenants and boosted them as impartial public workers. In Kaira, Mohanlal Kameshwar Pandya was the main farmers' leader: following Gandhi's tactical advice, he landed in prison for cutting down an onion crop which had been attached in lieu of revenue, and consequently became a local hero. As in Champaran, a small group of educated assisted in organization and publicity; though here Gandhi was able to draw on a recently founded Home Rule League and the Gujarat Sabha, of which he had just been made President. His main helpers were three Ahmedabad lawyers, Vallabhbhai Patel, Kalidas Jeskaram Zaveri, and Maganbhai Chaturbhai Patel; other local people —Deoshankar Dave of Umreth, Raojibhai Patel of Sojitra, Haribhai J. Patel of Broach, Mahadev Desai of Surat, who had recently joined Gandhi's entourage and assisted in village work in Champaran, and Anasuya Sarabhai, sister of a prominent Ahmedabad millowner; and

two Bombay business and newspaper men, Indulal Yajnik and Shan-
karlal Banker.[5] During the Ahmedabad *satyagraha* some of the same
names cropped up. The millworkers produced no leaders, and Gandhi's
helpers were Anasuyabehn, Banker, and Vallabhbhai Patel.[6]

In a year Gandhi had built a personal constellation of two local
groups who operated as middle-rankers under his direction. The
creation and operation of the constellation depended, however, on the
perception of each party in the relationship of the role of the leader and
his group. The qualifications for entry into the group and continuing
participation in it become apparent when we see how Gandhi and his
men viewed the enterprise. Gandhi saw himself not primarily as a
career politician, or even as a religious leader, but as one who had
wrestled with the meaning of truth for men as individuals and in
society. He participated in public life whenever he saw 'wrongs' which
he believed he could right by his idiosyncratic method of *satyagraha*.
His ideology of truth compelled him into political action, driving him
to seek power, not for personal aggrandizement but for what he
could do with it in society. Consequently, there were two main
characteristics he looked for in those whom he chose as his lieutenants.
Firstly, they had to be able to deliver the goods he wanted in any
particular situation. In 1917–18 this meant men with local knowledge
and influence, men whose occupations allowed them free time, men
who possessed the organizational ability and technical skills necessary
for public persuasion and collection of evidence. But, secondly, his
lieutenants had to be men who were amenable, who would work in the
way which was peculiar to him. Tight personal control was a marked
feature of his *satyagrahas*, even in South Africa. He elevated it to the
status of a *satyagraha* principle: as he said in 1919, 'he expected implicit
obedience and blind compliance with his orders'.[7] This was understandable as *satyagraha* was a risky business: ill-judged or ill-timed
resistance to laws could land a whole campaign in disrepute and
violence, contrary to Gandhi's ideals.

In practice, therefore, though Gandhi selected his lieutenants, the
range of people on whom he could draw was restricted to those who
exhibited these characteristics. In Champaran Gandhi needed men who
knew the locality, could interpret the Bhojpuri dialect, and had the
time and expertise to record peasants' statements. Local lawyers fulfilled
these requirements. Moreover, they submitted to his control—in
particular to his ban on any attempt to link the *satyagraha* with Home
Rule propaganda. The local ICS man acknowledged Gandhi's control
over them, and Rajendra Prasad recorded that 'Mahatmaji had sealed
his own as well as our lips and we were not permitted to deliver
public speeches either on the Champaran situation or in connection

with the Home Rule movement.'[8] It is significant in this connection that many of them were fairly young. Rajendra was 33, R. D. Sinha 31, Kripalani 29, A. N. Sinha 28, Ramnawami Prasad 26, and Sambhu Saran 25. Their career patterns were probably still flexible, or, like Sambhu Saran and Ramnawami Prasad, they may not have built up large practices by that date—hence their willingness to submit to Gandhi's direction.

Gandhi himself described the reasoning behind the choice of his main middle-ranker for the Kaira *satyagraha*:

Many people were prepared to follow my advice, but I could not make up my mind as to who should be my deputy commander. I then thought of Vallabhbhai. I must admit when I met him first I could not help wondering who this stiff-looking person was and whether he would be able to do what I wanted. But the more I came to know him the more I realised that I must secure his help. If it were not for his assistance, I must admit that this campaign would not have been carried through so successfully.[9]

Here again, Gandhi chose his lieutenant, but his choice was constrained by the necessities of the situation—'I realised that I must secure his help.' Vallabhbhai Patel was a Kaira Patidar, member of the caste of prosperous farmers who were disputing the revenue assessment; he was also a prominent Ahmedabad lawyer, member of the Gujarat Club, a secretary of the Gujarat Sabha, member of the Ahmedabad municipality, and brother of Vithalbhai, the Bombay politician. He was ideally placed to deliver the goods Gandhi wanted—organization at village level, combined with support and publicity among the politically aware of Gujarat and Bombay. As in Champaran, so in Kaira and later in Ahmedabad, having chosen his 'men', Gandhi kept tight control over them. In both places his control depended largely on his physical presence, though in Kaira he also used the Gujarat Sabha.

However, the qualifications for entry into Gandhi's constellation of lieutenants were not, in his view, adequate for continued participation in it. His abhorrence of western civilization and idealization of what he took to be traditional Indian civilization made him condemn the growing dichotomy between India's western educated and the majority of the population. The former, by virtue of their skills and experience, necessarily formed the largest part of the catchment area on which he could draw for lieutenants but, having admitted them to his group, he educated them to new styles of public activity and perceptions of the good society. He wanted the western-educated to throw off their false sophistication and aloofness from their compatriots, and to work for their country at all social levels in a variety of ways, many of which were not overtly political. Concurrently he hoped to arouse the

illiterate and apathetic to awareness of public issues and conscious participation in public life. From this stemmed his insistence in Champaran
that work among the peasants, to better their economic conditions, to
teach them to read, and to inculcate basic principles of public health and
hygiene, was true Home Rule work.[10] His instructions to volunteers in
Kaira stressed similar village education and urged them to go on foot
and to eat the simplest food, so lessening the gap between them and
their rustic compatriots.[11] Moreover, as President of the Gujarat
Political Conference, he insisted that its proceedings should be in the
vernacular, and that it should have a strong executive body to act on its
resolutions—hence its involvement in the Kaira *satyagraha*.[12] Gandhi
was determined that his educated lieutenants should not get away with
fine rhetoric but inaction, with comfortable security as a prosperous
social group though they preached patriotism, discipline, and reform.
Modification of attitudes, and of styles of life and political action, were
essential qualifications for continuing as lesser leaders in his circle.

Although Gandhi selected his lesser leaders, there was also a strong
element of self-selection present. In the process and relationship of
recruitment complementary initiatives from both sides were vital. For
example, in Champaran Pir Muhammad offered his assistance, and the
lawyer group went out of their way to cluster round Gandhi when
Shukul brought him to the district. In Gujarat Vallabhbhai had once
been sceptical of the rustic apparition in the Gujarat Club who preached
truth and soul force, yet in 1918 he was willing to cooperate with him.[13]
The forces which thrust individuals into Gandhi's orbit obviously
varied. It is difficult to know how men felt at the time because their
reminiscences tend to be coloured by Gandhi's subsequent public
repute; while contemporary comments by police and officials empha-
sised the more patent drives of self-interest. There is little doubt that
most of the middle-rankers in Gandhi's constellation realized that he
had something to offer in the particular arena in which they were acting
or aspiring to act. To the cultivators' leaders in Kaira and Champaran
he offered leverage in village life, showing them new ways of dealing
with rural authorities. To the local educated his campaigns were a
chance to ventilate personal grievances and to increase their influence in
the local community, whether indirectly by undermining the influence
of other powerful local groups like the Champaran planters, or directly
by connecting them with groups from whom they had been isolated.
For some of the lawyers at least, Gandhian *satyagraha* provided an
occasion to extend the local range of modern political awareness and to
increase their own importance in that arena. The local ICS officer noted
that Braj Kishore and Rajendra Prasad were 'prominent in the politics
of the province, and were anxious to give the movement the character

of a Bihar national undertaking'.[14] The same was probably true of Vallabhbhai in Gujarat, who was currently building up an opposition bloc in the Ahmedabad municipality to challenge official control. However, it seems unlikely that at this stage in their own or in Gandhi's career even these three calculated that alliance with him would give them prominence in all-India politics within Congress or in opposition to the *raj*.

Ideological and personal attraction towards Gandhi almost certainly blended with vested interest and personal ambition to drive these middle-rankers into his circle. Such an attitude towards their leader, though difficult to define or document, was almost essential if they were to subject themselves to the degree of discipline he required. When he recruited his lawyer henchmen in Champaran the only question he asked was whether they would be prepared to go to gaol! Gandhi's methods were novel and immediately relevant to the local situation, and consequently exciting to young men who felt that the politics of petition in Congress were both remote from their own situation and increasingly proving an ineffective enterprise. But Gandhi also benefited from a strain of idealism which had earlier propelled some of his lieutenants towards the Servants of India Society, or Theosophy. Rajendra Prasad was one such. He later described the attraction and challenge Gandhi presented in 1917, though he could not unravel the skeins of experience, idealism, and friendship with lawyers who had already taken the plunge, which brought him to the point of being prepared to go to prison in the course of Gandhian *satyagraha*.[15]

Although it is impossible to document each middle-ranker's reasons for making himself available to Gandhi, it is easier to trace the repercussions of the constellation's existence and joint experience on the participants. Some of Gandhi's lieutenants rose fairly rapidly thereafter to become leading politicians in their own regions and all-India figures of considerable weight. Most obviously, Rajendra Prasad and Vallabhbhai Patel moved from the middle rank, largely as a result of association with Gandhi at this stage in their careers. Both were equipped by higher education and legal training to operate in the modern political arena; both had been active locally in that arena before Gandhi's appearance in 1917–18. But association with Gandhi gave them a spring-board into all-India politics which they might otherwise have lacked because of the regions from which they came. The power structures of Gujarat and Bihar and the dominant issues in local public life were such that these areas had generated tepid interest in Congress politics and sent few representatives to Congress sessions; those few had carried little weight compared with men from Bombay, Poona, Calcutta, or Madras. Now Prasad and Patel rode to continental influence in the wake of a leader who began to break down the dominance of such places with a novel political appeal and technique, and was by 1920 recognized as one of the most powerful men in all-India politics.[16]

Gandhi's influence in the careers of Prasad and Patel was not just that he took them with him as lieutenants into all-India *satyagrahas* and Congress. He also trained them in a new style of political action, educating them to campaign on issues and to mobilize support over a far wider range than had earlier politicians. These were qualifications which put them at a premium in the rapidly changing political scene during the First World War and its aftermath. The importance of Gandhi's tutorship was particularly clear in Vallabhbhai's case. Kaira and Ahmedabad were followed by the Borsad campaign, the Nagpur flag *satyagraha*, and the Bardoli campaign. These established him as Congress' main organization man, capable of mobilizing a wide span of social groups and coordinating their actions in ways far beyond the capacities of the previous political generation. They were the foundation of his national leadership role in civil disobedience between 1930 and 1934. As Gandhi wrote of the Kaira experience, 'That Vallabhbhai found himself during the campaign was by itself no small achievement'.[17]

Yet factors of temperament, inclination, and the availability of other opportunities were also important in determining career patterns. Two more of Gandhi's henchmen in Champaran rose from the middle ranks, but by other routes—A. N. Sinha via the Congress machine and work in local and central legislatures, J. B. Kripalani through academic office and the Congress Party—though for both Champaran was their entry into active political work and their step to the middle ranks. By contrast, Braj Kishore Prasad, who in 1917 looked the likeliest candidate of Gandhi's Bihari group for a top rank political career, appears to have made little of the opportunity offered. Perhaps his legal practice was too established and his career expectations too defined to permit the necessary flexibility—although he did give up his practice during non-cooperation in 1921–22.

Others who assisted Gandhi in Bihar and Gujarat remained, like Braj Kishore, local and middle-rank politicians after 1917–18. They differed from Braj Kishore in that participation in local *satyagraha* often marked both their debut in political action and their elevation to the middle ranks, while he was already established as a local leader by 1917. Most of the Bihari lawyers, for example, had as a result of their training and education the requisite skills and interest for participation in modern politics, but were only peripheral participants in the political arena before 1917. Local *satyagraha*, followed by the Rowlatt *satyagraha* and non-cooperation, precipitated them into that arena: their response to Gandhi's plans opened the way to middle-rank status in local Congress politics. G. P. Singh became a member of the Muzaffarpur District Board, and in 1922 a member of the Bihar legislative assembly. R. D. Sinha established himself as one of Bihar's leading Congressmen and served in local government and on the Bihar legislature. Sambhu Saran and M. A. Dharnidhar similarly became leading lights of the Bihar Congress, while Gorakh Prasad was one of Bihar's leading Gandhians and directed the province's part in Quit India. In some cases ties of friendship and marriage strengthened the bonds of shared political loyalty and experience between them and other politicians. Sambhu Saran, for example, was a close friend of Rajendra Prasad and A. N. Sinha, and married Lal Bahadur Shastri's sister. Braj Kishore's two daughters married J. P. Narayan and Rajendra Prasad's eldest son. How far such ties originated in common commitment to Gandhi is unknown. They might presumably have served as mobilizing factors in the political careers of these men, had Gandhi not built up a local constellation, as might the extension of political power and opportunity following the 1919 reforms. But this is speculation; in fact, participation in *satyagraha* was their point of political 'take-off'.

More of Gandhi's helpers in Gujarat had been initiated into modern politics—through the recent activities of local branches of the Home Rule League—before they joined him. But Gandhi contributed to their training for local leadership roles, and several reappeared as middle-rankers after the specific local issues of 1918 had been settled. Several were deputed as organizers of the Rowlatt *satyagraha* in particular areas—Banker and Yajnik in Bombay, Haribhai Javerbhai in Broach, and M. K. Pandya in Nadiad. Pandya was also to become one of Vallabhbhai's main lieutenants in the Bardoli campaign.[18] Mahadev Desai took up a unique middle-rank role as Gandhi's private secretary, which was his departure point for considerable political influence, particularly in Gujarat. When he was arrested in November 1930 he was described by the governor of Bombay as 'at present most influential leader of Civil Disobedience in Gujarat after Vallabhbhai Patel'.[19] He was a particularly good example of the strength and self-confidence which participation in a constellation round a prominent leader could generate, though it took some years more in Gandhi's company after Kaira before he could write: 'I had little confidence in myself a month ago when Vallabhbhai was arrested, but the way in which the public is responding has filled me with self-confidence. I am addressing meetings daily the like of which I never addressed before in my life.'[20]

Others in Gandhi's constellation in 1917-18 seem to have dropped out of active politics once local *satyagraha* had ended, or at least to have fallen into the category of rank and file rather than lesser leaders.

Champaran's cultivator spokesmen do not reappear as known politicians, and Pir Muhammad and Ramnawami Prasad apparently subsided from political action. I have not found evidence that the others of those whom the police noted as Gandhi's assistants in Kaira retained their middle-rank position. The explanation of their disappearance while others remained prominent in the political field probably lies in their initial reasons for joining Gandhi's constellation, their personal ambitions and capacities in relation to available modes of political activity once the local protest was over The extent to which Gandhi trusted them and tried to keep them in play in politics may well have been a further significant factor. But precisely because they disappeared from prominence it is difficult to find evidence of their career patterns and to isolate the crucial factors which separated them from their peers who continued in the political limelight.

The operation of a personal cluster round a major leader also modifies the role and repute of the central figure—an important factor in this discussion because the repercussions of the group's actions on the career of the leader affect the way middle-rankers regard him, thus helping to determine the extent of his influence over possible recruits to his circle as well as its existing members. The fate of Annie Besant, who ceased to be an exciting and efficient political leader and gradually lost her constellation of admiring assistants, underlines the point.

Gandhi's local groups were essential for his emergence as an all-India political figure. On local issues, under close personal supervision, they delivered the goods he wanted. As the instruments of successful *satyagraha* they helped to create his public image as a novel and successful political leader. When, however, he began to campaign on wider political issues not so closely woven in the fabric of local life, he found them less effective instruments. Even in their own localities they were not entirely dependable: sometimes they proved too weak to be efficient local leaders, sometimes they modified his plans and went their own ways. For example, when Gandhi launched the Rowlatt *satyagraha*, even Rajendra Prasad hesitated until Gandhi was confined to Bombay before coming firmly out as a local organizer. Later he felt that *satyagraha* should not be extended to the Punjab, and he reported to Gandhi that he could only vouch for himself in Bihar as a staunch *satyagrahi* who would obey Gandhi unquestioningly.[21] During non-cooperation in 1921–22, Gandhi's Bihar lieutenants proved signally ineffective in securing the communal harmony essential to the campaign. Gujarat was more reliable during Gandhi's campaigns on all-India issues, largely because of his stronger personal connection with his home area. Yet even Gujarat erupted in un-Gandhian violence in 1919, and his henchmen were powerless to prevent it.

Outside their localities Gandhi's Gujarati and Bihari lieutenants were even feebler reeds during his all-India campaigns. They could, and did, help to sway Congress in Gandhi's favour, but when it came to political action in the country they had no direct control. At this point the inefficiency of the personal constellation as a recruiting mechanism and training-centre was displayed. It was too limited geographically to bear the burden of a continental campaign—a problem earlier politicians had encountered and attempted to solve by cross-regional alliances between major leaders and their constellations. Gandhi not only met the difficulty but also, to his consternation, found that his name had become a profitable band-wagon. His local *satyagrahas* had so boosted his public image, he and his lieutenants had so publicized his methods in and out of Congress, that men who wielded or aspired to wield influence in their own localities took advantage of his name and plans, often to further their own interests in local politics as the alleged spokesmen of the great man. 'Gandhi's men' operated throughout India in 1919 and in 1921–22, though many were outside his control and in some cases he disowned them. Even where local men did attempt to follow him, he was dependent on their goodwill and local influence for the conduct of his campaigns, because he lacked the sanctions he had possessed in the face to face politics of local *satyagraha*. By 1922 there were signs that the disintegration of his campaign and his vacillations in this dilemma were reducing his leverage and appeal. Gaol possibly saved him from a fate akin to Annie Besant's.[22]

Gandhi's role in the careers of his lieutenants in Bihar and Gujarat, and the repercussions of their actions on his career, indicate some important characteristics of India's political system at that date, and by extension that of other colonial areas where modern politics are in their infancy. The operation of his constellation illuminates the mechanics of a type of successful political leadership. A cluster of middle-ranker henchmen appears an essential element in the strength of the major leader who can deploy few social and economic resources of attraction and control in public life. He needs his 'men' both in and out of such political organizations as Congress. Outside, they are his organizers and publicists, where parties are weakly and intermittently organized, and limited—geographically and socially—in appeal. Inside, they engineer or sway voting patterns, particularly if there are no fixed numbers of participants or defined constituencies. Henchmen are important even where formal political institutions are strong and comprehensive: they are the more so where the 'big man' cannot build his strength on appeals to party members or constituents, or on the exercise of patronage in a party structure. But middle-rankers are also a liability. As Gandhi found, his 'men' and those who purported to be his 'men' were not always controllable. He lacked sanctions outside the face to face situation of the local campaign, in part because he was not the only departure point for a successful political career. Other recruitment mechanisms and avenues of advancement were open to potential middle-rankers when the arena was wider than that of local *satyagraha*—whether through the Congress organization or in the constellation of another 'big man'.

The cluster round a major leader is not the only pathway to political power. But it is an important addition to more formal avenues of political recruitment and advancement in certain situations, when political institutions are weak and limited in range, and when the forces thrusting people into the political arena are often local, and the political style of existing institutions often appears uninviting or inappropriate in the light of the interests potential participants wish to pursue. Operating as a supplementary recruitment and advancement mechanism, the constellation serves to mobilize 'new' people in the political arena. It can be the open door to a younger generation who see little chance of influence in institutions dominated by an 'old guard' and are increasingly disillusioned about the effectiveness of existing political tactics. It can pave the way to political influence for men from areas which have previously provided few representatives in formal political organizations where these, like Congress, have no rules to guarantee balanced geographical representation, and tend to cater for the concerns of the more developed parts of the country which produce the bulk of those interested in and equipped for modern politics. The personal constellation with its wide range of joint activity and interests can also mobilize groups who have previously seen modern politics as irrelevant to their particular grievances or ambitions. Gandhi's constellations in Bihar and Gujarat performed all these functions. By creating a group of middle-rankers he mobilized a predominantly young group, brought into play in modern politics two areas which were notoriously backward in that arena, and opened the eyes of such social groups as Bihar peasants and Kaira Patidars to the possible pay-offs of political agitation in their situations.[23] Action within his group was the political spring-board for some men who became middle-rankers in *satyagraha* and stayed on in politics to become middle-rankers in Congress.

Equally significant as those whose political careers dated from association with Gandhi in 1917–18 were the apparent failures among his lieutenants—those whom he temporarily elevated to the role of middle-ranker but who disappeared from political importance thereafter. The phenomenon of the middle-ranker 'drop-out' may indicate the degree to which a modern political system has not expanded sufficiently to comprehend concern for most major public issues. It reflects the concomitant perception of politics as a part-time activity, to be engaged in sporadically according to the question at issue, rather than as a pattern for a full-time career or even as a part-time but constant commitment. It suggests that the boundaries of public action are not clearly demarcated in men's minds when entry into and activity in the modern political arena are not standardized, and the pay-offs not assured. The 'drop-outs' are, however, a pool of potential political activists: they may well give resilience to a political system and permit flexibility of tactics by acting as reservists, available for call-up as local middle-rankers when the political situation demands large-scale direct action. To prove the point, one would have to look, in India's case, at Gandhi's later all-India civil disobedience campaigns and see if any of the 'failures' of 1917–18 reappeared as local organizers.[24]

Within India's political system Gandhi's constellation also had a significant educative function. Having gathered his lieutenants, he consciously educated them for leadership in new styles of politics. By contrast, political institutions tend to be inflexible, less capable of adapting to changing circumstances. Gandhi's impact on Congress in 1920–22, and subsequently on the style of Indian politics, suggests that the innovating individual surrounded by amenable middle-rankers is an important, perhaps a necessary, agent of adaptation and transformation within a political system which must learn to cater for the increasing diversity of needs thrown up in periods of rapid change, as when imperial authorities divest themselves of power.

The achievements of Gandhi's constellation illuminate the nature and workings of India's political system. Its weaknesses are equally informative. The pattern of Gandhi's leadership and the response of his middle-rankers in 1917–22 demonstrated the inadequacy of the personal constellation as a means of political recruitment and control. Because such a constellation is by its nature geographically restricted, its attractions and sanctions are also limited. As Gandhi discovered, when more people become interested in modern politics the personal constellation cannot channel and hold them: if the political system is to achieve a new stability it must develop effective methods of coping with such recruits. More formal political structures are necessary to provide avenues for advancement, rewards for the compliant, and sanctions against the deviant. Gandhi seems to have realized this, and was a prime mover in 1920–21 in the refashioning of Congress into a mass party. The British also acknowledged and contributed to the change by remodelling the political institutions which were dependent on their fiat. Congress leaders struggled with the growing problem until independence: their experiences hint that no final solution is possible for an organization which sees itself as a national movement and is not content with the role of a political party.

Study of 'Gandhi's men' between 1917 and 1922 suggests that the major leader, by attracting a cluster of middle-rank henchmen, performs vital political functions in the fluid conditions which characterize the early manifestations of modern politics in traditional societies, and the process of their expansion and formalization. He mobilizes and innovates where institutions cannot. If he succeeds his very success rebounds on him, demanding the creation of new political structures and styles, and his own adaptation to the changed political environment.

The observer of the erstwhile leader's fate must then ask a new set of questions about the role of the 'big man' and his constellation of middle-rankers. Does such a phenomenon still exist? How does the personal constellation work in relation to the new organizations and institutions? Does it manipulate, challenge, or stand aloof from them? Where now does the major leader gain his lieutenants, what can he offer them and what sanctions can he deploy against them?

Gandhi's relationship with Congress and the institutions of the reformed constitution after 1922 provides evidence for tentative answers to such questions. The foundation of political leadership began to shift, and the criteria for judging influence in politics changed as politics became increasingly institutionalized, expanded in range to comprehend more important public issues, impinging on wider areas of the community's life, and became a key arena from which people concerned with public issues could not afford to be excluded. As the nature of the major leader changed, so did his role in the careers of lesser leaders. Gandhi never fully adjusted to this change, despite his insistence on an efficient Congress organization firmly rooted in popular support. He never abandoned the agitational style of politics to which ideology and experience drew him, never became a party boss or constitutional tactician. Consequently, when the new institutional structures were fully operative, his influence over lesser leaders, their need of and, therefore, their response to him weakened markedly. But until the very end of his life the institutionalization of politics and the expansion of this political mode to comprehend the major issues in public life were in process rather than complete. Precisely at those points in the process when the institutions appeared constricting and inadequate men turned to Gandhi. Then, at least in his case, the constellation of middle-rankers round the major leader became again a nursery for some who rose to all-India stature, and many more who stayed in the middle ranks and manned the country's provincial political hierarchies.

12

THE LESSER LEADER AMID POLITICAL TRANSFORMATION: THE CONGRESS PARTY IN MYSORE STATE IN 1941 AND 1951

James Manor

This is a study of the careers of lesser leaders in the Congress Party of an Indian state on each side of the watershed which was Indian independence. The discussion focuses around two points in time: 1941 when Congress was a struggling opposition party to a princely regime which seemed well entrenched in power, and 1951 when Congress was entering its fifth year as an all-powerful ruling party under a parliamentary system. The political transformation which occurred in these ten years within the Mysore Congress roughly parallels that which occurred within the party in most British Indian provinces between 1920 and 1950. In order to understand this transformation, we shall examine why and how men entered politics, the backgrounds from which they came, their perceptions of themselves and the political environment, the roles that they played, and the resources and styles that aided or thwarted their advancement.

Mysore was the second largest of India's princely states, covering an area about the size of Scotland. It was also the most progressive state in princely India, rivalling British India in industrial and educational development, an even-handed judicial system, and freedoms of speech and the press. Its British-style administrative structure, if less extensive than in the neighbouring British province of Madras, was the model of the princely order. And since the nineteenth century it had maintained a legislature and local self-government boards, although it was far less generous than the British in extending power to these institutions.

Three social groupings held the centre stage in Mysore politics in this period. The Brahmins—highly literate, urbanized, and thus

	% of total population[1] (1941)	% of males literate (1941)
Brahmins	4.0	73.0
Lingayats	11.4	28.8
Vokkaligas	20.0	15.4
Total population	100.0	20.4

politicized—were very active politically, but lacked the numbers and wealth necessary for great political influence. Two populous and wealthy groups, the Lingayats and the Vokkaligas, divide the state into roughly equal parts in which they exercise dominance in rural areas.[2]

From the early 1920s a few dozen, mainly Brahmin, enthusiasts in half a dozen towns in Mysore met sporadically and called themselves the Mysore Congress. But they had no sustained programme of work, never contested elections, and were in no sense a political party. At the same time there existed a loose, informal, non-Brahmin political association which consisted of a handful of eminent professional men, most of whom were Lingayats and Vokkaligas and members of the state assembly. In 1937 these two groups merged into a single political force which combined the Congress label with the non-Brahmins' influence among their numerous caste fellows. The merger marked the beginning of serious party-building in Mysore.

In 1941, when we first encounter it, the Mysore Congress had just begun to develop an organizational structure beyond a handful of urban centres. Its only role was as the sole opposition to a princely government which refused to extend even a minimal degree of power to political parties. Its only real hope for power lay in the possibility of change from above, in the possibility that the coming of Congress Raj to British India would persuade or force the princely authorities to open the way for the local Congress as well. Hence much of the party's effort was focused on convincing the leaders of the national movement that Mysore Congressmen were true believers and genuine representatives of the masses. But in 1941 the end of British rule seemed much more than six years away. Hence the Mysore Congress had to rely for manpower on a limited number of volunteers with a stomach for sacrifice. Recruitment problems were further complicated by the reluctance of the princely government to extend its administrative tentacles into local-level political arenas to the same degree as British Indian governments. As a result two quite distinct political systems existed in Mysore in 1941: the government's administrative structure penetrating downwards from the state level, and the traditional idiom of politics at the local level.[3] Local magnates, untroubled by interference from above, lacked the grievances against the government which moved many of their counterparts in British India to cooperate with Congress.[4] They thus remained almost entirely aloof from politics beyond the local arena.

By 1951 quite striking changes had occurred. Congress had been the ruling party since late 1947 and a sophisticated party organization had come into being. The era of universal suffrage was to be inaugurated in a few months with India's general elections. To continue in power, the

party required a popular mandate from below. The main preoccupation of Congress leaders was thus to convince the rural populace that
their best interests lay with a Congress government. To achieve this
they sought out new recruits who could help to deliver votes. This task
was not difficult. As patronage from state-level office-holders began to
flow into rural parts, ambitious men in local-level arenas all across the
state came to realize that the new political system offered them tangible
resources for use in the locality. They overcame their former aloofness
and volunteered for Congress work. As they did so the local-level
arenas were linked with the state-level system of politics through
transactional alliances which they had forged with politicians at the
state level. For the first time it was becoming possible to speak of a
single, integrated, state-wide political system.

1941

(a) Brahmin publicist-clerk for the district Congress committee:

T. P. Krishnappa[5] was born about 1910, the eldest son of a Brahmin
family in Tumkur, the headquarter's town of one of Mysore's nine
administrative districts. His father was head clerk in the government's
district office, a job which was poorly paid despite its being the highest
rung on the ladder of the non-gazetted (lower level) civil service. His
father, a loyal government functionary, was unsympathetic to Indian
nationalism. But his mother, like many urban women of the more
literate castes, had heard of the Congress struggle in British India and
was deeply touched by stories of the suffering of nationalists at the hands
of the brutish foreigner. She was particularly drawn to the figure of
Gandhi because the puritanical strain in his teachings was so consistent
with the ethos which was prevalent among high-minded Hindu
women. In their home she often spoke warmly of Congress and poin-
tedly refused to second her husband's criticism of the nationalist
sentiments that had gained wide currency among high school boys in
the 1920s.

In those days there was no college in Tumkur, so when young
Krishnappa finished at the English-medium high school he enrolled
at Maharaja's College in Mysore City, seventy-five miles away. His
family was too poor to pay his way. So, as was often the case, he
arranged for a relative there, who was a gazetted, well paid civil
servant, to house and support him. But no sooner had he arrived at
college than his relative was transferred. This dashed his hopes for
higher study and further embittered him against the government
which had so ill-rewarded his father's labours. He returned to Tumkur
and took a low-paid job in a small print shop which was run by a

group of Brahmin nationalists. Through them he became involved in Congress activities in the early thirties. He did not do so out of a desire for personal power. He was a poor man and, as a Brahmin, could not hope to compete in electoral politics with men of more populous castes. For Krishnappa Congress work was an expression of his resentment against the government; it offered him a place in a historic movement which gave his life greater meaning in moral and religious terms.

After the non-Brahmin politicians entered Congress in 1937 the party sought to prove its claims to popularity in two ways: by public demonstrations (which often involved civil disobedience) and by electoral victories. Krishnappa—with only his literary skills, his knowledge of the town, and his enthusiasm to offer—proved useful on both counts. Anti-government demonstrations (a predominantly urban phenomenon in Mysore) relied for manpower mainly on youthful enthusiasts, since Congress was chronically short of money and patronage with which to mobilize people. Krishnappa used his contacts with younger people in the town and circulated underground leaflets to ensure good attendance at Congress demonstrations. He also passed these leaflets and reports of demonstrations to press correspondents, so that the news would reach readers in other towns and cities in Mysore and in British India.

Elections posed a slightly different problem. In theory each of the ten *taluks* (sub-divisions) of the district had its own Congress committee, which worked among the peasant masses, met frequently, and elected a delegate to the district committee, which in turn sent a representative to the party's state executive committee. In practice committees in almost all *taluks* were non-existent. District committees only came to life at election time, and then rather haltingly. The district's most eminent politician—almost always a lawyer of the locally dominant caste—would invite one or two leading dominant caste notables in each *taluk* to stand for election to the legislature or district board. These local notables, who were often unenthusiastic about association with Congress, consented to stand as nominal Congress candidates because they admired or were beholden to the district leader, who was often their lawyer. Once such tenuous links were forged, district Congress clerks like Krishnappa had the task of maintaining them by correspondence, at least until the election was over. Thereafter the clerks worked to persuade the press of the nationalist zeal of the successful Congress candidates and to sustain the fiction of a strong Congress organization, even after the party machinery in the district had lapsed once again into inactivity.

The image-inflating role was important to a party which needed to appear convincing to national Congress leaders and to the newspaper-reading public of Mysore. But it was not this which gave men like Krishnappa the status of leaders—albeit lesser leaders. It was their virtually complete control of the district office. They had this control because they were, quite simply, the only people willing to undertake the dull, arduous paper work which in 1941 offered no remuneration and little hope of future reward. Few members of the powerful rural castes were sufficiently educated and politicized to do the work, and those who were usually found well-paid positions via connections with wealthy relatives or fellow castemen.

This left things to the Brahmins. Their control of the office could become important when a politician in the district Congress set out to depose the presiding district leader. In such cases the contending factions were often of roughly equal strength and the outcome could turn on the publicist-clerk's ability to muster support through official party correspondence. Such struggles did not arise very often. But even when they did not, non-Brahmin district leaders usually paid heed to the publicist-clerk's opinions, to insure against future trouble. Men like Krishnappa lacked the wealth, professional eminence, and base in a populous caste necessary to advance into the forefront of the party. But while no one else volunteered for office duty, sheer hard work won them a place in the middle rank. It was not long, of course, before the future prospects of Congress brightened and ambitious men swelled the ranks of the volunteers. When that happened, non-Brahmin politicians were quick to pack the district offices with men bound to them by ties of kinship, caste, or strong personal loyalty. There was no room, then, for mere altruists like Krishnappa, and he returned to his print shop, where he can be found today.

(b) *Dominant 'caste' lawyer and district party leader:*

S. Nijalingappa[6] was born in 1902 into a prosperous family of the merchant section of the Lingayat sect. His early years were spent in Davangere, the flourishing mercantile centre of his district. During his high school years and then at college in the state capital, Bangalore (1916–22) he shared in the general student enthusiasm over Gandhi's first disobedience campaigns. He went on to study law at Poona, perhaps the most fervid centre of nationalism in the sub-continent, and enrolled in 1924 as a four anna ($\frac{1}{4}$ rupee) member of the Indian National Congress.

But the end of his student days and the opening of a legal practice in Davangere in 1926 brought great changes. His fellow merchant-Lingayats, who dominated the economy of the district, welcomed his entry into a profession which had previously been a virtual monopoly of the distrusted Brahmin. Thanks to their patronage and to his abilities, he soon became the most prosperous lawyer in the district. He greatly enjoyed his profession and the material rewards it brought him, and for a decade he pursued this new life to the exclusion of almost everything else. He moved his family into a spacious home, cultivated expensive tastes, and became an active member in a local British-style club for well-to-do gentlemen. He remained aloof from the politics of the nearly powerless local boards and state legislature, and from the non-Brahmin political association. Although he quietly helped to raise money in Davangere for the Congress non-cooperation movement in British India in the early 1930s he rejected pleas in those years from the mainly Brahmin Mysore Congress to join the state party.

By 1936, however, a number of Lingayats and Vokkaligas had entered the Mysore Congress and the merger of the Mysore non-Brahmin association into Congress seemed only a matter of time. Congressmen wooed Nijalingappa because he was considered the only Lingayat in his Lingayat-dominated district with the skills and connections to develop a popular base there for the party. After considerable hesitation he lent his name to Congress. Within a few months he was made president of the district committee and was elected unopposed as a Congress candidate to the upper house of the legislature. But for three years he was a decidedly diffident Congressman, whose activities for the party were limited to very occasional speeches at public meetings. He had joined Congress out of sympathy with nationalism and because it added lustre to his eminence. But he saw to it that it did not intrude on his life of patrician comfort, and when Congressmen in the state engaged in civil disobedience in 1937–38 he remained at a distance.

In 1939, however, a few of the Brahmins who, like T. P. Krishnappa, controlled the district Congress office initiated the first local civil disobedience movement. It was to dramatize the Congress demand for prohibition—an issue close to the heart of Nijalingappa's teetotal caste. Each day batches of Congress volunteers would advance with instruments of destruction upon the government-owned palm grove, with the aim of cutting the trees which provided the base for the local liquor, only to be arrested by the police. Nijalingappa at first refused to participate, but the campaign soon aroused great sympathy in the district and questions were asked about the reluctance of the most eminent local Congressman. The Brahmins, who could never hope to lead the district Congress, had cleverly forced Nijalingappa to a crossroad. He could prove his sincerity as a nationalist by courting arrest (which meant almost certain disbarment and an end to his income), or he could withdraw from Congress. Such an admission of hypocrisy—and on a very sensitive issue at that—might discredit him before Lingayats and the public at large.

Like many other men at such crucial moments, he consulted his family on the question. His father had died long before, and the advice of his mother, the great influence in his life and the senior figure in the family, weighed heavily. She was a woman of great piety and—like Krishnappa's mother—was drawn to the puritanism of Gandhi, whom she considered an *avatara*, deity incarnate. With the family's agreement, he went to jail. The Mysore government—not content with a mere prison term—disbarred him as well, thus removing the option of a return to his life of genteel detachment. By the severity of this reaction the government recruited to full-time Congress service a man with the influence to make Congress a formidable force in his district.

Nijalingappa's work as a lawyer equipped him well to lead the district Congress. It has been argued that lawyers attained prominence in the national movement because their training enabled them to comprehend the sophisticated issues of the illegitimacy of imperial rule. But the key to their success lay more in their knowledge, gained through involvement in litigation, of the factions and quarrels among notables in the district. This could serve as a guide in developing networks of support which were essential to success in elections and agitations. And, since the government had extended little power to district boards, district politicians had insufficient patronage at their disposal to develop strong networks of support among local magnates. In such a situation the services which lawyers like Nijalingappa had performed in the courts for clients throughout the district were often sufficient to develop support for the lawyer's party.

As long as substantial patronage remained unavailable to district politicians (i.e. until after 1947), political support could be developed on the basis of such factors as a man's professional eminence, the gentility of his manners, the lofty nature of his ideals, and his willingness to undergo personal suffering. Though a late and reluctant convert, Nijalingappa offered all these things. Together with his ties to his powerful mercantile sub-caste, they enabled him to organize Congress committees around a few clients in every *taluk* in the district and to stand above the resulting organization as the leader of the district Congress.

As leader of Congress in his district, Nijalingappa was chosen as its representative on the state-level party executive committee. But in order to qualify as anything more than a lesser leader in the state party, he had to become a strong influence within the executive. His social and professional background was very similar to that of the other members of the executive, but even when he held the nominal party presidency in 1945 he failed to gain admission to the inner circle of party leaders. This was because the state executive was dominated by members of the pre-1937 non-Brahmin political association which Nijalingappa had refused to join. Their resentment over that was compounded by suspicions over his commitment to the party as a result of his failure to court imprisonment for three years after he had joined Congress.

These senior leaders derived their complete control over the Congress organization (which enabled them to exclude Nijalingappa from their circle) from the predicament which confronted the party. The Mysore Congress was completely excluded from power by the princely government and depended for its ultimate success on the support of the national Congress leaders after a future transfer of power at the national level in India. These leaders were thus able to demand from Congress members in Mysore complete loyalty in order to present to the princely authorities and the national Congress leaders the appearance of the greatest possible unity and strength. As a result men like Nijalingappa, who might have wished to generate dissidence within the state Congress to lift themselves within the party hierarchy, found themselves thwarted.

After 1947, when the party had to depend on mass electoral mandates for its survival, these senior leaders were unable to maintain this sort of tight control over Congress. The scent of political spoils brought ambitious men from local arenas all over the state into the party, men who demanded a voice in decision-making in exchange for the votes they could deliver on election day. In that changed world the politician who could cater most effectively to the wishes of these local men gained ascendancy within the state party. In the mid-1950s Nijalingappa mastered the new rules of politics better than all his rivals and lifted himself out of the welter of lesser leaders to pre-eminence in Mysore politics.

1951

(c) Dominant 'caste' leader forced to adapt to the changing rules of politics:

H. M. Channabasappa[7] was born around 1910. Like Nijalingappa, he was a member of the merchant section of the Lingayat sect. But his ancestors had given up trade for agriculture and, by Channabasappa's time, the family were moderately wealthy landholders. After high school in Mysore City, about forty miles from his village, Channabasappa went off to Bangalore to study science and received his BSc degree in 1929. He spent the next three years in further study but in 1932 returned without a higher degree to manage the family lands.

This work was not sufficiently fulfilling, however, to a young man who had lived for nearly a decade in large urban centres and had become aware of the potentialities of popular politics. Within two years of his return to the family estate he had been elected as an independent candidate to the state assembly from one of the northern *taluks* of Mysore district. Two years later he won the right to represent an adjacent *taluk* on the district board. He achieved such quick success not because of caste dominance on these *taluks*—merchant-Lingayats, though wealthy, were far less numerous than the locally dominant Vokkaligas—but because at that early date there was no serious competition there for elective office.

With his sharp eye for political opportunity, it was not long before Channabasappa realized that, although membership of the assembly carried greater prestige than a place on the district board, the presidency of the board was the only post which offered even a modest amount of power in the politics of the day. But coveting the presidency and winning it were two different things. The incumbent was the most thoroughly entrenched local office-holder in the state—one B. S. Puttuswamy. Puttuswamy, a lawyer, had been president since 1930 and had developed a powerful organization throughout most of the district by dispensing personal favours received from the government in exchange for his staunch loyalism. As almost the only board president with personal patronage from the government at his disposal, Puttuswamy was able to draw a large number of local magnates into his organization. Most of these supporters were his fellow Gowda Lingayats—the dominant agriculturist caste across most of the district —who distrusted Channabasappa's merchant-Lingayats.

When most non-Brahmin politicians joined Congress in 1937, Puttuswamy remained an independent, loyal to the government. Young Channabasappa, seeing in the growing Congress movement a possible counterforce to the loyalist organization, became a Gandhian. Results were slow in coming, however. Puttuswamy left the presidency in 1940 but his organization swept a close relative in to replace him. On the day of the next presidential poll in 1944 a helpful Congressman in Mysore City kidnapped one loyalist board member, but Channabasappa still lost. It was not until the eve of Indian independence in 1947, when Congress fervour was mounting throughout the state, that he managed to become president.

It was only then that Channabasappa was able, through the use of his patronage powers as president, to lift himself to a position of moderate influence in the state Congress. And, as the 1952 elections approached, there seemed every reason to expect that he would use his clout as district leader to become a leading voice in the state party— perhaps even a cabinet minister. But the rules of the political game were changing and Channabasappa failed to discern three crucial facets of the transformation. First, having spent the better part of a decade battling with the loyalist organization, he tended to view politics as a struggle between Congress and its opponents. But by 1945 the key struggles were taking place *within* his party. Second, he failed to see that the advent of mass suffrage implied that account had to be taken of the more populous of the newly enfranchised castes. Finally, he had concentrated too much energy on developing his hold over the district-level Congress, ignoring the fact that the smaller *taluk* unit had become the crucial political arena. It was at the *taluk* level, where competition had intensified enormously, that he had to win election to the assembly and it was there that he foundered.

During the first four years of Congress rule the seats in the Mysore cabinet had been filled by members of the small inner circle of the pre-1947 Congress party. These men had proved themselves incompetent and unresponsive to the wishes of younger politicians. In addition, it was widely believed that the cabinet leaders were under the control of a rich Mysore City moneylender (Channabasappa's kidnapper friend from 1944) who was using his influence in government to line his pockets. These suspicions gave rise to a faction of young Turks within the state Congress to challenge this ruling group. In order to remove the moneylender as a rival within his district and to place himself in line for a cabinet post, Channabasappa joined the young Turks. He was naive enough to believe that the factional struggle would end after the selection of candidates, that once he received the party nomination he need only wait for the Congress wave to sweep him into office. But the moneylender set up an 'independent' rival against him, a man chosen for his personal loyalty to the moneylender and for his membership of the populous and newly enfranchised shepherd caste. The moneylender, whose own caste was dominant in the *taluk*, funded the rival lavishly and Channabasappa was beaten. In later years Channabasappa was to re-enter politics and rise to the cabinet rank which he now holds, but this would be possible only when he had adjusted his strategy to the transformation which had occurred.

(d) Party strategist without a power base who was too intelligent to be allowed to survive:

B. N. Gupta[8] was born just before the turn of the century into a mercantile caste family of modest means in Chittor District, which is in the Telugu-speaking area of Madras presidency, bordering on Mysore state. As a youth he went to Madras City to study and became involved with the group of Indian nationalists led by Mrs Annie Besant. Through them he met the Bengali leader Bipan Chandra Pal, who was impressed with the young man's intelligence and took him to

Calcutta where he became involved in the Congress organization. During the nationalist agitations of the early 1920s Gupta gained first-hand experience of the management of a complex political organization in a civil disobedience campaign. Soon after the agitations ended, he returned to Madras to apply the lessons he had learned to make his living from politics. He joined the Justice party which championed the cause of non-Brahmin advancement and he drew a modest income writing for the party newspaper, *Justice*.

In 1925 he was sent to Mysore as the paper's correspondent. He quickly realized the possibilities for a non-Brahmin party in Mysore and was instrumental in building the state's non-Brahmin association during the late 1920s and early 1930s. In 1934 he collected funds from leading members of the association and started a non-Brahmin daily newspaper for the state in Kannada (the language of Mysore, which he had only recently learned). Gupta's writing was lively and entertaining without being sensational or doctrinaire, and within a matter of months the paper was far and away the most popular journal in the state. He began a Kannada weekly with similar results and by 1936 Gupta was one of the most influential men in Mysore public life.[9]

His dealings within the non-Brahmin association were less satisfying, however. He had worked for some years to galvanize the loose assem-blage of district-level leaders who made up the association into a genuine political party, tightly organized and concerned with state-level issues. But they were too preoccupied with their district bailiwicks to respond. He had also hoped to be given a leading role in the associa-tion. But because he had no natural electoral base, because he was neither a Lingayat nor a Vokkaliga but a Vaisya (mercantile caste, comprising only a tiny portion of the Mysore population), and a Telugu Vaisya at that, he was not acceptable to the men of these dominant groups who controlled the association.

As a result, he left the association in 1936 and joined the predomi-nantly Brahmin Mysore Congress.[10] In that year the leaders of the Indian National Congress had for the first time encouraged Congress work in Mysore. Gupta believed that if the support of the nation's heroes could be shown to be a powerful force among the people of Mysore, then he would be able to persuade the non-Brahmins to unite with Congress in a single party of opposition to the princely regime. If this were accomplished, Gupta's work as a go-between might even earn him a position of prominence in the resulting organization.

The events of 1937 proved him a shrewd judge of the situation. With support of the National Congress leaders, the fortunes of the Mysore Congress soared. In the columns of his papers and in countless private negotiations, Gupta wooed the Brahmins with great vigour and finesse. And in October 1937 the merger of the two groups under the banner of Congress was accomplished. As the architect of the union[11] and general secretary of Congress, Gupta's political future seemed assured.

Unfortunately for him, the Mysore authorities were all too aware that he was the prime mover behind the new opposition. They seized on the technicality of his status as a citizen of British India and expelled him forthwith from Mysore.[12] He was to remain in exile until 1945.

In his absence the party grew in strength and the non-Brahmin leaders took firm control of the organization. When he returned in 1945 he was given a Congress nomination to the state assembly. The Congress legislators, remembering his abilities as a tactician, elected him deputy leader of the party in the assembly. This post placed him high up in the second rank of the party leadership, the first being reserved for the tight little circle of old guard leaders whom Gupta had brought together during the 1930s. During the last months of princely rule and the first years of Congress government after 1947, when the old guard leaders sat in the state cabinet, Gupta served in the assembly with distinction. His tact, his eloquence and, above all, his brilliance as a strategist made him an ideal legislative leader.

But, astonishingly, by 1951, when the first general elections loomed, Gupta had been cast into the political wilderness. As mentioned in the previous case-study, the main division within Mysore's Congress Party between 1947 and 1951 was between the old guard cabinet ministers who refused to share decision-making powers with younger party members and the young Turks who sought to replace them. Gupta had realized early on that the cabinet was too insensitive to the opinions of others. He warned the cabinet ministers repeatedly that this would lead to difficulties within the party. But a bearer of bad tidings was not to their liking and he soon found himself unable to gain access to them.

He realized that the cabinet must be replaced if the party was to remain strong, and he offered his aid to the young Turks. They were happy to make use of the insights of this clever tactician. But, when they had succeeded in toppling the first cabinet, they offered Gupta no reward. His intelligence and his ability as a negotiator made him a threat to other advisers to the new Congress ministers and they prevented him from gaining a post in the new administration. Gupta had no territorial or communal base within Mysore from which to re-enter politics. He was thus forced to take up a career in business, where his abilities served him well.

All four of the men discussed here entered politics before 1941 because it offered them excitement and a means by which to improve their lot in life. But the improvement which they sought was not so much an enhancement of their wealth or their control over concrete resources as a rise in status and *moral* influence[13] and the satisfaction of taking part in India's national adventure. They expected little in the way of tangible rewards at the time when they entered politics because the political system offered little. The princely government refused to extend concrete powers to elected officials, with the exception of the token provisions to district presidents. Nor did the expectation of future reward play a part in the entry into politics. Even as late as 1941, none of these men expected Congress to topple the government in their lifetime. Gupta has said that in the early 1940s a Congress politician was 'like an ant' before the power of the Mysore government.[14]

By 1951 Congress politicians controlled the government. Civil servants who had previously been all-powerful in the districts and *taluks* were being brought under tight control by elected representatives. The influence of government was being extended into areas of life which had previously been free of interference. The idealism of the struggle for self-rule had waned when the struggle succeeded. Men entered politics in 1951 in search of tangible power and the spoils which were becoming available.

Once a man effects an entry into politics, the question arises as to the amount of time he devotes to politics, the degree to which he gets involved. Here, too, clear differences emerge between 1941 and 1951. In 1941 it was impossible for any man to be a full-time politician, to make his living from politics. Public offices to which he might be elected paid only token fees and he could not make anything on the side through the disbursement of patronage, since access to patronage was almost wholly unavailable. And, because the party had no access to patronage, it received donations not from wealthy opportunists but from less numerous and far less wealthy altruists who shared their ideals. It was thus chronically short of funds and could not afford to pay full-time (or even part-time) party workers. Since party committees, the legislature, and local boards assembled rather infrequently before independence, it was only a very few people like Krishnappa in the district Congress office who were kept busy most of the time—and even he had to continue working at the print shop to earn a living.

By 1951 it was almost impossible for a politician *not* to be fully engaged and a great many people were beginning to make their living from politics. High public offices carried substantial salaries. People in lesser positions traded their loyalty to superiors for political spoils which they could then dispense further down the line to clients who responded with uncommon generosity. Every government post down to the level of the peon provided a living for someone who was useful to the dominant party in some remote way. The Congress coffers overflowed and a small army of full-time party functionaries was put on the payroll. The party, state assembly, and local boards now managed the affairs of state, and this required the constant involvement of their members. It was for this reason that Gupta did not revive his newspapers after independence and Nijalingappa did not return to his legal practice when his disbarment was rescinded.

The criteria by which men advanced their positions within the party changed dramatically between 1941 and 1951. In both these years, loyalty was demanded of men who wished to advance. But the focus of their loyalty changed over this decade. In 1941, when a fledgling Congress faced an overwhelmingly powerful government, the principal object of loyalty had been the party as a whole and the nationalist cause. By 1951 the party had become even more powerful than the government of 1941 and internal quarrels over the fruits of office inevitably developed. Under these circumstances loyalty could only mean loyalty to an individual or a faction within the party. A man (like Channabasappa during the election campaign of 1951–52) who was naive enough to want simply to be 'a loyal Congressman' found this impossible.

In 1941, when membership in Congress carried no tangible rewards and plenty of risks, men (like Krishnappa) who were willing to put in long hours of hard work for the party could be sure of a role of at least modest importance. The situation was fluid, and the needs of the party great, so that a hard-working man with genuine talent could leave his mark on the shape of Congress and of Mysore politics (as Gupta had done only a few years earlier when he helped to bring the party into existence).

By 1951 the powerful incentives for joining Congress had brought a flood of volunteers for even the most arduous tasks. In order to secure a place in the organization, a man had to possess links with influential men within the party. The organizational structures of the state Congress had developed considerably since 1941, so that there was little scope for a man of talent to alter their shape. Indeed (as Gupta's career indicates), a politician's talent could be a positive disadvantage as party leaders sought out unimaginative supporters in order to avoid being threatened from below.

It was useful in both 1941 and 1951 to have ties with groups of electors within a particular area which could serve as an electoral base. But the relative importance of an electoral base to career advancement changed during the intervening decade. In 1941 such a base could facilitate one's advancement within the party. This is clearly illustrated by the degree to which Nijalingappa benefited from his base among his fellow-castemen in his district and Krishnappa suffered because his fellow-castemen were numerically weak. But since election victories yielded no real power for the party and since advancement within Congress was largely governed by the whims of the half-dozen senior leaders who controlled the organization, a strong political base did not guarantee a man success. By 1951 the introduction of mass suffrage had fundamentally altered the whole logic of the political system. Congress could derive its power only from a popular mandate at the polls. As a result, power inevitably passed out of the hands of the senior leaders at the top of the party structure to men who could deliver results on election day, and electoral bases became a much more powerful asset than ever before.

The nature of an electoral base in 1951 differed from that of 1941 in two ways. First, it was different in size. During the 1940s, because the district board president was the only elected official with any influence and because the *taluks* (sub-divisions of districts) were still rather sleepy politically, it was most helpful to possess a district-wide electoral base. But by 1951, when the state assembly with its *taluk*-sized constituencies had been invested with sovereignty, an electoral base at the *taluk* level became most important (as Channabasappa learned to his sorrow in the 1952 election). This was a powerful element in the redistribution of power from upper to lower echelons of the party.

The second way in which the electoral bases of 1941 and 1951 differed was in the types of people who formed the bases and in the things which they expected of the man whom they supported. In 1941 the electoral base was composed entirely of people from the 4·06 per cent of the population who were enfranchised by virtue of wealth or education. Within a single district a man could usually win an election with a few hundred votes. He could reach that many through personal contact. And because voters knew that no politician possessed much concrete patronage power, they often lent support to candidates on the basis of intangibles such as Nijalingappa's professional eminence, genteel manners, and lofty ideals.

By 1951 everyone had the vote. Powerful men in local arenas could use their socio-economic position to control the votes of many. By then such men had begun to realize that votes could be traded for tangible spoils from the newly powerful legislators, and electoral bases came to be made up of networks of such transactional alliances. A candidate even in the small *taluk*-level constituency could not reach all voters personally and had to rely on such alliances with intermediaries who could deliver votes. The intangible qualities which were effective in 1941 declined radically in importance as politicians came to be judged by their generosity with spoils or at least their promises of generosity.

As a result of the transformation which occurred within the political system and the Congress party in Mysore during this decade, many of the men who had been active in 1941 had fallen by the wayside by 1951. For those whose ascriptive status and lack of wealth disqualified them (such as the Brahmin Krishnappa), this was unavoidable. But many others who possessed the proper status, wealth, and ability to develop a political base foundered because they could not adjust their perceptions to the changed rules of politics. Channabasappa in 1951 is an example of this, albeit a temporary example. His reappearance and success after 1951 indicate that by adapting his perceptions after an initial setback, a politician who possessed the other prerequisites for office could recover the ground he had lost.

The mention of perceptions raises the final problem of motivation, the problem of the relationship between the pressures which a particular situation places on a politician to assume a certain role and his decision to assume it. This is an exceedingly complex question which can only be touched upon briefly here. But it is important to emphasize that a politician's assumption of a particular role which serves his interests does not always imply a cynical attitude towards the moral commitments which are associated with that role. In some instances cynicism is present, as was apparently the case when Channabasappa became a Gandhian in order to win the district board presidency. But some men possessed the ability to adjust their innermost beliefs to suit the external situation in a chameleon-like manner. Nijalingappa serves as the archetype of this in Mysore. When the situation demanded that he abandon his role as the wealthy club-going lawyer to become the devoted Gandhian, he appears by all accounts to have done so wholeheartedly and to have carried his conversion to the extreme of breaking caste rules by feeding Harijans in his home. But in the late 1950s, when his control over the state Congress depended on his surrender to 'casteism' of the most extreme kind, he appears to have done so with completely genuine enthusiasm. Thus the transformation in the external political situation produced a wide range of internal transformations in the motivations of individual politicians.

13

KONDA LAKSHMAN BAPUJI:
A BACKWARD CLASSES LEADER OF
THE TELENGANA (ANDHRA PRADESH)

Hugh Gray

Konda Lakshman Bapuji, who at the peak of his career was a state minister and is an important Backward Classes leader, started life very inauspiciously. Even today, unlike most successful Andhra Pradesh politicians, Konda Lakshman has no base in district or municipal politics, neither is he a trades union leader. His power base is in co-operatives and his social base in his numerically widespread caste, the Weavers.

Konda Lakshman was born on 27 September 1915, in the village of Wankadi, Asifabad *taluq*, Adilabad district, in the Telengana region of the Hyderabad princely state. His father was also born in Asifabad *taluq*, and his ancestors came from nearby Karimnagar district. His father received no formal education, but taught himself to read and write and learnt Urdu and a little Persian in addition to his native Telegu. He was thus able to obtain employment as a postman in the Nizam of Hyderabad's service. He was promoted to clerk and then sub-postmaster. He was retired in 1941 at 55 years of age. Konda Lakshman's mother died in 1918, when he was three years old. He was the fourth of five sons and there was one daughter. The other brothers did not complete middle school.

In 1931 Konda Lakshman saw Gandhi, and subsequently as a sign of commitment to the Congress cause wore a Gandhi cap. In 1933 he was strongly influenced by one Ramswamy, who was visiting villages and urging his fellow Weavers to Sanskritize their habits and way of life, to wear the sacred thread of the twice born, and become vegetarians. Konda Lakshman remained a vegetarian until 1954, when he developed septic ulcers and on medical advice 'took bone soup and ceased to be a vegetarian'.[1]

At twenty Konda Lakshman passed his middle school examination. He wished to continue his studies, and left for Hyderabad, the state capital. This was a difficult period of his life as, although his father realized the value of education, he could give him little money. He was interested in sports and, as a successful wrestler, became known to a wide circle of young men, through frequenting Hyderabad gymnasia, particularly the Gajanam Vyayamshala, Haribouli, of which he is now president. He thus came to the notice of Hyderabad Congressmen as a potential youth leader.

After his matriculation, his father urged him to enter the postal service, but he was determined to continue his education and fasted for three days to win his father's consent. By selling books and with the help of wealthy Weavers and other Backward Classes patrons he was able to pay his fees to take the intermediate course at the Hyderabad City College, but as he found it difficult to maintain himself without continual help from friends, he decided to take up law, which promised quicker returns, and joined the law classes organized by the High Court. At this time he was recruited by Guntaka Narsiah Pantau, a veteran Weaver Congressman, to organize youthful members of the Padmashali sub-caste of the Weavers, throughout the Telengana, against 'forced labour extorted by Zamindars and Government Officers'. He went on to organize a Youth Front of students from the Backward Classes, directed against 'other youths belonging to Deshmukh and other Zamindari families' on whom he 'inflicted many successful defeats in cultural and sports activities'. On 24 October 1938 the Hyderabad State Congress launched a *satayagraha* campaign in association with the Arya Samaj. Konda Lakshman participated, was arrested and sent to prison, but soon released.

In 1940 he passed his third grade Pleaders examination. At this time Konda Lakshman was living in the house of a Backward Classes lawyer, Suraj Chand, who provided him with free board and lodging in return for coaching his sons. His father again urged him to return home and accept a job as assistant to a local pleader. He refused, and started to work as a junior for his patron, Suraj Chand, and another lawyer.

It was now, Konda Lakshman says, that he found his 'first political guru', Pandit Vinayek Rao Vidyalankar, a Brahmin (later a minister in the Vellodi and B. Ramakrishna Rao governments of Hyderabad state). Vidyalankar also helped him legally and provided him with all the copies of the 'Deccan Law Reporter'. He started to specialize in political cases, but 'never allowed the brokers in the profession to come near him although many advocates depended mainly on these brokers for their cases'.

His main political activity was the physical training of Congress youths in preparation for the liberation struggle. In 1939, with some friends, he went on a five hundred mile cycle trip to learn more of the geographical environment in which he intended to be politically active. On 3 June 1940 he heard a speech by M. N. Roy on the problems of Indian revolution. He was as strongly affected as he had been by seeing Gandhi when he was sixteen. Subsequently he translated M. N. Roy's pamphlet, *Methods of Organising Revolution*, into Urdu. Konda Lakshman had many Communist friends but remained unsympathetic to Marxist analysis, as concentrating on class rather than caste and because of its 'authoritarianism'. M. N. Roy became his intellectual guide and he grew to admire, above all other Congress politicians ('except for the dreamer in Nehru'), Subhas Chandra Bose. He felt that non-violent pressures would never change the Nizam's government or lead to its collapse.

In 1941, after joining the Andhra Mahasabha, he helped to organize public protest meetings against the rejection by the Nizam's Dominions Legislative Assembly of the 'Anti Child Marriage Act'. He also organized small hawkers' teams to raise funds by the selling of khadi cloth. In this year he became a member of the working committee of the All-India Padmashali Yuvajana Sabha.

In Andhra Pradesh there are fifteen Weaver sub-castes. Konda Lakshman was a Padmashali, but his aim was to bring all the Weaver sub-castes under one umbrella. When caste membership and occupation coincide, as in the case of most Weavers, a caste association can act as a trade union and fill the gap in trade union organization which exists in most Indian rural areas. In 1943, when Konda Lakshman became the first president of the Nizam Rashtra Handloom Weavers Association, he proclaimed its aim as to see that deserving Weavers got their yarn quota and to put an end to malpractices in the distribution of controlled yarn. The Association also demanded that the Nizam's government distribute yarn through them, but this was refused.

In 1943–44 Konda Lakshman appeared for the First Grade Pleaders examination, and in 1945 was able to register as a First Grade Pleader. In 1951 he was accorded an Advocateship by the High Court.

He became a formal member of Congress in 1945, and at a session of the Hyderabad State Congress met V. B. Raju (Brahmin) whose follower, and then collaborator, he was to remain for many years.

He had long been dissatisfied with peaceful political activities, and started to organize local defence committees throughout the Telengana, for revolutionary activities against the Nizam. In this way he established a connection with Nalgonda district, and in Pochampalli village (later to be the scene of the launching of the 'Bhoodan' movement) he set up a workshop for the manufacture of bombs and the distribution of arms and ammunition. He undertook to defend in court, free of charge, all his collaborators if they were arrested by the police and prosecuted.

Policemen came to arrest him in Hyderabad on 26 June 1947. His cook kept the police engaged in conversation while he escaped through the small door of the lavatory, used by the daily scavengers to come and go. He took refuge in the house of Uddhav Rao Chavan, who worked in the Nizam's police department, but sympathized with the freedom struggle. Later he moved to the house of Afzul Purkar, a Maharashtrian, who lived a few yards from the police residential quarters. Until he left the state he moved around disguised as a Muslim.

He left Hyderabad for Bombay on 19 August 1947, and raised money there to establish a training camp for young Congress militants at Sholapur. Shortly afterwards his bomb manufacturing unit at Pocham-palli was discovered and his associates arrested. On 4 December 1947 a bomb was thrown at the Nizam, and Konda Lakshman's name was placed on the list of accused and wanted people, for having given instructions in the technique of bomb-throwing to trainees at Shola-pur.

In February 1948 he left for Nagpur and unsuccessfully tried to establish a radio station there. In April 1948 he organized an All-India Conference of Padmashalis at Sindhawai in Chanda district, Central Province. He then moved to Madras, and again failed to establish the radio station, but finally succeeded in doing so in Mysore state.

On 27 May 1948 he married Dr Shakuntala Devi, an assistant professor of physiology, the Padmashali daughter of a middle-class retired rail official, from Nellore district (then in the Madras composite state, now in Andhra). He received no dowry, and 'between the parties of the bridegroom and the bride there was only a bargaining of hearts'. He considered it a great advantage that she was a doctor, as her services might be of great use in the armed struggle against the Nizam. After their marriage his wife obtained a transfer from Madras to Masuli-patnam General Hospital as assistant surgeon. Despite Konda Laksh-man's subsequent financial and political success, she continued her medical career, although always attentive to the needs of their three children and cooking for her husband, friends, and family.

From Masulipatnam, after the 'Police Action' of 13 September 1948, when Hyderabad was forcibly incorporated into India, Konda Laksh-man returned to Hyderabad, once the arrest warrants against him had been cancelled. He immediately busied himself with the cooperative movement and organized a hundred Weaver societies in a year and established an Apex Organization, under his leadership, to guide them. 'There was no important cooperative institution with which he had no direct or indirect connection.' In 1949 he became president of Sultan Bazaar Ward Congress Committee, and a member of the Pradesh Committee of the Congress Party.

From 1950 to 1957 'his achievements as a successful advocate on the criminal side, in Hyderabad, were unparalleled'. As his power grew in the cooperative movement, so did his legal practice. A choice for the future had to be made between his developing legal career and politics. In the late 1950s he gradually became a full-time politician and his legal cases were increasingly handled by his lawyer colleague and principal assistant, Ramulu, a fellow Weaver from Karimnagar district, who is still involved in Konda Lakshman's political activities and acts as his principal agent.

Inside the Hyderabad Congress Party there were two major factions, both led by Brahmins, Swami Tirth and B. Ramakrishna Rao. Many of those supporting Swami Tirth, like Konda Lakshman, had left the state to establish armed groups, make raids and carry on a military movement to secure the end of princely rule. B. Ramakrishna Rao's group pursued more Gandhian methods. Swami Tirth's group was referred to by enemies as the 'Congress of Thieves' (referring to a spectacular bank robbery reputedly carried out by his supporters to obtain funds, which were then placed outside the state) and B. Ramakrishna's group as the 'Congress of Capitalists'. By 1947 the two groups had split and both called themselves Congress. After the Police Action Sardar Patel came to Hyderabad to settle the differences between the two groups. Swami Tirth was asked to step down from the presidency of the state Congress, and a supporter of his, Sri Bindu (another Brahmin), who was acceptable to B. Ramakrishna Rao, was made Congress president, and the two groups of Congress reunited. According to B. Ramakrishna Rao, Sardar Patel considered Swami Tirth and his supporters (including V. B. Raju and Konda Lakshman) as 'dangerously left wing'.[2]

After the dismemberment of Hyderabad and the integration of the Telengana into Andhra Pradesh in 1956, Swami Tirth was eliminated from state politics as he came from the part of Hyderabad state which was incorporated into Maharashtra. By this time Konda Lakshman was a prominent member of V. B. Raju's faction, whose ideological aim was to oppose and destroy 'Reddy Raj' and to ensure that the true representatives of the masses—Brahmins, Backward Classes, and Harijans—came to power in the socialist interest of all state citizens. When the state of Andhra Pradesh was formed, V. B. Raju's faction supported Sanjiva Reddy (against Gopal Reddy and B. Ramakrishna Rao) and this time were on the winning side, with V. B. Raju again becoming a minister in the state cabinet.

At the first general election in 1952 for the Hyderabad legislative assembly, Konda Lakshman was elected from his home district, Adilabad. Subsequently, he organized a mass demonstration in Hyderabad of handloom weavers from two hundred and fifty organizations, demanding employment. As a result the All India Handloom Board received Rs 1,000,000 from the central government. Konda Lakshman had also demonstrated his powers of organization, leadership, and the strength of his Weaver mass support.

In the 1957 general election he was elected to the new Andhra Pradesh legislative assembly from Chinnakondur, Nalgonda district. He had decided not to contest again from Adilabad because of 'opposition there from feudals who controlled district factions within Congress'. In Nalgonda, at that time a Communist-dominated district, the Congress Party was weak, and Konda Lakshman perceived that he could rally mass support from the Backward Classes without the successful interference of Congress dominant agricultural caste rivals, whose village power had been weakened by Communist infiltration. There was little opposition to his receiving the Congress ticket as the seat was thought to be unwinnable. Subsequently the intrusion of this urban-based, Backward Classes lawyer was strongly resented by the Congress country gentry, and through Dr Channa Reddy, who had relatives in the district, they did their best to get him shifted. At the state level Dr Channa Reddy was leader of a strong faction, always opposed in state politics to that of V. B. Raju.

In 1959 Konda Lakshman was made a member of the All-India Advisory Textile Board. In 1960 he reached the height of his career and became Minister for Small Scale Industries and a member of the state cabinet. It was around this time that he ceased to be regarded as a member of V. B. Raju's faction and was considered as a political power in his own right, although he remained a friend and collaborator of V. B. Raju. At the same time his political career was seen as having limitations, as, despite his marriage, he remained a regional leader whose efforts to extend his power into the Andhra area, where others dominated many Weaver cooperatives, had failed.

In the 1962 general elections Konda Lakshman was defeated by the Communist (CPI) candidate, mainly through over-confidence, an inefficient field organizer, and his spending too little time in the constituency while he was rallying the Backward Classes throughout the Telengana to vote for Congress. The victorious Communist candidate was, however, quickly unseated in the courts. The Election Tribunal held as proved beyond all reasonable doubt four instances of bribery by treating the electors to *sendhi* or toddy, two instances of undue influence by the intimidation of voters, and two instances of caste appeals, to wean away the voters. The Tribunal declared the election of K. Gurunath Reddy to be void, but declined to declare Konda Lakshman Bapuji as having been duly elected. On appeal the High Court held that the conclusions reached by the Tribunal were correct. On the corrupt practice of caste appeal, the High Court found two cases proved. In both cases Reddis had been urged to vote for the Communist candidate on the ground that he was a member of their own community. Newspapers commented that this was the first time since independence that 'the corrupt practice of caste appeal' had been successfully alleged and proved in court to unseat a successful election candidate. In 1965, at the resulting by-election, Konda Lakshman Bapuji was returned with a majority of 27,000.

While out of the legislative assembly he returned to the cooperative movement. In 1962 he became president of Hyderabad Central Cooperative Movement, and in the same year created the Weavers Welfare Trust, which owns property worth Rs 2,500,000. It made a plan to establish Weavers' hostels in district towns, and the first has been opened in Karimnagar. The chairman of the Trust is Ramulu, Konda Lakshman's lawyer assistant.

In 1964 Konda Lakshman was elected a member of the All-India Congress Committee. In 1966 he was elected president of Andhra Pradesh Backward Classes Congress, a position he still holds.

At the 1967 general election, as the boundaries of his old constituency had been changed, he contested from the part of his old constituency which had been amalgamated with Bonghir. He again won and was again made a cabinet minister in Brahmananda Reddy's new Congress government.

In 1969 Konda Lakshman resigned from the Andhra ministry and became the first prominent Congressman to be associated with the demand for a separate Telengana state. He formed the Telengana Congress Committee, with the help of a few Congress and Independent members of the legislative assembly. He was then expelled from Congress by the Andhra Pradesh Congress Committee, but this expulsion was never confirmed by the centre and he continued to attend meetings of the All-India Congress Committee in Delhi. At the time of his resignation the chief minister, Brahmananda Reddy, is said to have remarked that there was no need to worry about the Telengana separatist movement as, if Konda Lakshman and Channa Reddy were going to try to work in harness, it was bound to fail. This they never tried, as neither was willing to recognize the other as a leader of the movement, and Dr Channa Reddy remained in firm control of the rival organization, the Telengana Praja Samithi (TPS). At times it was difficult to know if Konda Lakshman was fighting for a separate Telengana state or waging caste warfare against Dr Channa Reddy and the dominant agricultural castes. Although he opposed Brahmananda Reddy and the integrationists, he put up his own separatist candidates against those of the TPS at by-elections and also in some constituencies at the general election of March 1971, when the Telengana Praja Samithi won 10 out of the 14 Telengana parliamentary constituencies. All Konda Lakshman's candidates failed.

Later in 1971, when Dr Channa Reddy, following an agreement with Indira Gandhi, led the TPS back into the state Congress Party, Konda Lakshman returned as well and wound up his Telengana Congress Committee. He had no backing from the TPS or the integrationists, few followers, but a few powerful friends. At this time he was, and has remained, a solitary but feared politician, as he is thought to have the ear of Indira Gandhi, who generally sees him privately when she visits the state and accepts his invitations to speak at meetings. He became even more isolated on V. B. Raju's departure for the Rajya Sabha, where he is now deputy leader of the Congress Parliamentary Party.

Since his election loss in 1962 Konda Lakshman gives considerable thought to election campaigns. His approach is that of the strategist, and he maintains a file on the up to date power situation of every village in his constituency. He skilfully manipulates the caste factor. He considers that the tactics for winning elections vary from campaign to campaign. In 1967 he waged a noisy, theatrical, hard campaign, with many public meetings, processions, and entertainments. In 1972 he decided that he could win only by a soft campaign, so as not to arouse strong overt opposition. He was opposed by both local *Samithi* presidents in his constituency, and there were strong Congress forces behind one of his Independent opponents. He had to fight for his Congress ticket and, according to Anjiah, a member of the Pradesh Election Committee, 'I told them that a ticket could not be refused to a Backward Classes leader like Konda Lakshman.'[3] In his campaign he decided against shows, processions, and many public meetings. He carefully worked on the local antipathy between Reddis of the Gudeti and Mutati sub-castes and obtained Mutati support against the more numerous and hierarchially inferior Gudetis (Dr Channa Reddy's relatives in Nalgonda district, like himself, are Gudetis). He produced a personal manifesto and concentrated on getting it into the hands of every Backward Classes and Harijan voter. It contained photographs of himself with Indira Gandhi, and other photographs of Indira Gandhi in which the villagers she was talking to could all be clearly recognized as Backward Classes men and women and Harijans. To general surprise, Konda Lakshman won comfortably and again became a member of the legislative assembly.

In 1971 Brahmananda Reddy was asked to resign as chief minister and was succeeded by P. V. Narsimha Rao (Brahmin), who left Konda Lakshman out of his new state ministry. P. V. Narsimha Rao resigned

on 17 January 1973, as there was breakdown in law and order in
Andhra, following the demand for a separate Andhra state. On the
following day President's Rule was introduced for the first time in a
Congress state, and lasted until 10 December 1973, when Indira Gandhi
chose Vengal Rao (Velama) as her new chief minister. Once again
Konda Lakshman was not offered a ministerial post, and at the end of
1974 was still outside the state government.

The state has been Konda Lakshman's chosen political arena but he
has remained a regional leader who failed effectively to extend his
power over Weavers outside Telengana into the Andhra area, where
others continued to dominate many of the Weaver cooperatives.
Konda Lakshman's career shows the open nature of the Indian political
system for those who can escape, through education, from the villages
or the huts of the cities and have the necessary strength of character and
personality to thrust their way upwards. Although self-educated, a
similarly successful political career in Andhra Pradesh is that of T.
Anjiah (Toddy Tapper), the only Congress trade union leader in
Hyderabad to come up from the factory floor, who is now Minister of
Labour in the present Congress state government.

Most Congress state level politicians in Andhra Pradesh are recruited
from *panchayati raj*, the municipalities, trade unions, cooperatives, or as
active university student politicians are financially supported and incorporated into state level factions. Another way is through successful
protest movements like the TPS (e.g. the recent political career of
Madan Mohan).

Konda Lakshman's political friends are, and always have been,
Brahmins, Backward Classes, and Harijans. It is seemingly easier for
Brahmins (although they are fond of calling themselves the Jews of
India) to move from second to first rank in state politics and become
leaders of powerful state level factions and chief ministers. For Weavers,
Tappers, other Backward Classes, and Harijans, it is more difficult to
become powerful faction leaders, as their strength generally derives
from the backing of trade unions or cooperatives, not from the country
gentry ('the Doras') who dominate *panchayati raj* institutions and most
rural constituencies. Brahmin leaders of factions are able more easily
to draw from both sources of support and are not seen as presenting the
same threat to the structure of rural life.

Although Konda Lakshman seems a spent force, in Indian politics
one can never tell. If he is to become chief minister, it must be as a
compromise candidate (which is unlikely because of the strong emotions
he arouses) or because he is chosen by Indira Gandhi and imposed by
the centre. Some civil servants consider that he is the only state politician with sufficient emotional drive and strength of will to put through

fundamental land reforms against the interests of the country gentry and richer peasants. If Indira Gandhi decided she needed such an instrument, Konda Lakshman's chance might still come, otherwise he is unlikely to become more eminent than he is.

14

SOME LESSER LEADERS OF THE
COMMUNIST MOVEMENT IN KERALA[1]

C. J. May

INTRODUCTION

The study of political parties and movements in the Third World has tended to bring out how loose a structure they have and how much they are permeated by the traditional political and economic power relationships. The Congress Party in India, for example, is often seen as the summation of local power groupings and conflicts. It may be useful to look at an organization which is more formalized, institutionalized, and bureaucratized than many in this series. This examination may pose questions that may not be so visible in other contexts, especially about the extent to which the demands of the organization itself may determine the careers of its leaders. Ideology is probably more real and discipline more important for Communists than for most politicians. The party can, therefore, do more dictating to members as they will be readier to accept allocated roles. The further question is raised as to how far and in what ways the Communists may be special, on the one hand, and how far they have to take the colour of the society and the political system, on the other.

BACKGROUND

Kerala is a narrow coastal state tucked into the south-west corner of India. The population of some 20 millions is densely packed together, depending mainly on agriculture, especially the cultivation of rice, coconuts, and tapioca, with some tea and rubber plantations in the hills, and a number of agrarian-based industries, such as coir, cashew-processing, and weaving, with only a modicum of modern industries but with about half the total population literate (the highest level in India), a well developed—indeed runaway—tertiary sector of government servants, teachers, and, above all, petty shopkeepers and the like. The population is about three-fifths Hindu, with somewhat more than a fifth Christian, clustering mainly in the south central part of the state, and rather under a fifth Muslim, mainly in the north central part. The Hindus are divided into castes, of which the largest are the Nayars among the upper castes and the Ezhavas among the lower. Not dissimilar divisions, as well as sectarian groupings, are found among the

Christians, and to a lesser extent among the Muslims. Under the British, Kerala was divided into three parts, the directly ruled Malabar district in the north and two princely states, the large Travancore in the south and the small Cochin in the middle. The latter two were joined in 1949 and the State of Kerala was formed in 1956. Kerala is divided administratively into districts, *taluks*, and villages.

The history of the Communist movement in Kerala may be divided roughly into four periods. The first, from 1930 to 1940, saw the effective entry of Congress into Kerala, the rise of the Congress Socialists, and the start of the trade union and peasant movements; the period ends with the emergence of the Communist Party. Ideology and organization were unsystematized. These were economically the years of depression. The second, from 1940 to 1951, begins and ends with the party underground for some three years: ideology and organization were systematized, severely tested, and adapted; some of the party's most famous struggles were fought; independence came in 1947—and after four years the party finally digested the fact; these were the years of war-time and post-war economic fluctuations. The third, from 1952 to 1964, was a time of increasing parliamentary work, culminating in the 1957-59 Communist-led government: there was a sustained rise in party and trade union membership; the apparent consolidation of a revised ideology ended, however, in a split into the 'right' CPI and the 'left' CPI(M), the 'Marxists', who took the bulk of members and voters, if not leaders. The fourth, from 1964, saw the two parties increasingly differentiating themselves: the state government was held by the Marxists with CPI and other support from 1967 to 1969, and subsequently by the CPI with Congress and other allies.

I shall outline the careers of six lesser leaders.[2] It is difficult to define precisely a middle level. With one exception, I have excluded ministers and members of national party committees, but several of those chosen have played very important parts in the history of the movement. Although a collective biography would be more useful, even these rather arbitrarily chosen biographies may give indications about the movement and the political system. I have chosen three Ezhavas, all from an aspiring middle-class background, all from small towns, all fairly well educated, all members of the legislative assembly (MLAs) in 1957; but one comes from each of the three regions of Kerala, they entered politics at different times, one is now with the CPI, one with the CPI(M), and the other has left politics. For further contrast, I have included three other Communist politicians who are not Ezhavas, one again from each of the regions of Kerala, two now in the CPI and one in the CPI(M), one unusual in being a businessman, one a former manual worker from a great heartland of the party, and one from the Scheduled Castes. Obviously, there are major distortions: I have, for example, not included anyone of the Nayar caste or anyone primarily concerned with the peasant movement. In a concluding section I shall list the main recruitment grounds for the party leadership, their main roles, and the major resources. I shall not try to integrate these factors and the periods of the movement's history into an elegant pattern, but some tentative observations can be made about political careers within the system.

1. M. Kumaran

The Thiyyas are the North Malabar equivalent of the Ezhavas. Traditionally they claim a superior social status to the Ezhavas of South Malabar and are matrilineal. At the end of the nineteenth century and at the beginning of the twentieth a powerful middle-class group emerged in the professions, especially in government service and in business, but the majority remained poor, generally in agriculture. M. Kumaran's family was 'middle class', his father a carter with four carts. Born in 1920, Kumaran, after his high school education, became an untrained teacher in an aided elementary school. The teachers at these private schools were severely exploited, with low and uncertain wages and the constant threat of dismissal. A union was built up, led by some secondary trained teachers who were forced by the depression to work in elementary schools[3] and were associated with the left wing of Congress. By 1939 the union was strong enough to call a widespread strike. About sixty teachers[4] were finally dismissed or suspended; only five of them were untrained, of whom one was M. Kumaran, who had been active in the union organization in one of its main strongholds.

Like most of the Congress Socialist Party, Kumaran joined the Communist Party in 1939–40. He rose fast, perhaps because most of those above him were jailed. He was soon *taluk* secretary. Although he took part in trade union work, peasant struggles, anti-Japanese campaigns, and cholera relief work, he was mainly concerned with party organization. By the time of the 1948 underground period he held the important post of district secretary. Few of the party were longer underground; he was eventually caught and jailed for seventy days.

When the party emerged from jail and underground, he became a member of the district secretariat (on the face of it, a lesser position). He entered local government. He was on a *panchayat* for ten years and for a further six years on the municipal council that succeeded it. He was elected to the district board, but, although one of the most senior Communists on the board, he did not hold office. He was an MLA from 1957 to 1959. At a time when the Communists had decided not to allow the creation of any new high schools anywhere in the state, Kumaran somehow succeeded in getting one for his constituency—a measure of his influence within the party. With the formation of Kerala in 1956, he remained a member of a District Secretariat. In 1953 he married, when he was 35, late for a Malayali but common among active party workers at this period.[5]

He had long been on the 'right' of the party, and he went with the CPI at the split. He was one of a large number of CPI leaders from Malabar who found themselves virtually without a party, for the mass of the membership and electoral support went to the CPI(M). He edited a party magazine for a short period and later became a District Secretary. At the last election (1970) he became an MLA again.

One may speculate about his career. In the first years he rose fast to become district secretary. He was on the leading committees of the state. Yet, in 1956–57, he was chosen as an MLA and neither joined the secretariat of the state nor became a district secretary. Indeed, he served under a man who had previously served under him. His base was in the party organization, but it is perhaps true to say that he did not rise as far as others. It may be that he had no mass front base; it may be that he was side-tracked into local government or into the Assembly; it may be that there were more leaders than top level jobs.

2. T. K. Krishnan

The Ezhavas were perhaps more oppressed in Cochin than in other parts of Kerala. T. K. Krishnan's grandfather was in agriculture, but his father worked for a Christian pappadom-maker in Kunnamkulam. The Christians dominated the population and trade of this small market centre in the north of Cochin. He set up on his own and his business became the biggest in the town, but later lost ground to others, and he eventually gave it up. His eldest son, T. K. Krishnan's brother, had meanwhile passed the secondary school-leaving examination, financed by government scholarships. He went to Ceylon—one of the great escapes for Malayalis, especially from this part of Kerala. He joined a private firm and rose to become general manager. He was able to pay for his brothers' education. One became an engineer; T. K. Krishnan became the first Ezhava lawyer from the *taluk*; the youngest brother manages a bookshop, one of the best in Kerala, owned by the son of a former minister in the Communist government. Krishnan's family is a good example of the successful middle class rising through trade, foreign employment, and education into the professions.

The Ezhavas were not merely economically depressed; they also suffered social discrimination, which was symbolized by their exclusion from temples and neighbouring roads. The Cosmopolitan Hostel for the local Christian college was, in Krishnan's time, cosmopolitan only for high caste Hindu students. Whereas the growing Ezhava middle class of Travancore had formed a strong caste association, the SNDP Yogam, at the turn of the century, it had not gained much support in Cochin. Attempts were made to remedy the situation. Under the influence of a prominent young lawyer, T. K. Krishnan[6] became a member of the board of directors of the Cochin SNDP while still at high school. This was his entry into public life.

He went to Trichur, the district town, for his college education, where he came into contact with the developing Communist movement. He joined the party in 1942, was active in nationalist and student politics, and became the secretary of the state Students' Federation.

At the end of the war the Communist Party made its most determined effort to channel communal forces as a part of a general strategy of forming the widest possible alliances. Although there had been a previous attempt by the leftists to take over the existing communal association, and although there were to be other attempts, this was the only time that they set up their own separate organizations, notably the Cochin SNDP, of which Krishnan was a *taluk* secretary. Other leaders, in particular E. M. S. Namboodiripad, entered existing organizations. The party later condemned the whole operation. The demands for social reform were clearly progressive; yet such an exclusive focus and exclusive organization were no longer appropriate.

In 1948 Krishnan took his law degree in Madras, but soon moved to Bombay as a journalist. In 1951, on his return to Kerala, he fought the election from his local constituency and became one of a substantial group of Communist MLAs elected in spite of a ban on the party. He has won five out of the six elections since then and, apart from the years 1960 to 1967, he has been continuously an MLA. As part of his duties as a party member rather than as a central concern, he has been associated with the trade union and peasant movement. He was also the moving force in organizing one of the few successful cooperatives in Kerala, the Indian Coffee Board Workers Cooperative, which runs its own coffee houses.

Krishnan began to practise as an advocate in the district headquarters soon after he became an MLA. His practice prospered sufficiently for him to have a junior. At the age of 34 he married a college lecturer.

Hardgrave writes of the period since 1951: 'the "middle-class intellectual B.A. Advocate" has become the archetype of the Communist party member in Kerala'.[7] He cannot possibly mean that the majority of party members are lawyers. It is, however, true that a third of the Communist MLAs in 1957 had a law degree. This must have been the result of a deliberate decision; presumably the party thought at that time that this would secure them the most effective representation. T. K. Krishnan can be considered a typical lawyer MLA. Yet, although he has progressed within the Assembly party, becoming, for example, Chief Whip, and although he was detained with other CPI(M) leaders, he has never been on the state committee and is not one of the topmost leaders.

3. R. Prakasam

The area where the Ezhavas were both best organized and economically most advanced was the southern Travancore region round Quilon. Weaving and coir manufacture were generally organized as small-scale industries; later, tile-making, and especially cashew processing, brought some prosperity to the area. Among the traditional elite of the Ezhavas were the ayurvedic (indigenous medicine) physicians; Prakasam's father came from a line of ayurvedic physicians. He went to the local high school, and then to the high school in Trivandrum, the state capital, where he was encouraged by the English headmaster. Although he went on to college, the Travancore government subsequently refused to employ him because of his caste, so he went to Malabar and joined the Madras government service. Family affairs forced him to return to Travancore, and then, because of his experience, the Travancore government felt compelled to give him a job, albeit a poor one. He was the third Ezhava to enter Travancore government service. He worked his way up to sub-registrar, and in one place the high castes rioted against his appointment. His rare honesty attracted the attention of the Dewan (the Maharaja's chief minister) and he was promoted to the state capital.[8]

Four of his sons followed him into government service, one by way of an American doctorate into a very senior post. He wanted Prakasam, who had a brilliant scholarship-studded progress through school and college (culminating in a MA at the prestigious Madras Christian College), to try for the Indian administrative service examination. Prakasam refused, however, for he had been intellectually attracted to Marxism while a student in Madras. After taking part in student politics in Madras, he returned to Attingal, his home town.

The Communist Party in Travancore had been centred on the coir industry belt round Alleppey, with outposts in other towns and industrial areas like Quilon and Trivandrum, but they had little influence over large tracts of the state. Trivandrum district, however, proved to be fertile ground for the party in the early 1950s. In the north of the district, round Attingal, the traditional industries of coir and weaving were facing a serious decline. Prakasam helped to organize unions among these and other workers. There was also an anomaly in the local land tenure. Although *jenmis* (landlords) had been generally abolished in Travancore in the nineteenth century, a few, in particular the royal family, were allowed to keep their lands. Attingal formed one of these pockets. This feudal tie caused much resentment, especially over rents. Building on such grievances, the Communist Party quickly grew in influence and they won the municipal election in 1953—one of only three towns won by the Communists. Though still in his mid-twenties, Prakasam became municipal chairman. One of his duties was to pay respects, traditionally dressed—or rather undressed—to the Maharaja when he visited the town. Not only was Prakasam the first Communist, but he was also the first Ezhava to be municipal chairman. Some local party members wanted a show of defiance, but Prakasam compromised: he paid the town's respects but, unprecedentedly, presented a list of demands, including a demand for a reduction in agricultural rents. He was later to touch the Maharaja for funds for municipal projects: he even suggested that a maternity home should be named after the Maharaja's mother, correctly anticipating a large donation.

Prakasam was elected an MLA in 1954, re-elected with a big majority in 1957, but in 1960, in the wake of the overthrow of the Communist ministry and against a strong Congress candidate (his own cousin, who had been a state minister), he was defeated. At this stage his political future still looked bright. He had gained wide experience and was one of the younger members of the state council—the highest body in the state party. Nevertheless, he dropped out of the party and out of politics, occasionally lending a hand at election time for one or other of the Communist parties. He joined his father-in-law's firm. He had married the daughter of one of the big Quilon industrialists just after he became an MLA. He denies that this influenced his decision to leave politics. He turned down the offer of a job in the family firm at the time of his marriage; instead, he spent his honeymoon in jail as a result of a strike. It seems, from his account, that he left the party for intellectual reasons, just as he had joined it, a weary disillusionment taking the place of the earlier enthusiasm well before his final election defeat. Perhaps his career is an example of the ambiguities of the relationship between the rising middle class, especially the Ezhava middle class, and the Communist movement; perhaps he was an early casualty of the heart-searching that accompanied the split in the party.

4. H. Manjunatha Rao

Unlike the three previous subjects, H. Manjunhatha Rao belongs to one of the smallest castes in Kerala, an immigrant group of Brahmins. More significant, they were a trading caste and Manjunatha Rao finally followed in the family line. There cannot be many other bullion merchants who have stood as Communist candidates. His career throws some light on the attitude of the Communists to businessmen.

Manjunatha Rao was born in 1909 in Calicut, the district headquarters of Malabar and a long established trading town. At college he was active at first in sport and later in the nationalist enthusiasm of the late 1920s and 1930s. In 1930 he took part in the salt *satyagraha* and soon became one of the most prominent left-wingers in the Malabar Congress, a member of the All-India Congress Committee, president of the town Congress, and treasurer of the Provincial Congress Committee. These young Congressmen read about and admired rather indiscriminately the Irish, Garibaldi, the Indian patriots, and the Russian revolution. Their ideas gradually became clearer.

Manjunatha Rao was one of a small group who, with the foundation of the Congress Socialist Party in Malabar in 1935, began forming trade unions in Calicut. He continued to take a prominent part in this trade union and nationalist work, taking his share of jail and restrictions. On one occasion, confined to his house, he went to a public meeting disguised as a Muslim lady in purdah. He was at the foundation conference of the CPI in Kerala, and was in jail from 1940 to 1942, and again from 1947 to 1952. After 1952 he took up business as a gold merchant, until 1962, when government restrictions meant that he would have been able to continue only through smuggling. He then worked as a manager for a rising South Indian trading company, where he was able to arrange for the employment of two other leaders of the Communist Party. Manjunatha Rao continued in politics, sacrificing much time that should have been spent on business, but mostly it was local level politics. He was a member of the municipal council from his Congress days and served, with a short break, for thirty years. In 1962 he became the first mayor of the newly formed Corporation. He remained president of the union that was particularly his own, the Municipal Workers (in 1948, when the Communist Party was banned and he was in jail, the union had gone to Congress through a simple calculation of self-interest, but in 1952 it returned at once to the Communists). Manjunatha Rao was never on party committees above the district level. In 1957 he was a state assembly candidate and was quite narrowly beaten in a three-cornered contest, but he was dropped in the following election for a candidate who was stronger in caste terms, who was more actively engaged in the trade union movement, and who had previously fought the parliamentary seat.

It was fitting that Manjunatha Rao should take the salute at the 25th anniversary Independence Day parade in Calicut. He was one of the outstanding young nationalists who had helped build up both the

Congress and the Communist Party in Malabar. When independence had been achieved and the party had accepted it as a fact, Manjunatha Rao retired into business and local, part-time politics. The party had only a limited use for him. Unlike Congress, which was closely and openly locked into the business world, the Communist Party had only a very small number of business supporters.[9] They were useful, on the one hand, in their access to money and, on the other hand, as a demonstration of the success of the broad front strategy, standing as symbols of the 'smaller', national bourgeoisie who, at this stage, would support the Communists. They were backed, generally as Independents, in a few difficult assembly seats, or more often in local, especially municipal, politics, where the party was trying to build up support from a weak position by alliances.

5. P. A. Solomon

Bullion merchants are not generally considered the stuff that Communist parties are made of; the party should be the vanguard of the working class. In Kerala, no section of the working class has played so important a part in the Communist movement as the Alleppey coir workers, with their rich contribution of lives, legends, and leaders. Although the bulk of the coir workers were Ezhavas, several of the prominent leaders were Christians (and a few Muslims). P. A. Solomon came from a family that had originally been Syrian Catholic but became Latin Catholics when they moved to a village near Alleppey.[10] His father, after a period in Bombay where his own uncle had a furniture business, at first ran a business importing stationery from Bombay, but, when this failed, ran a carpentry business, sometimes working himself, sometimes employing two or three workers. Solomon was born in 1917. His elder brother had a full education and became a Sanskrit pundit, but his career was not successful. Solomon's education stopped shortly after primary school, but his father took Malayalam papers, and even Hindi and Tamil magazines, so that there was encouragement to read. He later learnt English at a night school run by the trade union. He had got a job in a large Indian-owned coir factory through a relation who was a contractor there. He was a clipper, finishing off the pattern on the mats, among the higher paid workers in the industry.

After some three years he joined the union, which was gaining strength, and he soon rose within it. During the great coir workers' strike of 1938 he was convenor of the Publicity Committee, was arrested, and lost his job. He had joined the local Congress and the Congress Socialist Party. When the Communist Party was formed, he became the first secretary of the crucial Alleppey unit. After about a year he moved to Cochin state to help organize both the party and the trade unions, as the local trade union organizers had been arrested. This is one example of the way in which Communists from one part of Kerala frequently worked in other parts, breaking out of the boundaries of the old political arenas, so that the Communist Party can correctly claim to have been the first organization to have a genuinely all-Kerala leadership. It should perhaps be mentioned that one of the unions that Solomon organized was that of the toddy tappers. This occupation was caste-bound, being exclusively Ezhava; yet both Solomon and the original organizer were Christians.

Solomon returned to Travancore after about a year, and was responsible for building up the union of the plantation workers. By 1946, when the union was banned, it was well organized and powerful, with twelve separate branches in the hilly region. During the times of repression Solomon concentrated on party work: until his arrest he was one of the leaders who re-established the party after the Punnapra-Vayalar rising; during the 1948–51 period he escaped arrest. In the 1948 state assembly elections he was one of the small number of Communist candidates (they were all defeated). He was always on the top state committees of the party, although never on the national committees. In the trade union movement, however, he was a member of the national committees, as well as holding leading positions in Kerala. In 1958 he became a member of the Rajya Sabha, the upper house of the Indian parliament—a job reserved at that time exclusively for important party leaders. At the time of the split, like most trade union leaders, he went with the CPI. He was the manager of their daily newspaper for some time, recently retiring to take up local party work in his wife's village. He had married, at the age of 37, into a well known party family.

Solomon is a good example of the Alleppey coir workers who became leaders of the party. The fact that he is not an Ezhava stresses the importance of class rather than caste. A significant minority of the leadership of the Communist Party in Kerala was drawn from manual workers. This is in sharp contrast to other parties and indeed to the Communist Party elsewhere in India.[11]

6. M. K. Krishnan[12]

The most oppressed section of society in India are the former untouchables, the Scheduled Castes or 'Harijans', formerly slave agricultural labouring castes. They are still predominantly agricultural labourers in Kerala and, despite government attempts to ameliorate their position, still backward and exploited. A small munber have been able to take advantage of government schemes and have gained generally minor positions in government or in the political parties. The constitution reserves a number of seats in the legislatures for the Scheduled Castes; the various governments in Kerala have felt it incumbent on them to appoint a token Scheduled Caste minister. The first Scheduled Caste minister to have more than the Harijan Welfare and Community Development portfolios was M. K. Krishnan, who was also the Marxist Minister of Forests in 1967.

Krishnan won government scholarships which took him through to the BSc class. Born in 1924 in Cochin state, both his parents were agricultural labourers. During his period at college the Communist Party were helping to build up a communal organization for the largest Scheduled Caste—the Cochin Pulaya Mahasabha—which was to be the training ground for almost all the Scheduled Caste leaders who have emerged in the Communist Party. It was perhaps the first serious effort to organize the Scheduled Castes in Kerala. It encountered considerable difficulties—direct, sometimes physical, opposition, the problems of organizing scattered, exploited, and frightened agricultural labourers, and the deeply embedded differences of consciousness, epitomized by the remark of one high caste Communist leader that the members of the Scheduled Caste were 'a different sort of people'.[13] Krishnan was active in this movement. He had already been impressed by the nationalist militancy of the Communist students and soon joined the party. He took part in the last of the major campaigns against the exclusion of low castes from temples and their environs. He organized a union of agricultural labourers in his own village. For a time he was secretary of the Pulaya Mahasabha, until he had to follow his predecessor underground. He remained in a neighbouring state, employed as a chemist in an oil mill, until the ban on the Communist Party was lifted.

He returned to Kerala to work full-time for the party. He led a number of unions, including the toddy tappers, shop employees, and agricultural labourers. From 1953 onwards he was a member of the local *panchayat*, and was for a long time its president. He was a member of the district committee of the party, but in 1959, when the top state committee of the party was expanded and included for the first time members of the Scheduled Castes, it was two other former officials of the Cochin Pulaya Mahasabha who were chosen, an ex-state minister and an ex-MP. At the split they joined the CPI, but Krishnan and the mass of the Scheduled Caste voters joined the CPI(M). The Marxists have deliberately put greater emphasis on the most oppressed sections of the countryside, the agricultural labourers, the Scheduled Castes. Since 1964 Krishnan has twice been elected an MLA, has become a member of the much smaller state committee of the 'new' party, and was for a time a minister. He is now the secretary of the party in a district where the great Marxist strength mainly relies on agricultural labourers and where the party is trying to build up strong unions among them.

CONCLUSION: RECRUITMENT GROUNDS, ROLES, RESOURCES, CAREERS, AND CASUALTIES

If one turns from the minutiae of the careers, one can observe certain patterns. In this concluding section I shall list the recruitment grounds, the roles, the resources, and finally some conditions of advance among the leadership. In theory, one should distinguish between the 'entry stations' into public life and the 'recruitment grounds' for the party.[14] On the one hand, there was no separate Communist Party until 1940, so that up till then one had to enter politics via another organization; on the other, even after independence, when a 'career' in politics began to look more tempting, many were not directly recruited into the party. One cannot enter directly a cadre party or any party that is selective about its membership. It is generally the front or ancillary activities that first mobilize people. Of the six leaders in this study, two were first drawn by union activity, two by caste movements, and one by the student movement; only one appears to have moved directly into the nationalist struggle. He was typical of a generation of Malabar Communists who entered the nationalist movement, then joined the Congress Socialists and finally the CPI. In practice, however, the entry stations often served as the recruitment grounds. It would, moreover, be wrong to suggest that for any individual there was necessarily a single recruitment ground. M. Kumaran, for example, passed through the teachers' movement and the national struggle; both Krishnans through communal organizations, the student and the national movements.[15]

Perhaps the most important recruitment ground has been the national struggle. The larger and more enthusiastic wing of the Congress Party in Malabar and significant sections from Travancore and Cochin moved into the Communist Party. Clearly, this avenue was closed with the advent of independence, or at least with the party's acceptance of it, that is at the end of the second period. Similarly, in practice, this period saw the closure of a second ground, the communal movement. Communal associations were strong in Kerala and the caste associations, especially of the lower castes, were voicing demands that any modernizing party would support, but, with the change of the rules of the political game at independence, they became more dangerous politically and more reactionary socially. Even though the odd recruit might be made as an MLA or an MP, they did not become leaders. The teachers' movement, and the teaching profession in general, was a major source, especially in the earlier periods, but it may also have dried up as the party lost exclusive control of the movement. (On the other hand, the movement among lower government servants —NGOs, non-gazetted officers—has perhaps become a new source of leadership.) During the pre-independence period the student movement threw up many leaders for the party in Kerala, as well as for other parties. After independence, the Communists gradually lost the initiative among the students to Congress; in the latest period students have provided many leaders for Congress. None the less, although some felt that the party neglected students in favour of the 'basic' classes, the party has continued to recruit some leaders from the student movement. It should be added that, even though it was suggested that Prakasam was attracted by intellectual reasons, it was the student movement that canalized this feeling. Of the two most important mass movements, the trade unions, with their special ideological place and with their well established organizational structure, have continuously provided leaders at all levels of the party from among the workers themselves; the peasant movement seems to have provided, so far, only local level leaders, for the upper leadership appears to have been recruited elsewhere and drafted into the movement more or less at the top. Recruitment from other parties was common in the first two periods—indeed, the whole original party came in this way, but the last group came from another party in 1948. Afterwards, leaders from other parties were generally treated as allies; they might even be offered ministerships, but were never accepted into the party itself. The movement has now lasted over a generation, so that it has started to reproduce itself, party families just beginning to provide a few, as yet middle-level leaders. It is difficult to distinguish among these recruitment grounds any that can be ascribed as specific to top, middle, or lower leadership.

Just as recruitment grounds may overlap, so may roles. The top leaders have tended to be identified primarily with a single role; at the middle level there is perhaps the most overlapping; at the lower level there is a mixture of single-role and multi-role leadership. The role that is specific to a movement—as opposed to a more fully formed party— is the agitational role, the ability to rally supporters, generally requiring a combination of oratory, energy and personal magnetism. It was most noticeable in the first two 'heroic' periods, when the most glorious exploits of the party took place; it is doubtful whether any one will again achieve the legendary position of, for example, A. K. Gopalan.[16]

From Lenin onwards Communists have emphasized the importance of ideology; a role that may be regarded as distinctively Communist—

certainly in the Kerala context—is that of the ideologue. The function of this role is to place particular events and developments within a wider context, to integrate them into an overall pattern, and to pick out the broad tasks for the party. At a lower level the role is responsible for all internal and external propaganda. The supreme Kerala example is E. M. S. Namboodiripad.[17]

Another role whose importance has been stressed by Communist writers is the organizational. In the Kerala context this has meant primarily, on the one hand party organization, on the other trade union and peasant organization. Other parties and political groupings in Kerala have had an organization, but whereas it is commonly the primary role of Communist leaders it is very rarely so among other leaders, except in two organizational sub-roles that were not well developed in the Communist movement—communal organization and party factional organization. There can be no doubt that Communist organization was qualitatively different from that of other parties. It was one of their greatest strengths. P. Krishna Pillai may be taken as the typical organizer.[18]

It was the final role, the parliamentary, that mainly established the reputation of non-Communist politicians as leaders. One may distinguish three sub-roles: the local governmental, the legislative-ministerial, and the political-managerial. The first two are self-explanatory; by the third term I mean the exercise of skills in gaining and keeping electoral or legislative allies and confounding the opposition. Although many Communist leaders have taken up these roles, they have not been their main role—or at least not the role that established their reputation. Only one leader came to the top through the legislative-ministerial role, but at the middle level of leadership it may be more important; T. K. Krishnan is an example.

I would suggest that the second and third roles have been distinctively Communist. The first and second, the agitational and the ideologue, have concerned a smaller number of leaders and they have been mainly at the top levels, while the parliamentary has tended to be the primary role of those at the middle or low levels.

Even more than roles or recruitment grounds, the 'resources' have been inter-linked. It is extremely difficult, even in individual cases, to separate the different resources and almost impossible to work out the weight that should be given to each. I shall simply list the main obvious ones. I will deal, first, with resources that could play a part both in the entry and in the later career, and, secondly, with those that are only important in the later progress. In many cases it is not possible to say if a resource is an asset or a liability; the rules of the game may change at different periods or in different arenas. The well-known agitator may be the first to be put in jail, while jail itself may be a source of prestige, but can mean being cut off from one's power base. The fact of being a middle class lawyer may contribute to being chosen for the assembly, but may inhibit a career in the party.

Men and treasure, two resources that are important in other parties, have been less important in the Kerala Communist movement. The *condottiere* figure, selling himself and his troops, has had no place and nobody has bought himself into the leadership. Personal links, personal background, and social background, however, have certainly been important. The personal links of kinship, marriage, friendship, discipleship, and occupation are perhaps the hardest to assess. The personal background would include sex (very few women have been leaders), age, education, and skills (the first three subjects were probably chosen to be MLAs partly for this reason), and outside reputation (charisma is an extreme form). Political analysis has generally focused on the social background. Community and caste have been exhaustively discussed. It is a big advantage, at least in electoral politics, to come from the largest caste, as in the case of the Ezhavas, and a disadvantage to come from a small caste, as in the case of Manjunatha Rao. M. K. Krishnan's career was probably helped by the Marxists' decision to give greater attention to the Scheduled Castes. Class has also been much discussed. Solomon came from the working class, which was an advantage in a Communist movement. Marxists would probably suggest that M. K. Krishnan's advance was due to his class (agricultural labourer) background rather than his caste. Geographical area is important when an organization has developed mainly in certain strongholds. In these areas one is more likely to join the party. Generally, it seems to be an advantage to come from such areas. Most of the top and middle leaders probably come from these strongholds. It may sometimes be a disadvantage; one reason that T. K. Krishnan did not advance in the party could have been that there were already too many leaders in his district. Similarly, it may sometimes be an advantage to come from a weak area; there is no competition, as may be seen in the case of Prakasam. A final factor is social standing or position. A. K. Gopalan, for example, came from a traditional elite family.

The other group of resources that are important for the career rather than the entry into politics relates mainly to the organization. First, there is experience, that is the performance of particular roles. Not only is the length of experience important, but also the variety. It may be an advantage or a disadvantage to have a wide experience. Kumaran may have suffered from not having a 'mass front' base, or he may have suffered from being in local government, which may be incompatible with advance within the party. Secondly, there is the office held at any particular moment rather than the past experience. District secretaries are traditionally seen as very powerful figures in the party. Thirdly, there is prestige, dependent largely on sacrifice in jail, underground, money, or personal terms, and battle honours for having participated in the great campaigns: for example, Solomon in the coir workers' strike or Kumaran in the teachers' strike. Fourthly, there are personal links within the movement, including patronage and favouritism. This is a murky area, for Communists do not like to acknowledge these phenomena. Fifthly, there is loyalty, and, sixthly, there is what may be called ideological grasp, which is important in Communist parties. Finally, there are three further resources that have probably been very important in the advancement of leaders. In the first place, time. In the careers I have alluded to this factor. It seems that one must be a full-time worker to qualify for the higher leadership. Prakasam left politics completely; Manjunatha Rao retired to local politics. Yet T. K. Krishnan shows that it is possible to pursue certain careers and still advance, but only within the parliamentary field. In the second place, there is the crucial fact of ability. It is difficult to gauge, but all the top leaders seem very able, at least in their primary roles. In the third place, there is priority. Many of the top leaders got to the top by being there first. E. M. S. Namboodiripad and A. K. Gopalan, for instance, were in leading positions almost from the start of their political careers. There is a real danger that both Communist parties may eventually be led by old men.

It may be suitable to conclude with a few observations on the factors that have helped or hindered careers within the system. Casualties have occurred for three reasons. Physical casualties have occurred initially because of repression and latterly because of old age. Ideological casualties have taken place at every major change of line in the party. 'Careerist' casualties particularly affected the student movement and the early years of the individual politician's career, especially with the responsibilities of family and marriage. The leaders' careers have been within a hierarchy and some of the chief factors affecting progress have been the constraints common in any organization. There are the problems of specialization. There is the limit of the number of vacancies at the top, even though it is possible for the number to expand, as happened with the new party constitutions in 1954 and 1958 and at the split in 1964. There are 'vacuums' ('priority', from the organization's point of view), for example, in developing an arena like Prakasam, 'openings' such as occurred for Kumaran when other leaders were jailed, 'bunching' when there are too many leaders at a particular point, which may have affected Kumaran and both the Krishnans, and similar phenomena.

It should be stressed, however, that although individuals have doubtless used the movement to advance their careers and also to satisfy other needs outside politics, the system is such that the party has used individuals far more. The Communist movement in Kerala has in many ways been a successful organization. It has been bureaucratic and rational, formalized and specialized, perhaps even Leninist. The organization's demands have shaped people's careers and used the individual resources in the performance of its own roles.

15

FIVE SINHALESE NATIONALIST POLITICIANS

James Jupp

Ceylon (now Sri Lanka) has enjoyed over forty years of parliamentary democracy, based on universal suffrage and with a consensus established between the major parties in parliament and the major cultural groups within society.[1] I have argued elsewhere that 'at independence it had a class of established politicians drawn from the professional classes and landed aristocracy . . . and deeply committed to parliamentary methods'.[2] I intend here to study a group of five Ceylonese politicians who might, superficially, be thought of as exceptions to this general rule. They all joined with S. W. R. D. Bandaranaike in the coalition which won a landslide victory in 1956. This victory marked the turning point in Ceylon political history from 'post-colonialism' to 'majority nationalism'.[3] The five politicians concerned, W. Dahanayake, Philip Gunawardena, I. M. R. A. Iriyagolle, K. M. P. Rajaratne, and R. G. Senanayake, were known primarily for their strong commitment to the Sinhala language and to Sinhala nationalism.[4] They did not, therefore, accept the notion of compromise between communities, and particularly between Sinhalese and Tamils, which characterized politics under colonialism and during the years of United National Party rule between 1947 and 1956. Nor, it subsequently appeared, did they accept the trend towards a two-party system which became increasingly marked in independent Ceylon.[5] Further, in distinguishing them from the dominant politicians, all of them in varying degrees and at different times not merely rejected 'western' culture but also criticized 'western' institutions, especially parliamentary democracy. They might variously be described as 'Sinhala nationalists', as 'communalists', as 'traditionalists', as 'indigenous radicals'. Or they might be dismissed as political eccentrics unable to fit into a well developed and disciplined two-bloc electoral system. Although Dahanayake was briefly prime minister, while all the others held ministerial office at some time, they were 'middle-ranking' politicians in the sense of being unable to establish themselves firmly within the narrow circles which came to dominate the leadership of these two blocs.[6]

It is at once clear from the social origins of the five that they came from the same general backgrounds which characterized most Ceylonese politicians. There have been virtually no working-class or peasant members of parliament elected since 1931, and certainly none of the five could be so described. The 'traditionalists' were largely middle and upper-middle class people, educated in English and to the tertiary level. A tiny handful of Sri Lanka Freedom Party politicians has emerged with genuinely 'traditional' backgrounds, in the sense of coming from the Sinhala-speaking rural lower classes.[7] Only with the inclusion of T. B. Tennakoon in Mrs Bandaranaike's cabinet of 1970 has any of them reached the level of national leadership. Although all five of those being studied made a major and often successful appeal to the rural masses in the Sinhala language, they did not belong to the masses themselves. R. G. Senanayake was 'born into politics' as a member of the family which dominated national affairs from the 1930s to the 1950s.[8] W. Dahanayake, although Ceylon's only middle-class prime minister, went to St Thomas' College, Mount Lavinia, the 'Eton of Ceylon'. Gunawardena and Iriyagolle were educated at Ananda, the Buddhist Theosophical Society public school designed to give an alternative to the Christian education enjoyed by members of the Ceylonese upper classes.[9] K. M. P. Rajaratne, the only one of the five educated after independence, took his degree at the University of Ceylon at a time when studies were still conducted exclusively in English. Thus all five, like all other Ceylonese politicians until recently, were born into classes which were able to give them the English-language education which cut them off from the 90 per cent of the masses who could not speak the language of colonial politics and administration.

There have been only a limited number of roads into politics in Ceylon, and in this respect all five have had fairly conventional backgrounds. A normal requirement has been a sound local position, based on a good family which either has a large economic stake in the locality from which the politician is elected, or has a good reputation and high social standing. Two of the five, Senanayake and Gunawardena, had suitable 'aristocratic' backgrounds, in the sense of coming from families with substantial estates. The Senanayakes made their wealth from graphite mining and were, consequently, wealthier than the Gunawardenas, who were traditional owners of landed property. Both held 'personal' seats for many years: that is, votes were given to them regardless of their changes in party allegiance. Although twice unseated for statutory offences, Gunawardena was able to hold on to Avissawella between 1936 and 1970, putting his wife in to take his place in 1948 after he had been disqualified from sitting for seven years for his part in a strike. His brother, Robert, held the neighbouring constituency for much of the same period, both being regarded as Marxist socialists. Equally, Senanayake had his stronghold in the

Dambadeniya district, surrounded by his close Senanayake, Kotelawala, and Jayawardena relatives in the coconut plantation belt between Kelaniya and Dodangaslanda, much of which was owned by themselves and their Bandaranaike rivals. Gunawardena and Senanayake were natural entrants into the political arena. Senanayake was the son of F. R. Senanayake, who had opposed the British as a Sinhalese nationalist in 1915.[10] Philip Gunawardena's father, a village headman, had also been arrested during the wave of repression following the communal riots of 1915. Senanayake was the nephew of Ceylon's first prime minister, D. S. Senanayake, the cousin of the second and third prime ministers, Dudley Senanayake and Sir John Kotelawala, and a relative of the current leader of the opposition, J. R. Jayawardena. With the last named, however, he maintained a life-long feud. Senanayake and Gunawardena both had the necessary leisured background for those naturally destined for the political elite. Gunawardena spent ten years overseas at universities in America and Britain, while Senanayake was educated at Pembroke College, Cambridge. Neither ever needed to use their degrees. In true 'Edwardian' style they went into parliament, Philip at the age of thirty-five and Senanayake at thirty-three, without any need to earn a living. Senanayake's election in 1944 was to a seat previously held by his brother-in-law. In 1956, in winning Kelaniya, he allied with one set of relatives, the Wijewardenas, to defeat another kinsman, J. R. Jayawardena. Senanayake and Gunawardena were, then, typical of the small number of those born to politics, educated under the British, and elected to the colonial legislature. Senanayake took the 'Right' road of allegiance to the United National Party; Gunawardena the 'Left', of leadership of the Marxist Lanka Samasamaja Party. The puzzle is not how they got into politics, but how they progressively mismanaged their careers to the extent that their own loyal local retainers eventually threw them out of their personal fiefs in the 1970 general election.

The other three represent a second road into politics which became increasingly popular after S. W. R. D. Bandaranaike's victory in 1956.[11] With the new emphasis on the Sinhala language, those lower in the professional scale began to come into political prominence. They were often more proficient in Sinhala than the upper-middle classes, who frequently spoke English as a mother tongue and had to relearn the native language of their constituents, as did Bandaranaike himself after his return from Oxford in 1925.[12] Dahanayake, Iriyagolle, and Rajaratne were all drawn from the teaching profession, which formed the backbone of recruits into the nationally conscious political class created by the spread of mass education and the ballot box revolution of 1956. Although Dahanayake's upbringing was largely in English, he was foremost in forming a pressure group agitating on the language issue in 1956. He normally addressed parliament in Sinhala, well before this became usual. Iriyagolle was even more centrally concerned with the language as a teacher, writer, and translator. Rajaratne was to emerge as the most fanatical of the three. As the only one to enter politics after independence it was natural for him to adopt the Sinhala nationalism which came to form the basis of the consensus after 1956. But Dahanayake and Iriyagolle were able to do so rather more easily than the westernized aristocrats who formed most of the leadership of the United National Party which governed after 1947, and even of the Sri Lanka Freedom Party which replaced it in 1956.

Although the three middle-class nationalists were not born into politics, they all had a strong local base. Dahanayake's father, *Muhandiram* D. S. P. Dahanayake, was well established in Galle, the major town of the overwhelmingly Sinhala Buddhist Southern Province.[13] From this area came many of the Buddhist revivalists of the first half of the century and the powerfully organized temperance movement which marked the beginning of mass support for nationalism.[14] The connection with Galle has proved lifelong. Only very briefly in mid-1960 did Dahanayake lose the majority in Galle which he had first secured in 1947. His initial return to the House of Representatives followed eight years of membership of the Municipal Council, of which he became the first elected mayor. Although changing his party seven times, Dahanayake has never really lost the loyalty of his native town. Alone of the five he survived the 1970 general election. Thus, while it is generally true that political 'notables' in Ceylon, as elsewhere, rely on a rural base, he has been able to build a local urban machine. He has his own party at the municipal level, which has frequently controlled the majority on the Galle council. This caters for the local Muslim minority as for the Sinhala Buddhist majority, making Dahanayake one of the few examples of a 'city boss' in Ceylon politics.[15]

Iriyagolle and Rajaratne also possessed a strong local base in traditional rural areas. Iriyagolle was born in the village which bears his name and is in his stronghold of Kuliyapitiya, which he won at the elections of 1947, 1952, 1956, March 1960, and 1965, although running under four different labels. Equally, Rajaratne was brought up and educated in the area of Uva Province, which he was to hold on several occasions and in which his wife was also to be elected. Thus, as with the great families, so with the middle-class professionals, a strong local and family base was a vital asset in securing entry into politics and insuring against defeat. Apart from R. G. Senanayake, who achieved the record in 1956 of winning two seats at once, all five were geographically limited to their home areas. As with other Ceylon politicians, they had to appeal to local loyalty, which was often much stronger than loyalty to a party or programme. Had they not had such firm local bases, it is quite possible that the five would have been submerged by the rapidly consolidating party system well before 1970.

Whether aristocratic or 'national middle class', the five were all of Sinhala race, Buddhist religion, and Goyigama caste.[16] They came from the community which has provided all prime ministers and a majority of ministers and members of parliament. There were thus no social barriers against them rising to the highest offices in the land, and Dahanayake briefly became prime minister in the chaos surrounding the assassination of Bandaranaike in 1959.[17] Gunawardena, Iriyagolle, Senanayake, and Dahanayake certainly saw themselves as potential prime ministers, especially during the breakdown of the party system in 1960. By birth, education, upbringing, race, caste, religion, there was no vital difference between any of the five and those who earned a more secure place at cabinet level in the major parties. To some extent, then, their relative failure to stay at the top must be attributed to reasons of personality. It is difficult to assess the importance of their often idiosyncratic behaviour. There are few extensive biographies of them and the major account of Philip Gunawardena's life is intended to praise him.[18] Nor, indeed, are there many critical biographies of Ceylonese politicians against which their careers and behaviour could be gauged.[19] There are very few studies with a sound psychological basis of the 'Sinhalese character' and none at all of political participants.[20] Such studies as have been made stress the contrast between security within the family and communal group and insecurity outside these groups. On the national scale this may be translated as security within a broad sub-nation and hostility towards those who are not part of it. Thus Sinhala nationalism contained two dimensions: hostility towards the colonizing British and fear of the Tamil nation which, although a minority in Ceylon, had thirty million members close at hand in South India. The Buddhist revivalists associated with the American Theosophist Colonel Olcott and Anagarika Dharmapala criticized western values and British rule.[21] Of the five, Iriyagolle is closest to this tradition, as he was personally invited by Anagarika Dharmapala to edit a Sinhala newspaper of the Buddhist revivalist movement. Through his father, R. G. Senanayake might well have been influenced by the movement's contacts within his own family. But, like the remaining three, he shows more signs of the second aspect of Sinhala nationalism, the almost paranoic belief that other communities, and particularly the Tamils, are dedicated to the destruction of the Sinhalese. His reported statement that he would like to wear slippers made from the hide of the last Indian Tamil is hardly in the nobler tradition of the Buddhist revival.

The Buddhist revivalist movement was at its height during the formative years of all but Rajaratne. Dahanayake, Gunawardena, and Iriyagolle were all old enough to have clear memories of the aftermath of the 1915 riots when, for the first and last time, the British launched mass repression against Buddhists. Gunawardena's father, a respected local headman, was arrested, as was Senanayake's.[22] Iriyagolle, Gunawardena, and Rajaratne were all educated at Buddhist Theosophical Society schools, which had been founded specifically to advance the cause of Buddhist revivalism. Senanayake came from a family deeply committed to the associated revivalist and temperance movements. The Senanayakes were regarded as patrons of the Ramanya Buddhist sect, which was considerably more radical and nationalist than the conservative Kandyan Siam *nikaya*. Dahanayake grew up in the heart of the area in which the revivalist movement had its strongest hold. Thus all were born into and brought up within the national revivalist tradition, in contrast to S. W. R. D. Bandaranaike himself, all of whose family were Anglicans and who made a political decision in adult life to adopt the Buddhist religion, the Sinhala language, and the national dress. Thus, although Senanayake began his political life as a conservative in the United National Party while Gunawardena was a Marxist in the Lanka Samasamaja Party, both eventually became famous for their fanatical and at times almost insane advocacy of Sinhala hegemony.

Dahanayake, a former Marxist, and Iriyagolle, the conservative rural notable, shared a common love for the Sinhala language. They both pursued rather similar policies as ministers of education charged with strengthening the national element in a system still strongly affected by its colonial and Christian origins. Rajaratne, Senanayake, and Gunawardena vied with each other for the most blood-curdling phrases against the Tamils and Catholics, although on many national and international issues they had very little in common. All five were drawn by their backgrounds and outlook to Bandaranaike when his programme concentrated primarily on Sinhala nationalism. However, they drew so far away from his Sri Lanka Freedom Party when it adopted socialist measures that four out of five of them ended their political careers serving the conservative United National Party. The fifth, R. G. Senanayake, refused to rejoin the party founded by his uncle only because of the deep personal hatred which he had for most of its leaders, and particularly his own relative, J. R. Jayawardena.

If the early influence of Sinhala Buddhist revivalism is easy to trace, it is much more difficult to deal with the evident personal idiosyncracies which characterized all five in varying degrees. It is arguable that western psychiatric terminology may not apply to oriental societies.[23] Even if it did, no one possesses enough first hand knowledge of the five to be able to analyse them in the manner used by Alan Davies in his *Private Politics*.[24] By British standards Gunawardena, Senanayake, and Rajaratne were almost paranoic demagogues, while Iriyagolle and Dahanayake were, at best, lovable eccentrics. Yet the ringing oratorical phrases in which they denounced the real or imagined enemies of their race may not be sufficient guide to the concrete policies which they implemented while in office. Oratory is an art in Ceylon, and political meetings are a major form of popular entertainment. Philip Gunawardena, in particular, was a past master at them. Of Philip it was said that 'he spares nothing in venom, nothing in sting or in virulence in the coining of these biting phrases'.[25] The same might be argued of R. G. Senanayake's increasingly shrill denunciation of Indian Tamils in the 1960s, or of Rajaratne's apparent belief that American imperialism was involved in a conspiracy against the Sinhala nation, Iriyagolle's fervid puritanism and anti-westernism, or Dahanayake's attacks on British institutions and the use of the English language.

All these oratorical devices contain strong hints of insecurity and had the political function of appealing to age-old Sinhalese beliefs in the isolation of their race and religion in a Hindu Indian region and its vulnerability to the religion, culture, and economy imported from the powerful societies of Europe ever since the Portuguese arrived in 1505. There is much in common between many of the arguments for Sinhala hegemony put forward by the five and those which became almost common currency after 1956 among politicians of all major Sinhalese parties. Attacks on the Tamils, the Indians, or the west are evidence of an ability to swim in the mainstream of Ceylonese politics, rather than of eccentricity. It can, however, be argued that each of the five had certain personal characteristics which, while quite common in Ceylon and elsewhere, made it hard for them to fit into a disciplined party political system increasingly concerned with social and economic problems rather than with communal appeals. Psychologically the most interesting and the most easily characterized is Philip Gunawardena. His whole political style from the earliest incursion into Marxist politics at least until his entry into the United National Party government in 1965 was that of open onslaught, personal attack, and being the 'bogey man' of Ceylon politics. From being a powerful figure in the land, with a strong trade union following in the transport industry, the 'father of Ceylon Marxism' became, by the end of his life, a pathetic and isolated captive of the very conservative politicians against whom he had fought for years. His virulently expressed hatred of Mrs Bandaranaike did not prevent her from becoming prime minister. His lifelong feud with the LSSP leader, N. M. Perera, did not prevent Perera from becoming finance minister and retaining the great bulk of organized LSSP support. His espousing of Sinhala nationalism did not keep a single important ally for him, nor did his continued appeal as a labour leader keep his union organization from disappearing. In the end his own loyal villagers turned against him and replaced him by an almost unknown SLFP candidate who had only recently defected from the UNP.

Gunawardena's personality seems to have been the major factor in this tragic decline. On joining the Bandaranaike government in 1956 as its 'socialist conscience', he 'was unable to attract to himself a single friend or sympathiser. Every month, unerringly, laboriously, he added to the list of his enemies by the brusque word flung across the Cabinet table. . . '26 There was a political as well as a personal dimension to Philip's isolation. He was beset by the conservative forces in the Sri Lanka Freedom Party associated with R. G. Senanayake, W. Dahanayake and the Buddhist monk Buddharakkitha (called 'Buddy Racketeer' by Gunawardena). It was Buddharakkitha who was subsequently convicted of planning the assassination of Bandaranaike. Eventually the great majority of the cabinet 'went on strike', refusing to meet until Gunawardena was removed. Bandaranaike was forced to comply, and Gunawardena was removed early in 1959. His reform of land tenure through the Paddy Lands Act of 1958 had deeply annoyed conservative landowners, including (it was said) Mrs Bandaranaike's relatives, the Ratwattes. Gunawardena was also hated for his support of striking members of his own transport unions. His removal was seen by the entire Left as proof of the conservative domination over Bandaranaike, and both the Communists and the LSSP withdrew their support from the government. Yet it is obvious that Philip was an impossible colleague. He had already served a prison term and been unseated in 1948 for his action during a previous strike. He had split the LSSP in 1950, taking his allies into a Viplavakari Lanka Samasamaja Party which allied with the Communists in 1952. He had been the first Marxist to adopt a policy of 'Sinhala Only' and moved progressively from his former comrades on this issue. After leaving the government he fell out with his niece, Mrs Vivienne Goonewardena, an LSSP leader, and in 1960 with his brother Robert. His attempts to form a communal party in 1960 in alliance with extreme Buddhists was a failure and its component parts had gone their separate ways within a year. Thus, at every turn Gunawardena's life is characterized by refusal to accept authority or obey the law (a necessary attribute under the British but less acceptable after independence), refusal to cooperate with colleagues on an equal basis, personal antagonism and vituperation against almost every important figure in established politics, the maintenance of a machine on a patronage basis in which he could not be challenged by equals, and the adoption of a completely eclectic ideology which makes one doubt whether ideas were ever anything more to him than rationalizations for his personal fears and antagonisms.

All this suggests, however impressionistically, a profoundly insecure and neurotic personality expressing itself in continuing hostility to everything and everybody. The two major ideological positions held by Gunawardena, his anti-imperialist Marxism and his anti-Western Sinhala nationalism, were both negative and hostile in the sense of being concerned with destroying enemies. In office, his one creative work was the Paddy Lands Act, while in every other respect he was frustrated. His personal following remained substantial in the major areas of Low Country Sinhala Buddhist predominance which had nurtured the Buddhist revival. But he proved quite incapable of building a new party upon it and he saw his rural support drift away to the SLFP and his labour following to the LSSP within five years of leaving Bandaranaike's government.

R. G. Senanayake also experienced a similar fall from high office to political irrelevance. He also left only one major monument, the China-Ceylon rice for rubber barter agreement of 1953, which still forms a major element in Ceylon's trade. In most other respects he, like Gunawardena, was quite an impossible colleague, whether within the restraints of party discipline or of cabinet loyalty. Not only was he 'born to politics' but he was also 'born to power'. His uncle, D. S. Senanayake, made him his parliamentary secretary in 1947, and his cousin, Dudley Senanayake, made him a minister five years later. Yet his excellent family connections did not prevent him from leaving the government over its 1954 agreement for formalizing the citizenship of Indian Tamil estate workers, from harrying the government for two years, or, eventually, from being expelled from the United National Party. He directed most of his venom against J. R. Jayawardena, whom he eventually defeated in the 1956 election by deliberately running against him at Kelaniya as well as standing in his own seat of Dambadeniya. He was able to win his way into Bandaranaike's cabinet as easily as into that of the UNP, and became a leader of the anti-Gunawardena right wing. Yet his adherence to the SLFP did not mean a conversion to party loyalty. He fought against its electoral pact with the Marxists in 1960 and was left out of Mrs Bandaranaike's cabinet as a result. He never held office again. In 1961 he was expelled from the SLFP for joining an opposition attack against the corruption of its ministers. He ran as an Independent in 1965, returned to the SLFP, left it again in 1968, and launched a specifically Sinhala communal party, the Sinhala Mahajana Peramuna, which was wiped out with him in the 1970 general election. Senanayake, like Gunawardena, was extremely belligerent in his relationships and public utterances. But he was also specifically a racialist and the nearest thing to a Fascist, in European terms, that there has been in Ceylon politics. Although he had the best of connections and the strongest of local bases, there was no room in politics for Fascism or undisciplined *prima donnas* by 1970.

K. M. P. Rajaratne echoed in many ways the themes of personal insecurity expressed through communalism and racialism. His political career began in the SLFP and ended with the United National Party. With the abolition of the Senate under the new constitution of 1972, he lost his parliamentary position altogether, having already been defeated in the 1965 general election. Rajaratne's career, short though it has been, has been just as marked by strife and dissension as those of Gunawardena or Senanayake. Appointed as a parliamentary secretary by Bandaranaike in 1956, he resigned almost at once in disagreement over the pace of making Sinhala the only official language, rapid though that was. He was unseated on an election petition shortly afterwards and, like Gunawardena before him, was replaced at the ensuing by-election by his wife who was, if anything, a more fanatical Sinhala nationalist than himself. In 1958 Rajaratne played such a major role in the agitations surrounding the race riots between Sinhalese and Tamils that he was detained under emergency regulations for three months. His new political party, the Jathika Vimukthi Peramuna (National Liberation Front) was proscribed but this did not prevent its reappearance and the re-election of Rajaratne in the two elections of 1960. His troubles, however, were not over. He was sentenced to prison for involvement in riotous behaviour arising from the anti-Tamil campaign of 1958. He began a fast in the House of Representatives in an attempt to secure a pardon, was removed from the House, began to serve his term but had it commuted by the Governor-General. Once again he was returned to parliament, and after his defeat in 1965 was appointed to the chairman-ship of two public corporations in exchange for the support which his party had given to the United National Party. Rajaratne and his wife were renowned for their extreme hostility to the United States, the Catholic Church, the Tamils, the English-speaking elite, and all the traditional enemies of the Sinhala Buddhist majority. Whether this can be taken as an indication of personality disorder, or was merely an extreme expression of views which were commonplace during the period between 1956 and 1965, is a matter of debate. Certainly by 1965 there was little room in politics for the extreme expression of com-munalism associated with the Rajaratnes. As the failure of R. G. Senanayake and their temporary ally, Philip Gunawardena, suggests, that particular approach, so powerful in the late 1950s, had become bankrupt.

Dahanayake and Iriyagolle do not show the same fierce hostility towards their opponents as the other three. Iriyagolle was more victim than aggressor and his consistent pillorying by the English-language press and the English-speaking intelligentsia did much to make his period as minister for education unfruitful. He, too, made ill-judged statements on occasion, including an attack on the Buddhist clergy in 1969 which caused great embarrassment to the government and forced him to make public apologies.[27] Rather than being a communalist in the militant sense, Iriyagolle was an old-fashioned conservative of rural Sinhala background, deeply concerned with morality, religion, and language. Brought into Bandaranaike's government as a parliamentary secretary in 1956 as the representative of a group urging the language issue, he resigned to form a Samajawadi Mahajana Peramuna (Peoples Socialist Front) which ran forty candidates unsuccessfully in the March 1960 elections. Iriyagolle learned by his defeat and promptly joined the United National Party, which made him president of its Youth League, the mass electoral organization. Iriyagolle, in contrast to the other four, thus spent the latter part of his political life in one of the major parties and was made minister for education on its return in 1965. But his conservative and traditional attitudes brought him into conflict with the universities and it was during his term of office that the militant student movements which ultimately led to the revolt of 1971 were created and expanded.

Dahanayake had also found education to be an area of major conflict. But his greatest test, and one which he failed completely, came after the assassination of Bandaranaike in 1959. Dahanayake was unwillingly made prime minister in the belief that this was Bandaranaike's wish. He was faced with a growing revolt within the SLFP, which had leaders more centrally placed than himself. Eventually he expelled most of his ministers from the cabinet without warning them in advance. His scratch cabinet, which held office pending the election of March 1960, was the weakest and most unrepresentative in Ceylon's history. Dahanayake was accused of building up a secret service, of extending favours to those involved in the assassination, and of using government facilities to launch his new party, the Lanka Prajathantrawadi Pakshaya. The LPP, which continued in existence until after the 1965 election, was primarily concerned with religious and cultural issues. It opposed the report of the Buddha Sasana Commission, which wished to reform the Buddhist clergy, opposed the nationalization of the school system, and supported the repatriation of Indians. On these issues it was engaged in debate with other small and newly created parties led by Gunawardena, Iriyagolle, Rajaratne, and S. W. R. D. Bandaranaike's cousin, S. D. Bandaranaike. Dahanayake's electoral defeat and the fairly rapid revival of the SLFP under Mrs Bandaranaike, suggested that none of these sectarian formations had any real political future. By 1965 Dahanayake was virtually an ally of the United National Party, which he joined on becoming minister of home affairs. His penchant for party changing was not quite exhausted, however, and on the crushing defeat of the UNP in 1970 he once again declared himself an independent, ostensibly in criticism of the continued membership of the new Sri Lanka in the British Commonwealth.

Although obviously of somewhat different personality, what characterizes the five is their political incompetence. In a crisis they normally behaved in a way guaranteed to isolate themselves from any potential support. All were too ready to rush off into a new party of their own foundation rather than to work within the existing and steadily strengthening two-party system. With the exception of Rajaratne, all had learned their politics in colonial times, when no disciplined parties existed. None could readily submit to cabinet or ministerial discipline, although they were not alone in Ceylon politics in this regard. All climbed on to the bandwagon of Sinhala nationalism but none was able to take advantage of communal appeals for very long. In the crisis election of March 1960, all were to be found standing on essentially communalist platforms in the hope of repeating the landslide victory of Bandaranaike in 1956. They failed, and by 1965 pure communalism had become discredited as a main plank. All the major parties, including the Marxists, had incorporated such items as 'Sinhala Only' and the republic into their platforms. The alliance between Mrs Bandaranaike, the LSSP, and the Communists in 1964 changed the issue. Increasingly the communalists were flogging a dead political horse. Rather than putting them on the radical Left, where they and most communalists had been in 1956, the continued adherence of the five to the Sinhala revival in its extreme form put them on the conservative side. By 1965 the SLFP had greatly modified its nationalist appeal by adopting economic and social policies akin to those of the Marxists. Politics polarized between Right and Left, leaving groups and individuals with a choice of joining one major bloc or another or remaining politically isolated. Had the five remained with the SLFP, which they all supported in 1956, they might well have constituted a leading element in the party which was victorious in 1970. But neither their personalities nor their ideologies, their tactics nor their political insight, was appropriate. Politically they ended either in the wilderness or in the pockets of those they had fought throughout their vigorous political youth.

16

ROLES AND CAREERS OF
MIDDLE-RANK POLITICIANS: SOME
CASES FROM EAST BENGAL

G. W. Choudhury

This paper deals with the roles of a few middle-rank politicians in East Bengal during the period of united Pakistan (1947–71). Without going into any theoretical discussion about 'middle-rank politicians', I shall begin by making some comments on political dynamics in East Bengal, now Bangladesh. It is not possible to analyse the role of any political leader, of middle or any other rank, in East Bengal without making some reference to the political realities prevailing there at the time.

The political process in united Pakistan had features common to many newly independent Afro-Asian countries. The national movement had been carried on in the name of the people and of democracy under the leadership of a popular hero, *Quaid-i-Azam* (the great leader) M. A. Jinnah, who transformed the movement into a mass one, making it possible for politicians of all ranks to play their parts. After the success of this movement Pakistan adopted a parliamentary form of government modelled on Westminster. But there was no sound base for democratic order in Pakistan and democracy in Pakistan was totally unsatisfactory: the country had no general election and no well organized political parties during the era of so-called parliamentary democracy (1947–58); provincial elections held during the period were rightly described as 'a farce, a mockery, and a fraud upon the electorate'.[1] Though democracy was the driving force behind the creation of Pakistan, and though the country's political system began as a parliamentary form of government, it soon degenerated into a civilian dictatorship (1953–58) and then a military one (1958–71).

Pakistan had a federal *constitution* but not a federal *government*. The central government, thanks to the unsatisfactory working of parliamentary democracy up to 1958 and then to the rise of a military dictatorship, was dominated by a ruling elite composed of top civil and military officials, none of whom were from East Bengal. The political order in Pakistan, particularly since 1958, gave hardly any scope to Bengalis for effective and equal participation in national affairs. They had no share in the decision-making process. The East Bengalis could only react but could never take effective action on any vital national issue, whether it related to economic matters, external affairs, or problems of defence and security.[2]

There was a parliament, there was a cabinet, but the participants in the decision-making process were from neither parliament nor cabinet. They were bureaucrats or army officers. There were some brief intervals when the political order was to some extent dominated by the politicians. Thus, when after Jinnah's death Liaquat continued to be Prime Minister and a weak personality like Nazimuddin was made Governor-General, the roles of political leaders, including middle-rank politicians, were more substantial. It was during this period also that Bengali cabinet ministers like Fazlur Rahman had a share in the decision-making process. Similarly, when Suhrawardy, founder of the Awami League, the present ruling party in Bangladesh, became Prime Minister in 1956 and continued in office for thirteen months, the roles of politicians, including Bengali politicians, became prominent. Except for such brief intervals, however, the political system gave little scope to Bengali politicians. The result was a dearth of political leaders. The political process through which, in a democracy, a junior- or middle-rank politician enters the political scene, makes his mark, and gradually moves upward or proves unsuccessful beyond a certain stage, was lacking.

There was recurrent conflict in Pakistan between those who wanted able leaders to exercise supreme power irrespective of popular support and those who considered it more important that the prime minister or provincial chief ministers should be supported as widely as possible by political parties.[3] Even while popular governments were in operation, political leaders were constantly under the threat of emergency rule (under the emergency powers of the various constitutions) or disqualification from political life under the Public and Representative Offices Disqualification Act (PRODA).

With this background to the political system in Pakistan, I shall now examine the roles of political leaders in East Bengal. Politics in East Bengal under united Pakistan were influenced by a number of factors operating outside the province; these outside forces were at the centre. The power of the centre to appoint and dismiss provincial governors had great impact on politics in East Bengal during the era of parliamentary democracy, and after the emergence of military rule East Bengal politics were virtually controlled from the centre. It was in opposition groups that the roles of politicians, including middle-rank politicians, could be performed more effectively.

I shall therefore begin my discussion of the roles of middle-rank politicians in East Bengal by selecting one from the Awami League.

The Awami League was the first opposition party in Pakistan. It was formed in Dacca in June 1949, 'representing both genuine social protest and political ambitions of frustrated Muslim Leaguers'.[4] H. S. Suhrawardy was its real founder. Suhrawardy, who was premier of Bengal in 1946–47 and played a significant role in the movement for Pakistan, fell from favour in the Muslim League high command; he lost his seat in the constituent assembly, on the ground that he was not a resident of Pakistan. He applied himself to working for communal peace with Gandhi in Calcutta. He returned to Pakistan in 1949 and organized the first group opposed to the ruling Muslim League.

Sheikh Mujibur Rahman, the former Prime Minister of Bangladesh, and Zahiruddin were the two student leaders closest to the Suhrawardy group of the Muslim League in Bengal before independence. Zahiruddin came from an upper middle-class family in Calcutta. He received his undergraduate education at Islamia College, Calcutta, and then at Calcutta University where he obtained a law degree. In the movement for Pakistan in Bengal and Assam, Islamia College played a role similar to that of Aligarh University in Northern India. Zahiruddin was an able speaker; he could speak fluent Bengali and Urdu as well as English. He was highly successful in organizing student support for Suhrawardy on the eve of the general election in 1946, when there was a tussle between the Nazimuddin group and the Suhrawardy group inside the Bengal Muslim League. Zahiruddin and Mujib were of great help to Suhrawardy, who won control of the League and became premier of Bengal in 1946.

While both Mujib and Zahiruddin thus assisted Suhrawardy in the party leadership struggle and in the 1946 election, Mujib had a much wider base of support in the rural areas of East Bengal whereas Zahiruddin's political base was confined to the urban areas of greater Calcutta. Zahiruddin was a prominent student leader in Calcutta; when Jinnah visited Calcutta on the eve of the elections in 1946, Zahiruddin proved an important asset to Suhrawardy, organizing a mass rally of Calcutta Muslims and keeping them spellbound by his excellent oratory, mainly in Urdu. But Mujib was of greater value to Suhrawardy in election campaigns in the rural areas of East Bengal. Both were close associates and devoted followers of Suhrawardy during the great upheavals in Calcutta in 1946–47. It was during this period that Mujib and Zahiruddin also developed the special friendship between them which continued to exist even when the former became the father of the new nation of Bangladesh while the latter had to be given 'friendly protection' at Dacca Central Jail after the creation of the new state.

How was it that Zahiruddin, with his better educational background and perhaps also with greater patronage from Suhrawardy, could not go beyond the status of a middle-rank politician? Zahiruddin is not a 'son of the soil' in East Bengal, while Mujib has powerful local roots. For Zahiruddin, the shifting of the political scene from Calcutta to Dacca was not advantageous. His roots were in West Bengal; he became a 'political refugee' in the new environment at Dacca, where Nazimuddin became chief minister of East Bengal. Suhrawardy and his followers were politically harassed and soon organized themselves into the first opposition group. Zahiruddin, however, had no constituency in East Bengal, while Mujib began his agitational politics in his home province and began to attract attention.

In 1954, the ruling Muslim League was defeated and the United Front won a landslide victory over the League. The United Front had three main constituents: the Awami League, the Krishak-Sramik Party of A. K. Fazlul Haq, and the Nizame-i-Islam Party. The victory of the United Front was due mainly to the charismatic appeal of Fazlul Haq over the East Bengal Muslims; the Awami League and its boss, Suhrawardy, were junior partners, while the Nizame-i-Islam was of little importance. Zahiruddin was not chosen for any seat in the election because, as has already been pointed out, he had no obvious or natural constituency. But when the elections to the second constituent assembly (which was also the federal legislature in Pakistan at the time) took place in 1955, Zahiruddin became a member. Election to the federal legislature was by indirect election by members of the provincial legislatures. By this time the United Front was divided, the Awami League having broken away by challenging Fazlul Haq's leadership. Suhrawardy now had an absolutely free hand in selecting his candidates from the Awami League so there was no difficulty in securing Zahiruddin's nomination.

As a member of the constituent assembly when the constitution of 1956 was framed, Zahiruddin proved his worth as an able speaker and soon made his mark in the assembly. His speeches for the opposition were far superior to those of many of his colleagues, including Mujib, who was also a member. But Mujib began to emerge as a top leader by his vigorous championing of Bengali causes inside and outside the assembly.

When, in 1956, the Awami League finally came to power at the centre and in East Bengal, after many years in the political wilderness, Suhrawardy became Prime Minister of Pakistan and his party nominee, Ataur Rahman Khan, became chief minister in East Bengal. A cabinet minister at the centre was always regarded as much more important than a provincial minister. Yet Mujib became a provincial minister under Ataur Rahman Kahn while Zahiruddin was chosen by

Suhrawardy as education minister in his central cabinet and continued in that position until Suhrawardy's cabinet was forced by President Iskender Mirza to resign in October 1957. As the youngest member of the cabinet Zahiruddin proved a success, yet his political role virtually came to a halt with the dissolution of the Suhrawardy cabinet.

On 7 October 1958 the democratic process was suspended in Pakistan, with the establishment of military rule which continued till December 1971. During the first two and a half years of Ayub's rule, all political parties were banned and many political leaders, including Mujib, were put in jail. Zahiruddin was not arrested; he was treated rather gently by the military regime. In the meantime regionalism became the dominant factor in East Bengal politics and men like Zahiruddin could not feel very happy in the changed circumstances. Although an Awami Leaguer, Zahiruddin, like his political patron Suhrawardy, was a nationalist rather than a Bengali regionalist.

When political parties were revived in 1963–64, the Awami League was also revived. By this time Suhrawardy had died and Mujib became the supreme boss of the revived Awami League; even Ataur Rahman Khan, who had been chief minister in East Bengal, was ousted from the party. Zahiruddin continued in the party but no longer as an equal colleague of Mujib; Mujib now took Suhrawardy's position in the party and Zahiruddin remained faithful to him.

For several years, up to 1970, Zahiruddin's role in the Awami League was that of a middle-rank politician. As long as Suhrawardy was alive and supreme boss of the Awami League, Zahiruddin had an important role; with the death of his patron, he was at the mercy of Mujib. The latter excluded almost all important old Awami Leaguers but he retained Zahiruddin, first because he was no threat to his supremacy and, second, because of their longstanding personal friendship. Zahiruddin realized that his political future in East Bengal depended on the goodwill of Mujib and was content with his secondary role.

During the first and last general elections in united Pakistan, Zahiruddin was given a seat in an area of Dacca where there were a large number of Urdu-speaking voters, mostly Biharis. Zahiruddin, with his fluent Urdu, had no difficulty in securing election. During the civil war of 1971 the army authorities made several attempts to win the support of the Awami League members of the national assembly. Zahiruddin was approached several times, but consistently refused to collaborate. He is reported, however, to have said that he believed in one Pakistan under the 'six-points' programme of the Awami League. This was 'crime' enough, once the demand was for total independence. Soon he was dubbed a collaborator—the easiest method of political elimination. It was in this situation that Mujib, because of his long-standing friendship, gave him 'friendly protection' by arranging some tolerable accommodation at the Central Jail. Thus ended the career of a political leader who, in his formative stages, seemed brighter than Mujib and who was no less close to Suhrawardy. Zahiruddin's main limitation was that he was not a 'son of the soil'—an expression which had great significance in the region-ridden politics of East Bengal.

By 'region-ridden' politics I mean that the people of East Pakistan became more and more conscious of region rather than religion, which had been the main link with West Pakistan. Bengali sub-nationalism based on regional feelings began to develop in East Bengal within Pakistan just as Muslim nationalism began to develop in the 1930s and 1940s within the Indian national movement in the final stages before independence in 1947. In the new political situation as it began to develop in East Bengal, men like Zahiruddin did not have much scope: he did not belong to the region and he was committed to the ideal of a united Pakistan. One may ask why Zahiruddin could not have built up a political base in East Bengal with the support of West Bengali Muslims and Urdu-speaking Biharis. There were two main reasons for his failure to do so. First, West Bengali Muslims preferred not to maintain any separate identity and were largely successful in integrating with East Bengali Muslims. The West Bengali Muslims were never tired of demonstrating their loyalty to emerging Bengali sub-nationalism; they would follow undisputed Bengali leaders like Mujib or Bhashani rather than Zahiruddin, who might have been regarded as 'an outsider' because he used to speak both Urdu and Bengali. To speak Urdu was already a political crime in East Bengal by the 1960s. Secondly, association with Biharis would have been political suicide for Zahiruddin because the Biharis always identified themselves with the West Pakistani ruling elite rather than with the Bengalis.

Zahiruddin, therefore, had to be content with the role of middle-rank politician. He was far-sighted and wise: he realized, unlike many other Urdu-speaking people in East Bengal, that only by identifying with the dominant group, the Awami League, or a 'leftist' party, could he play at least some role in politics in East Bengal. Zahiruddin, because of his close association with Suhrawardy, was not acceptable to the leftist forces; neither was he a leftist by conviction. He was a centre politician; for him the Awami League was the only available party but he could not rise above the middle rank because of his weaker political base. Bangladesh today needs honest and able political leaders like Zahiruddin. In the future he may yet have the opportunity he deserves; he is still in his forties.[5]

I shall now discuss the role of another middle-rank politician who began his career as a Muslim Leaguer, joined the Awami League in the mid-1950s, subsequently joined Fazlul Haq's Krishak Sramik Party, and finally Ayub's Convention Muslim League in the 1960s. Like Zahiruddin, he was also put in jail on a flimsy allegation of 'collaboration'. Hashemuddin Ahmed comes from Mymensingh, the largest district of East Bengal, which provided ruling authorities in East Bengal for thirteen out of the twenty-three years of united Pakistan— Nurul Amin as chief minister for seven years (1948–54), and Abdul Monem Khan as the all-powerful governor under Ayub for six years (1963–69). Like most of the Muslim intelligentsia of Bengal in the 1940s, Hashemuddin joined the Muslim League during the movement for Pakistan but failed to rise above the rank of district leader before independence. In the 1950s, when the Muslim League ministry in East Bengal under Nurul Amin (who in 1971 became the vice-president of Bhutto's truncated Pakistan) became most unpopular, Hashemuddin joined the opposition forces and became an Awami Leaguer. In the 1954 election, when the United Front defeated the Muslim League, Hashemuddin was elected a member of the provincial legislature but not included in Haq's short-lived cabinet.

When, in 1955, opinion in the United Front was divided and some Awami Leaguers sought to move a vote of non-confidence in Fazlul Haq's leadership, a smaller group in the party continued to support Fazlul Haq; Hashemuddin was one of them, and he was expelled from the League. When, however, after a period of central rule through the governor, parliamentary government was restored and a provincial cabinet formed by Haq's Krishak Sramik Party, anti-Haq Leaguers were excluded while Hashemuddin was given the portfolios of Food and Agriculture as well as Judiciary and Legislative Affairs.[6] He became an important member of the cabinet and even began to emerge as a powerful figure in East Bengal politics. But the provincial cabinet had no majority backing in the provincial legislature and throughout its fifteen months in office never dared to face the legislature—an unprecedented phenomenon in a parliamentary democracy. Hashemuddin was not associated with the later stages of this disgraceful state of affairs; he resigned from the cabinet some months before it fell.

This ended an important phase of Hashemuddin's political career. When, in 1956, an Awami League government was formed there ensued a bitter struggle for power with the Krishak Sramik Party which culminated in riots inside the legislature, resulting in the death of the deputy speaker.[7] Hashemuddin, because of his change of loyalties, had not been able to regain his position in East Bengal politics when military rule came in 1958.

With the revival of political parties in Pakistan under Ayub's

Political Parties Act of 1962, various leaders who were not debarred under PRODA either joined their old parties or formed new groups, or changed their loyalties and joined new parties. Hashemuddin, true to his record of changing political affiliations, joined that faction of the Muslim League led by Ayub Kahn, which was known as the Convention Muslim League. From 1963 Hashemuddin began to emerge once more, now under Ayub's quasi-democratic political order. He was soon elected secretary of the Provincial Convention Muslim League. As the ruling party in Pakistan, the Convention Muslim League, though without popular support in East Bengal, exercised political power and influence. Hashemuddin showed his talent as a good organizer of the party: notwithstanding its unpopularity in East Bengal, the provincial party under Hashemuddin was quite active and vigorous.

It was during the presidential election in 1964 between Ayub and Miss Jinnah that Hashemuddin was able to attract the attention of Ayub, who was much impressed by Hashemuddin's ability. Hashemuddin was one of the few political leaders who dared to face the big crowds in East Bengal on behalf of Ayub. Ayub told me in August 1964 that he regarded Hashemuddin as a potential leader of East Bengal, and I got the impression that Hashemuddin would be selected by Ayub as one of his cabinet ministers after the election.

Hashemuddin's success in Ayub's campaign and his coming closer to Ayub, however, sealed his fate with regard to any further promotion. The provincial governor of East Bengal, Abdul Monem Khan, could not tolerate any other politician rising to eminence or coming closer to the President; he considered such a man a potential threat to his own supremacy. Ayub was so dependent on Monem Khan for his authoritarian rule in East Bengal that he would not offend him, and Monem Khan, taking advantage of Ayub's need for his ruthless and tyrannical rule in East Bengal, was able to eliminate any of his political rivals in the ruling party. There was a joke in East Bengal during this period that, if a Convention Muslim Leaguer wished to commit political suicide, the easiest and surest way would be to see Ayub more than once without Monem's consent.

Such was the fate of Hashemuddin. After the presidential election in 1964 Hashemuddin contested a Mymensingh seat in the national assembly. Thanks to the indirect method of election, very few from any opposition party could expect to be elected, especially since Monem was noted for his success in winning elections in East Bengal. Yet Hashemuddin, who was given the ruling party's ticket and who himself belonged to Mymensingh district, lost to the opposition party in the election. It was Monem's home district also, and there is no doubt that the opposition candidate had his full support and blessing, so determined was he to eliminate Hashemuddin from the political scene. Hashemuddin made representations to Ayub but with no result. Thus ended the second phase of Hashemuddin's political career. Twice he had the chance to rise to the top level, but twice he failed.

In a genuinely democratic system both Zahiruddin and Hashemuddin might have risen higher; they had the potentialities for political leadership but these were unfulfilled—in part at least because of structural changes for which they were ill-placed. But, while Zahiruddin was impeded by factors beyond his control, Hashemuddin's case was perhaps different. He was less dedicated at any stage to the Awami League or to any other party. He changed parties not out of conviction but in response to the temptations of short-run advantage. His trouble was not lack of resources for a political career but excessive opportunism accompanied by a series of miscalculations. Unlike Zahiruddin, Hashemuddin had a solid political base; if he had dedicated himself to any one particular party, his career might have been more successful. Like Zahiruddin, however, he was at the same time committed to the ideal of a united Pakistan; to that extent, with the rise of Bengali subnationalism, there were limits to his advancement.

It is a remarkable fact that when he was freed from jail in early 1974 Hashemuddin got a big ovation from the public. The political scene in Bangladesh is currently very fluid. The desperate economic situation may cause a major political upheaval. If Mujib's government collapses a new set of leaders will emerge; whether Hashemuddin will have any further political role is yet to be seen.

Both the Muslim League and the Awami League were parties of the centre; each at some stages was more than a political party in the strict sense of the term: rather, they were national bodies working for the establishment of separate national states—Pakistan and Bangladesh. They could, therefore, accommodate politicians of varied creeds and convictions. To conclude this chapter I shall refer to the careers of two politicians belonging more clearly to the left and right in East Bengal. Neither of them has been able to rise above the status of middle-rank politician, yet they played significant roles in East Bengal before the creation of Bangladesh. They are Muzaffar Ahmed of the pro-Moscow National Awami Party and Ghulam Azam of Jamat-i-Islam.

Muzaffar Ahmed was a lecturer in commerce. He resigned from Dacca University in protest against an ordinance made by the Muslim League ministry on the eve of the 1954 elections debarring teachers from contesting. He was given a ticket by the United Front from the quota of the Awami League and had no difficulty in winning a seat by defeating the education minister of the Muslim League cabinet. He continued to be an Awami Leaguer, but when Suhrawardy, as Prime

Minister, began to defend Pakistan's military alliances with the West, a section of the Awami League under the leadership of Moulana Bhashani revolted and broke away from the Awami League to form the National Awami League Party in June 1957. Muzaffar, with his left leanings, joined the new party and at one stage was very close to Bhashani; he was his secretary during his tour abroad in 1954–55 and became an intellectual spokesman for the party. As the Communist Party in Pakistan was banned from 1953, the National Awami Party was the main leftist party in both East Bengal and West Pakistan. Although as a member of the provincial legislature Muzaffar did not make much impression as a speaker, as a close associate of the chief of the NAP he played a significant role behind the scenes during the whole of the turbulent pre-Ayub period.

During the early martial law period, Muzaffar, like many other political leaders, was put in jail; in the 1960s, however, he re-entered politics and soon rejoined the NAP. By the mid-1960s the NAP, like Communist parties in many other countries, was split into pro-Moscow and pro-China factions.[8] Muzaffar, who was a close associate of Bhashani, was unhappy about the latter's support for China and his support at one stage for Ayub's foreign policy. Muzaffar joined the pro-Moscow group and soon became chief of the group in East Bengal. But by this time the Awami League enjoyed a dominant position. As the chief of a smaller though well organized party, Muzaffar's role was not spectacular. The NAP had some hold over students, who had always been a powerful pressure group in East Bengal. The self-styled 'Professor' Muzaffar's role was confined to issuing regular press statements on various national issues and addressing public meeting, much smaller gatherings than those organized by the Awami League.

During the political movement in 1958–59 against Ayub, Muzaffar and his group joined the combined opposition forces—the Democratic Action Committee. Muzaffar attended the Round Table conferences convened by Ayub in early 1969 but made hardly any impact either inside or outside the conferences. He and his party took part in the general election of 1970 but won no seats; in the provincial legislature they won two or three seats.

During the civil war in Bangladesh Muzaffar, like many other leaders, took shelter in Calcutta; he also made trips to Moscow to secure Soviet help and support. As the Soviet Union supported Bangladesh, Muzaffar and his group became more prominent in Bangladesh after liberation, The Soviet press and propaganda media also tried to magnify the role of the Communist Party of Bengal and, indirectly, the role of Muzaffar and his group. If Bangladesh ever becomes a member of

Brezhnev's 'Socialist Commonwealth' Muzaffar may have a big role to play, but the chances are very small.

Mujib, in his present political predicament, has made an alliance with the pro-Moscow Communist Party and with Muzaffar's National Awami Party. This alignment is mainly directed against the dormant rightist elements and the pro-Peking leftist forces; Mujib has given orders to 'shoot at sight'[9] the pro-Peking groups. Muzaffar, in the context of the growing Sino-Soviet rift and its impact on South and Southeast Asia, is giving all-out support to Mujib to crush the pro-Peking leftist forces. It is, however, too early to predict which forces are likely to be liquidated in turbulent Bangladesh. In any event, Muzaffar, with his limited abilities, has little prospect of rising above the middle rank as a politician.

Ghulam Azam belonged to the rightist Jamat-i-Islam Party which, like other rightist or communal parties, is banned in Bangladesh and he is now a political refugee in London. A former lecturer in political science, he was by conviction and training an orthodox but not unenlightened political figure in East Bengal. After the creation of Pakistan, when religion was supreme in Pakistan politics, leaders like Ghulam Azam had a role to play. He was a vigorous champion of an Islamic state in Pakistan. When, in 1956, the separate or communal electorate was replaced by a joint or secular electorate by the national assembly, Ghulam Azam waged a powerful campaign against the decision. That was the beginning of his active role in East Bengal politics and, although he was not a member of the legislature, Ghulam Azam and his party attracted some big gatherings by appealing to religious sentiment in rural areas.

When the military regime put an end to all political activities, Ghulam Azam and his group could not be entirely silenced. They carried on a vigorous campaign against Ayub's social reforms, e.g. the Family Law Ordinance banning polygamy, and family planning. But when region rather than religion began to dominate East Bengal politics a political party like Jamat-i-Islam found its scope limited.

During the election of 1970, the fate of Ghulam Azam and his party was the same as that of all other parties in East Bengal: total defeat by the Awami League. Ghulam Azam contested a seat in which there were large numbers of Urdu-speaking voters, but the Awami League selected Zahiruddin for this seat and he had no difficulty in making Ghulam Azam forfeit his deposit.

Jamat-i-Islam and its leaders are dubbed 'collaborators' in Bangladesh today, and there is no immediate prospect of their flourishing. No doubt the age-old Hindu-Muslim antagonism has been revived in 'secular' Bangladesh and communal riots between Hindus and Muslims have already occurred; anti-Indian feelings are also present. But the prospect for any leader or party which supported the army's action in Bangladesh are rather bleak. A revival of the old Islamic spirit is not inconceivable, but to make it a political force new leaders and groups will be needed; these may emerge in due course if the democratic process is established and allowed to continue. But the position of leaders like Ghulam Azam, whose party had, directly or indirectly, supported the Pakistan army, seems hopeless, at least in the near future.[10] At the same time it is worth noting some very recent reports of renewed support for Ghulam Azam's party; there are also references to 'unholy' alliances between extreme pro-Peking leftist forces and the Islamic rightist forces.

17

THE FORMATION OF THE POLITICALLY ACTIVE STRATUM: EVIDENCE FROM THE CAREER ORIGINS OF PARTY ACTIVISTS IN AN INDIAN CITY

Thomas Pantham

In all societies, ranging from the least to the most democratic, the politically active stratum is a less numerous group than the politically relevant stratum, which, in its turn, is only a part of the total population. Hence the processes through which and the criteria according to which new members enter, or are recruited into, the politically active stratum are significant features of political life in all societies.

Studies of the recruitment of political professionals and activists usually employ the 'social basis' approach, which seeks to identify the socio-economic strata from which they are drawn. Findings from such studies show that (in the absence of specific class-based recruitment being carried out by such agencies as political parties) the upper-status groups in the society tend to get over-represented within the politically active stratum.[1]

Social background data on political professionals and activists, however, only help describe the pool of socio-economic eligibles for political recruitment. They do not help us understand why not all individuals from within this pool of eligibles actually get recruited into active political roles. They also do not enable us to know how or why some individuals from outside this pool manage to become political activists. Hence, for a fuller understanding of the recruitment of political professionals and activists, we need to complement analysis of their socio-economic backgrounds with explication of the processes through which they have been socialized and recruited into active political roles.[2]

Data on the political socialization and recruitment of political activists in a given locale or country not only explicate the origins of their individual political careers but also throw light on the nature of the politically active stratum which they collectively form and of the larger political community which they sustain. Thus, a society in which entry into the politically active stratum is restricted or controlled legally and/or socially would be operating a system different from that of a society that grants open, multi-route entry into its politically active stratum.

In a new nation like India, the very emergence of a national democratic political community is shaped by the political socialization and
recruitment of its 'pioneer' politicians and political activists. Obviously,
political socialization-recruitment processes which enhance and
perpetuate the divisive beliefs of the 'little communities' would be
antithetical to the emergence of a national political community,
which, at a minimum, is held together by the shared expectations of
the diverse peoples. In a new nation, therefore, the entry-into-politics
question is of crucial importance. Knowledge of the formation of the
politically active stratum and of the larger political community in such
a society is the knowledge of who enters when, how, and with what
expectations.

From a larger study of the consensus-building role of political
parties in an Indian city (Baroda City in Gujarat state), the present
paper reports the findings on the early political socialization and
recruitment of their organizational activists.

THE SETTING OF THE STUDY

Baroda City is a district headquarters, and has a population of
470,000.[3] It may be described as a fast developing university-industrial
city.[4] Until independence, Baroda was a princely state, ruled by the
Gaekwads under the paramountcy of the British Crown. While in the
British-ruled provinces the national movement was conducted by
the Congress Party, in the princely state a forum of citizens, called the
Praja Mandal, strove for responsible government.[5] The Praja Mandal
and Congress cooperated and coordinated each other's activities until,
after independence, the former merged into the latter.

In 1949 the Baroda Maharaja became the first of the princely rulers
to agree to the integration of his state into the Indian Union. Baroda
was accordingly merged into Bombay Province, which, after the 1956
states' reorganization, became the bi-lingual state of Bombay. Subsequently, as a result of 'linguistic-provincial opposition movements'
in its Gujarati- and Marathi-speaking areas, the state was bifurcated (in
1960) into two unilingual states, viz. Gujarat and Maharashtra. The
movement for Mahagujarat (Greater Gujarat), it may be noted, was a
mass movement, which brought together, under the banner of the
Mahagujarat Janata Parishad, the landholding farmers, students,
businessmen, and the non-Congress parties, notably the Praja Socialists and the Communists.[6]

From 1958 to 1961 the Mahagujarat Janata Parishad was the ruling
coalition in the Baroda municipal body. Both before and after this
brief period, however, Congress has been the dominant party in the
local political system. The 1969 Congress split did not immediately

upset the machine-like power structure in Baroda, whose political boss, mayor (Dr) Thakorbhai Patel, remained aligned to the Congress-O, which continued to be the ruling party in the state till May 1971. In the mid-term Lok Sabha election held in March 1971, the Baroda seat was won for Congress-O by Maharaja Fatehsinghrao Gaekwad of Baroda, convenor of the Concord of Princes, a minister in the state cabinet, and chancellor of Baroda University.[7] After the surprisingly good performance of the Congress-R in the 1971 Lok Sabha election, many leaders and activists of the Congress-O shifted their allegiance to the Congress-R, which was also joined by several members from the Socialist, Praja Socialist, and Swatantra parties. In Baroda, as a result of changes in the party affiliations of the mayor and his 'team' of municipal corporators, Congress-R became the ruling party in the municipal corporation on the eve of the 1972 state assembly election. In this election Congress-R won all the three seats from Baroda City.

Our interviews were taken immediately after the 1972 election. In all we interviewed 310 leaders and activists belonging to the various political parties which operate in Baroda: Congress-R, Congress-O, Jana Sangh, Swatantra, National Labour Party (Shramjivi Paksha)[8], Communist Party of India, and Communist Party of India (Marxist).[9] Our respondents belonged to the following categories of party activists: (a) party representatives elected to the municipal corporation, or to the parliament or the state legislature; (b) members or permanent invitees of the city-level executive bodies of the several parties; and (c) party workers, who, though not holding any of these positions, were deemed by 'party knowledgeables' to be playing important roles in the organizational life of their respective parties.

Our respondents did not constitute a random sample of all the members of the different parties. They were, rather, the top and middle-level activists, who, formally or informally, ran the real organizational life of their parties in the city. We are, however, inclined to think that the actual number of respondents interviewed from each of the parties fairly reflects the relative strength of their active supporters in the city. We also feel that our study population constitutes the upper and middle layers of the politically active stratum in Baroda City.[10]

In order to understand the processes of their initial political socialization and recruitment, we asked our respondents for recall information about their first interest in political matters, first political activity, first entry into a party, and subsequent changes in their party affiliation. From their responses to our several open-ended questions, we reconstructed the following twelve illustrative narratives, which will be followed by tabular analysis of data pertaining to all of our respondents.

1. Congress-O, activist (i) (Patidar)

My father was in government service. He was a *khadarite*. When I was about 15 years old (1935) I joined the Ramdas Vyayamshala run by Baburao Koti. There we had physical exercises and political discussions. Two years later, I became secretary of the Baroda Vidyarthi Mitra Mandal (a students' union). In 1940 I left college and joined the civil disobedience movement. As I was only 19 Gandhiji sent me to work in a village (Sankheda) where I taught in a school. In 1942 I worked underground for 10 months, and in the following year went to jail . . .

2. Congress-O, activist (ii) (Barber)

I first became interested in politics when I read about the Bardoli Satyagraha (1928). I was 12 years old then. About that time, some older leaders of the Praja Mandal entrusted me with the work of distributing *Navjivan* and the pamphlets brought out by the Praja Mandal, which were all banned by the British. In 1935 I became secretary of the Baroda Vidyarthi Mandal. We organized camps, study circles, and social activities. In 1942 we took part in the Quit India Movement, and I was jailed for 11 months. . . .

3. Congress-O, activist (iii) (Patidar; woman)

When I was studying in the 6th standard (1937) our teacher, Karunashankar, opened an *ashram*, in which we did praying, spinning, and singing of patriotic songs. . . . At the Wardha session of the Congress, I lived with Gandhiji and met many other Congress leaders like Sardar Patel. . . . I took active part in the '42 Movement, when I even gave some public talks. . . . Later on my social work centred on adult education and Harijan welfare. . . . Joined the Congress in 1950.

4. Congress-O, activist (iv) (Patidar)

My grand uncle, Sardar Gopaldas Desai, was a president of the Baroda State Praja Mandal. My father was also active in the Freedom Movement. In 1939 there was a riot on the occasion of Sardar Patel's visit to Baroda. As the then president of the State Praja Mandal, he had given a call for the introduction of responsible government in the state. The Maratha princes opposed his visit and did not allow him to give any public speech. I joined as a volunteer in the group, mostly Gujaratis, that welcomed the Sardar. I was only 14 then. . . . In 1942, along with other workers like Bhailalbhai Contractor, I joined in picketing liquor shops. . . .

5. Congress-R, activist (i) (Brahmin)

At the age of 15 (1940) I joined the Vidyarthi Mandal in Bhavnagar. It had leftist leanings. We discussed about the Freedom Movement and about building up a socialist India. I then joined the Congress Seva Dal and the Congress Socialist Party. . . . Arharya Narendra Dev and Indulal Yajnik influenced my thinking. In 1948 I took part in a railway strike in Saurashtra and was jailed. . . . I was a founder member of the Socialist Party in Gujarat.

6. Congress-R, activist (ii) (Scheduled Caste)

In 1935, inspired by Dr Ambedkar, I started a branch of the Dalit Sangh, of which I became a joint secretary. I was then a municipal scavenger. My community had lots of problems with the municipal administration. We approached Mr H. R. Gokhale of the Socialist Party, who advised us to form a union. This we did and I became its general secretary. In 1951 I got elected to the municipal board, but had to resign my position as I was told that a court case was being filed by some Congressmen against my eligibility for an elective position in the municipality, of which my wife was an employee (as a scavenger). My wife and I then 'effected' a divorce, as a result of which she was able to continue in her job and I was able to get re-elected in the next election. . . .

7. Congress-R, activist (iii) (Brahmin)

My father was a deputy collector. In 1944 Vir Savarkar came to Baroda and founded a branch of the Hindu Mahasabha, in which I joined as a founder-member. I was then a lawyer and president of a Vyayamshala (Gymnasium) . . . Realizing that the Hindu Mahasabha was at the root of Gandhiji's murder, I left it and joined the Congress in 1952. . . In 1962 I joined the Samyukta Socialist Party and won a municipal seat on its ticket. . . . I joined the Congress-R in 1969, since as an SSP worker I had stood for the socialism that Mrs Gandhi began to implement in 1969.

8. Congress-R, activist (iv) (Sunar)

My political career dates back to 1939, when, as a worker in a textile mill in Bombay, I joined the Communist Party, led by Mr S. A. Dange. I was jailed for 3 months for taking part in the Freedom Movement. In 1940 I was jailed for 9 months for my involvement in a Communist-sponsored labour strike. Eight years later I did party work in Baroda and was imprisoned for a year and a half. After my release I continued my work on the trade union front and joined the Praja Socialist Party. . . . Joined Congress-R in 1971 along with Mr Sanat Mehta. . . .

9. Communist, activist (i) (Brahmin)

At school I came in contact with a communist worker, Mr Narendra Oza, who was working in the student movement. I read some party literature and joined in 1941. The Communist Party, I saw, worked for the poor, for whom I too wanted to work. In college I worked in the student movement, and later on began my work on the trade union front. During 1949–50 I had to work underground. . . . Was held in custody for two days for protesting against the Rashtriya Swayam Sevak Sangh (RSS) when Gandhiji was murdered . . . was jailed during the Mahagujarat Movement . . . and was detained during the Chinese agression.

10. Communist, activist (ii) (Brahmin)

The years from 1934 to 1938 were the years when the Congress Socialists, the Royists, and the Forward Bloc were contending to capture the youth. I read their publications. Prior to that I had read Vivekananda and Savarkar. I had also been moved by the terrorist movement of Bhagat Singh. When I was 14 (1936) a fellow-student returned from Bombay with some Communist literature, which I read. I also became a member of the Rationalist Study Circle which had Communist leanings. . . . I joined the Communist Party in 1939 and worked in the student movement. . . . I was then sent to Surat for party work,

where I joined college to complete my studies for the LLB degree. After passing
LLB I ran away to Ahmedabad, where I worked for 6 months. I was again
deputed to Surat, where I organized the Red Flag Movement. . . . I returned
to Baroda in 1948 . . .

11. Jana Sangh, activist (i) (Brahmin)

When I was young I was a reader of *Kesari* and other Savarkar literature. I
became convinced that the British had to be driven out from our country.
When the Prince of Wales came to Bombay in 1921, I joined the *morcha* that
went to oppose his visit. In 1931 I joined the Hindu Mahamandal at the suggestion of a friend who was teaching at the Arya Kanya Mahavidyalaya. I was then
practising law and was secretary of a *vyayamshala*. . . . As the Mahamandal
ceased to operate as a party, I joined the Jana Sangh in 1951 and became the
first president of its unit in the city.

12. Jana Sangh, activist (ii) (Brahmin)

When I was about 15 (1939) I joined the RSS and, as a student, was involved in
Vidyarthi pravriti (work among students). The RSS taught us patriotism and
discipline, which also form the base of the Jana Sangh of which I am a founder-
member in Baroda. In 1948 I was jailed for 8 months for protesting against the
allegation that the RSS was involved in Gandhi's murder.

AROUSAL OF INITIAL INTEREST IN POLITICS

In order to bring some order into the recall data provided by our
310 respondents about their early political socialization and recruitment,
I shall now undertake a tabular analysis of the time and the agents of,
and the events associated with (i) the initial arousal of their political
interest, and (ii) their subsequent entry into party activism.

The political events associated with the arousal of initial political
interest among the party activists are shown in Table I. (It should be
noted that the activists' party affiliations shown in Tables I to VIII refer
to their first parties, and not to their present parties.) As Table I shows,
more than half the total number of our respondents were introduced
to politics in the context of the freedom movement. It had the greatest
impact on Congress recruits. Party formations and party-related
activities (e.g. activities of the RSS) accounted for the initial political
socialization of two-thirds of the Jana Sanghis, and about a quarter of
the Socialists and Communists.

Table II presents data regarding the agents responsible for the arousal
of first political interest among the activists. On the whole, more
references were made to political workers than to school or family.
References to family members were made more frequently by Congressmen and the Swatantrites than by the recruits to the other parties.
Not surprisingly, therefore, about 40 per cent of the two Congress
groups and the Swatantra group did in fact grow up in politically
involved families (Table III).

TABLE I. Political Events which first Aroused Political Interest (%)

	SW	JS	UC/ PJM	CR	SP+ LP	CP	Other	All
			First party affiliation					
Freedom movement	53	19	81	57	44	33	★	57
Mahagujarat movement	20	6	–	14	6	–	★	4
Election campaigns	13	8	7	7	13	–	★	7
Agitations & trade union work	–	–	2	7	13	44	★	8
Party-related activities	13	67	10	14	25	22	★	23
Total	99	100	100	99	101	99	★	99
N†	15	36	102	14	16	27	8★	218

SW = Swatantra Party; JS = Jana Sangh; UC = Undivided Congress
PJM = Praja Mandal; CR = Congress-R (led by Mrs Indira Gandhi); SP =
Socialist/Praja Socialist Party; LP = Labour Party; CP = Communist Parties.
★ Too few cases for analysis.
† The total N is only 218 because of the exclusion of cases with missing data.

TABLE II. Agents responsible for first Arousing Political Interest (%)

	SW	JS	UC/ PJM	CR	SP+ LP	CP	Other	All
			First party affiliation					
Family/relatives only	40	16	20	36	16	9	★	20
School/gymnasiums only	20	21	9	29	16	4	★	13
Political workers only	20	29	23	21	26	74	★	30
Family & school	–	5	2	7	5	–	★	3
Family & political workers	–	8	16	7	5	9	★	11
School & political workers	–	13	21	–	21	–	★	14
Family, school & political workers	5	3	7	–	–	–	★	4
Newspapers, books ect.	15	5	2	–	11	4	★	6
Total	100	100	100	100	100	100	★	101
N†	20	38	96	14	19	23	7★	217

★ Too few cases for analysis.
† Cases with missing data have been excluded.

TABLE III. Political Activity of Parents or Near-relatives (%)

| First party affiliation | Political activity of parents or near-relatives | | | | |
	Active	Not active	NA	Total	N
Swatantra	40	60	–	100	30
Jana Sangh	28	72	–	100	54
Undivided Congress/					
Praja Mandal	40	56	4	100	136
Congress-R	41	59	–	100	22
Socialist and					
Labour Parties	24	76	–	100	25
Communist Parties	18	82	–	100	33
Other Parties	★	★	★	★	10★
All	34	64	2	100	310

★ Too few cases for analysis.

As reported in Table IV, nearly three-quarters of the total developed their first interest in politics when they were under 18 years of age. Compared to the recruits to the other parties, the Jana Sanghis and Congressmen had initially been socialized for politics at an earlier stage in their life. In the case of the Jana Sangh, this is due to the close links it has with the RSS, into which admission is open even to children. The earlier socialization of the entrants into the parental Congress had to do with the freedom movement, which exposed them to politics in their childhood or early adolescence. Twenty-eight per cent of the party activists received pre-adult apprenticeship in such political and semi-political associations as the Congress Seva Dal, the Youth Congress, the RSS, students' associations, the *Bal Sena* (Children's Army), *Vanar*

TABLE IV. Age of First Political Interest (%)

First party affiliation	Under 13	13–17	18–20	21+	Total	N†
Swatantra	33	33	19	14	99	21
Jana Sangh	51	31	18	–	100	45
Undivided Congress/						
Praja Mandal	29	48	17	7	101	108
Congress-R	25	56	6	13	100	16
Socialist and Labour						
Parties	17	46	13	25	101	24
Communist Parties	23	39	19	19	100	26
Other Parties	★	★	★	★	★	10★
All	30	43	16	10	99	250

★ Too few cases for analysis.
† Cases with missing data are omitted.

Sena (whose members engaged themselves in playing monkey tricks on the colonialists during the freedom movement), gymnasiums, and the *Sathidal* (a cultural wing of the erstwhile Praja Socialist Party).

The biggest percentages of such pre-adult apprentices found within are the Jana Sangh and the parental Congress groups (Table V). None of those whose *initial* recruitment took place into the Congress-R had had any pre-adult apprenticeship. This shows that the 'new' Congress (i.e. the Congress-R) has been instrumental in mobilizing a new type of political activist. The furrowing of the recruitment fields of the undivided Congress and the Jana Sangh has been done by their own 'front associations', i.e. the RSS in the case of the Jana Sangh, and the *Bal Sena*, the *Seva Dal*, the Youth Congress, etc., in the case of Congress.

TABLE V. Pre-adult Political Activity of Party Activists (%)

| | First party affiliation | | | | | | | |
	SW	JS	UC/ PJM	CR	SP+ LP	CP	Other	All
Joined political or semi-political associations or camps	10	41	37	–	20	18	★	28
Did not join political associations but took active part in politics in an *ad hoc* manner	23	17	19	27	16	9	★	18
Neither	60	37	34	73	64	61	★	45
NA	7	6	10	–	–	12	★	8
Total	100	101	100	100	100	100	★	99
N	30	54	136	22	25	33	10	310

★ Too few cases for analysis.

RECRUITMENT INTO FIRST PARTY

In all, 30 per cent of the activists were under 21 years of age when they joined their first parties (Table VI). For another 37 per cent, their initial party recruitment took place when they were between 21 and 30 years old. Compared to the recruits to the other parties, the Jana Sanghis and the Congressmen (parental Congress) launched their party careers at an earlier stage in their life cycle.

Table VII documents information about the years in which the activists were first recruited. This is significant in so far as it tells us of the performance of the mobilization-recruitment function carried out

TABLE VI. Age at the Time of Joining First Party (%)

	Under 21	21–30	31–40	41+	NA	Total	N
Swatantra	10	50	30	10	–	100	30
Jana Sangh	28	39	28	6	–	101	54
Undivided Congress/ Praja Mandal	45	29	19	7	1	101	136
Congress-R	5	23	23	50	–	101	22
Socialist & Labour Parties	20	40	16	24	–	100	25
Communist Parties	18	61	18	–	3	100	33
Other Parties	★	★	★	★	★	★	10★
All	30	37	21	11	1	100	310

★ Too few cases for analysis.

TABLE VII. Year of Joining First Party by First Party Affiliation (%)

First party affiliation	Before 1947	1948–1962	1963–1968	After 1969	NA	Total	N
Swatantra	–	63	30	7	–	100	30
Jana Sangh	–	35	35	30	–	100	54
Undivided Congress/ Praja Mandal	42	44	12	1	1	100	136
Congress-R	–	–	–	100	–	100	22
Socialist and Labour Parties	12	32	12	44	–	100	25
Communist Parties	24	42	18	12	3	99	33
Other Parties	★	★	★	★	★	★	10★
All	23	40	17	19	1	100	310

★ Too few cases for analysis.

by the different parties in different times. During the pre-independence period, this function was carried out *par excellence* by the Congress Party. Out of our 310 respondents, 72 were first recruited into party activism during that period. Fifty-seven out of these 72 were recruited by Congress or the Praja Mandal. The rest were recruited by the Congress Socialist Party (which, until independence, functioned within Congress) and by the Communist Party. With the emergence of several new parties after independence, the function of political mobilization-recruitment came to be undertaken on a competitive basis.

The years from 1948 to 1962, during which period the first three general elections were held, saw the emergence, among others, of the Socialist Party (1948), the Jana Sangh (1951), the Praja Socialist Party (1952), and the Swatantra Party (1959). During this period 123 of our respondents made their first entry into party activism. The competitive nature of political recruitment in this period is revealed by the 1948–62 column of Table VII. The new parties thus had a recruitment impact in Baroda. During 1956–60, as I said earlier, the Mahagujarat movement served as a spur to oppositional politics in Gujarat. The movement spread the idea that opposition parties are needed to check and correct the ruling party. Many of the respondents belonging to the Swatantra, Socialist, and Communist parties had, in fact, taken active part in this movement, in whose cause some of them had even been to jail.

The years from 1963 to 1968 saw a tilting of the mobilization-recruitment balance in favour of the non-Congress parties. Of the total of 53 recruits for this period, only 30% joined Congress, the remaining 70% being claimed by the other parties. During the 1948–62 period, by contrast, Congress and opposition parties had shared the recruits more or less equally (i.e. 49% for Congress, and 51% for the opposition parties). The Congress-R, which emerged as a result of the 1969 split in the parental Congress, caused the initial recruitment of 22 of our respondents. Some fresh recruitment has also been done by the National Labour Party (cf note 8).

TABLE VIII. Mode of Recruitment into First Party (%)

	SW	JS	UC/ PJM	CR	First party SP+ LP	CP	Others*	All
Self-decided entry	31	18	8	35	5	22	★	15
Continuation from previous involvement	–	33	30	–	–	3	★	19
Entry occasioned by parents and/or near relatives	10	10	14	6	14	–	★	11
Entry occasioned by political workers and/or friends	62	45	56	59	86	75	★	60
Total	★★	★★	★★	★★	★★	100	★	★★
N†	29	49	120	17	22	32	8	277

* Too few cases for analysis

★★ Totals exceed 100 because some respondents referred to both parents/near-relatives and political workers

† This Table is based on a reduced number of cases because of the exclusion of cases whose mode of entry was not ascertained

The role of political parties in the recruitment of political activists comes into sharper focus in Table VIII, which documents data on the agents of recruitment. Only 15% reported self-decided entry. Such self-recruitment was reported more often by those who initially joined the Congress-R, Swatantra, and Communist parties. None of the recruits to the two Communist parties (combined in the Table) said that his entry was occasioned by family-members. This suggests that they are unaccepted, out-group parties in the local community.

Nearly one-fifth of respondents said that their formal adult 'entry' into the party was a mere continuation of their pre-adult political involvement. Another 60% said that their first entry into a party was occasioned by political workers and/or friends. Some recruits to the parental Congress, the Congress-R, and the Swatantra Party said that they had been drafted or coopted by rival leaders during periods of intense factionalism in their respective parties. Many activists of the Labour and Communist parties were recruited by leaders of trade unions.

CHANGE IN PARTY AFFILIATION

Of the 310 respondents, 70 have changed their party affiliation at least once. The relationship between the first and present party affiliations of the individual activists is shown in Table IX. It can be seen that the parental Congress Party, the dominant builder of India's political consensus, has given of itself to all the other parties. It was responsible for the initial mobilization-recruitment of 44% of the composite total of our six sets of party activists. Some of the activists in each of the opposition parties have initially been mobilized for the national symbols of the political system and recruited into what has historically been its central institution.

In India the institution of a centralizing government by the colonial rulers preceded the crystallization of national identity, forged and sustained by a dominant party, which, in its turn, preceded the development of a competitive dominant party system.[11] The sequential order of these sub-processes of political development has mitigated what would otherwise have been a severe crisis of national identity.[12] The Indian National Congress not only emerged before, but also contributed personnel and experience towards, the formation of specific interest-based opposition parties.[13] This sequential and relational aspect in the development of the party system in India was not confined to elite-level politics in Delhi or the state capitals; as our data show it permeated into cities like Baroda and, possibly, into the villages.

The Communist group has drawn to it a few activists from the undivided Congress and the Socialist parties and has given of itself to

TABLE IX. Relationship between First Party Affiliation and Present Party Affiliation (%)

Present party affiliation	First party affiliation									Total	N
	SW	JS	UC/PJM	CO*	CR	LP	SP	CP	Other		
Swatantra	78	–	15	–	–	–	7	–	–	100	27
Jana Sangh	–	79	13	–	1	–	1	–	4	98	67
Congress-O	2	–	98	–	–	–	–	–	–	100	50
Congress-R	7	–	55	2	19	–	9	4	4	100	108
Labour Party	–	3	45	3	–	38	–	10	–	99	29
Communist Parties	–	–	7	–	–	–	3	90	–	100	29
All	10	17	44	1	7	4	5	11	2	101	310

* CO = Congress-O.

the Congress-R and the Labour parties. It has, however, neither given nor taken from the Swatantra or the Jana Sangh parties. In this sense there is a real distance between the Communist group, on the one hand, and Swatantra and Jana Sangh, on the other.

While the parental Congress gave of itself to all other parties, the Congress-R has been able to draw activists from all but two (the Jana Sangh and Labour parties) of the party groups shown in Table IX. An examination of the historical process whereby the Congress-R built up its dominance in Baroda in 1972 shows that it was engaged in a zero-sum game. The Congress split—which in Delhi provided for a replacement of the 'ins' (the powerful syndicate within the Congress decision-system) by the 'outs'—in Baroda (as elsewhere in Gujarat) brought the two into an utterly competitive game, in which each side could gain only at the expense of the other. There were in the Congress-R game: (i) entrants from the periphery of the public decision-system in Baroda (viz. members of the Socialist, Samyukta Socialist, and Swatantra parties); (ii) some 'displaced elites', who hoped for a come-back (e.g. an ex-mayor and a suspended president of the City Congress Committee); and (iii) the 'ins' (e.g. the incumbent mayor and his team) who obviously sought to preserve their positions of power.

MOTIVATIONS FOR ENTRY INTO PARTY WORK

Owing to limitations of space, I shall treat only briefly of the entry motivations mentioned by our respondents. Ambition for a political career and/or expectations of material gains were acknowledged by some of the activists of each party, more so of the Congress-R, the parental Congress, and the Swatantra Party. Some of the responses were:

> To come up in life.
> To be eligible for the party's ticket in elections.
> Mine is one of the few very highly educated families in the whole of my community, which is a backward community. But no one in my family had a decent job until I joined the Congress. My two sisters and I now have jobs as per our qualifications.
> Instead of asking me why I joined the Congress then, you should ask me why I had not joined it earlier. The fact is that in 1952 my application for a Congress ticket was turned down on the ground that I had not been an active worker before. Mr X, who was given the ticket in preference to me is today a very big man. He has gone far ahead of me. My political career has been put back by at least 10 years because I had not joined the party earlier.

The two major motivational groups within the parental Congress were those motivated for moral considerations and for social contacts.

They joined the party mostly during the freedom struggle, not so much to promote any partisan ideology, as 'from a sense of dedication or merely from sheer excitement and exhilaration'. Some of the more frequently mentioned 'reasons' were: 'To fight for independence' and 'To do social service.' A lawyer as well as a doctor who joined Congress after 1967 said 'My best friends are in the Congress.'

The type of dedication and excitement seen in the recruits to the parental Congress during the freedom struggle was also discernible among the Jana Sangh recruits. Their patriotic fervour and nationalistic zeal, however, centred around a party-related redefinition of the Indian nation. Some of the Jana Sanghis said they started their party activism for the purpose of restructuring the Indian polity on 'newer' foundations, viz. *Bharatiya Sanskriti* and *Maryada* (Indian culture and tradition). Some of the Jana Sangh recruits 'explained' their party entry in the following manner:

Rashtrabhavan and *Hindutva* (patriotism and Hinduness).

To spread RSS thought in politics.

The Congress has been following a policy of appeasement of Muslims. I felt the Congress needed a strong opposition.

The motivational ideologues among the recruits to the Swatantra Party gave such reasons as:

I own property and I believe in property rights.

I want a system of free licences and free permits.

Congress will lead the country to communism unless it is opposed by a strong party.

Recruits to the Socialist and Labour parties were motivated either by ideological considerations or out of appreciation for the trade union work of their parties. Some Labour Party recruits said they were averse to Communist methods. One of them said he preferred Gandhian techniques, while another disliked the attitude of the Congress-R towards the workers.

The Communists said they had been motivated for bringing about 'workers' and peasants' rule', 'people's democracy', 'removal of capitalism', or 'economic emancipation through political struggle'. They said they learned these things from the workers' meetings addressed by trade union leaders. Two Communist activists read some Communist literature and held talks with Communist jail-mates during the Mahagujarat Movement and came to realize that 'major changes can be brought about only through a revolutionary party'. Another gave a more elaborate explanation for his choice of the Communist Party in the following words: 'For so many years, leaders like Vinoba Bhave and Jayaprakash Narayan have been waging a peaceful revolution. But what have their appeals to the owners resulted in? . . . I am convinced that if anything is possible, it is only through revolutionary means.' Yet another Communist worker gave the following brief reply: 'Nobody cared for us poor workers until we formed our union.'

Some of the fresh recruits as well as some of the converts to the Congress-R were influenced by their factional leaders. Those who 'defected' to the Congress-R just on the eve of the 1972 assembly election said they did so as they could not withstand the 'powerful stream of national politics'. One Muslim deserter from the Congress-O said his party had not been particularly helpful to his community during the 1969 communal riots,[14] while another Muslim said he had become disillusioned when the Congress-O entered into electoral alliance with the Jana Sangh in 1971. A few Congress-R converts from Swatantra said they left their previous party as it was inactive and ineffective. By and large the Congress-R converts sought to present themselves as motivational ideologues. One simply said: 'I believe in equality—social, economic and political.' The typical answer of the converts from the Socialist parties was: 'The Congress-R has started implementing such socialist programmes as we have been advocating all along. Hence, we felt, we must join to strengthen the democratic and progressive forces in the country.' One Congress-O deserter said 'For 22 years, the Congress has been talking socialism, but its implementation has so far remained on paper. Nothing was ever done that displeased the capitalists and the vested interests. Now, for the first time, Mrs Gandhi is taking some bold steps to reduce inequality.' The 'bold steps' that many Congress-R converts and recruits mentioned were: the nationalization of banks, the abolition of privy purses, the ten-point economic programme and, of course, the promise of *garibi hatao* (eradication of poverty).

POLITICAL CAREER MOBILITY

A quarter of our respondents have held, or currently hold, elective positions in parliament, state legislature, or municipal body (Table X). As expected, there are more such elective office-holders in the two Congress parties than in the other parties.

Information was obtained also about the offices or positions that the activists occupied within their present or previous party organizations. Those who held prominent organizational positions in their parties, like the presidentship or secretaryship of ward or *mandal* units or any positions in such higher level units as the city- or state-level committees, were coded as 'political career prominents', and the rest as 'non-prominents'. All those who represented their parties in parliament, the state legislature, the municipal corporation, or the primary education board were regarded as political career prominents, irrespective of their holding or not holding any party organizational positions. The results so obtained are shown in Table XI.

If we combine the current and previous holders of prominent political offices (Table XI), we find that the Congress-O claims the biggest proportion. This means that it has more political veterans than the other party units. Although all the Congress-O veterans do not at present hold important political offices, almost all of them occupy important positions in several social welfare, educational, and economic associations. These positions were given as political patronage by those leaders of the erstwhile dominant party who are presently in Congress-O. Some of the associations and organizations in which more than one Congress-O worker held office were: the State Road Transport Advisory Board, the Babajipura Sarvodaya Mandal, the Remand Home, the Bharat Sevak Samaj, the Khadi Board, the Youth Hostel Association of India, some cooperative housing societies and banks, a

TABLE X. Experience of Contesting and Winning Public Elections

| | Present party affiliation | | | | | | |
	SW	JS	CO	CR	LP	CP	All
Contested and won	19	3	30	48	–	10	25
Contested, but never won	15	22	10	11	10	10	14
Never contested	67	75	60	41	90	79	62
Total	101	100	100	100	100	99	101
N	27	67	50	108	29	29	310

TABLE XI. Political Career Prominence

| | Present party affiliation | | | | | | |
	SW	JS	CO	CR	LP	CP	All
Current holders of prominent political office	30	42	40	44	10	14	35
Former holders of prominent political office	19	12	30	20	–	10	17
Non-prominent (i.e. those who have never held any prominent political office)	52	46	30	36	90	76	47
Total	101	100	100	100	100	100	99
N	27	67	50	108	29	29	310

few educational trusts, some trade unions, a women's association, and a women's cooperative provisions store.

Two top Baroda Congress-O leaders, Bhailalbhai Contractor and Chandrakant Mehta, hold offices in quite a few of these and other organizations. Active involvement in them over the years has fostered a camaraderie and a sense of personal loyalty among the Congress-O activists. Some of them have been so tangibly attached to the party's state- and city-level leaders that it is not easy for them to extricate themselves from their earlier loyalties and join the Congress-R. Some of them, in fact, do not envisage any better scope for themselves in the 'new' Congress. One of our very prominent Congress-O respondents gave the following explanation of his career predicament: 'We are considering the matter of joining the Congress-R. Our principles and ideology are the same. The question is whether or not the Congress-R would give us *honourable positions*. After all, we *have held* positions in politics and social work. But the early entrants into the Congress-R have already taken their positions in the political career queue. Will they allow us an *honourable entry*?'

In a comparison of the socio-economic characteristics of the political career prominents with the non-prominents within the several party units, we found that a greater proportion of the career prominents within the dominant party than within the other parties came from marginal and minority communities. In other words, the dominant party, more than the other parties, coopted leaders of the lower social strata and of the minority communities into top leadership positions.[15] Illustrative of this process are the following accounts of the political career mobility of (i) a Muslim leader who is presently in Congress-O and (ii) a scheduled caste leader who is presently in Congress-R.

(i) I was a probationary *mamlatdar* in 1949. Two Congress leaders, Messrs Maganbhai Patel and V. N. Modi, advised me to resign from government service and start legal practice as a prelude to a political career. I followed their advice, and, in 1951, won a municipal seat on the Congress ticket . . . I was defeated in the next municipal elections, but was nominated by the party to the Primary Education Board. . . . In 1962, I got elected as an MLA and . . . I lost in the 1967 general elections, whereupon I was appointed to 'this' office.

(ii) In 1945, I was studying law with the intention of starting practice in the following year. Mr Pranlal Munshi, a lawyer and Praja Mandal leader, advised me to join the Praja Mandal as a prelude to my career. He had known me well as I had helped organize the first and second Harijan conferences in the state. I had also gone with him as a volunteer to the Haripura Congress session. I joined the Praja Mandal in 1945 and, in the following year, started my legal practice and was made a member of the District Local Board. . . . In 1951-2, as I was denied the party's ticket, I left the Congress and fought unsuccessfully on a PSP ticket. Soon after that, I was persuaded to return to the Congress, and was nominated to the city's Primary Education Board. .... In 1958, I became a municipal councillor . . . and, in 1967, president of a Congress ward committee. In the following year, on my losing in the municipal elections, I was again nominated to the Primary Education Board.

These illustrations and what I said above in introducing them should not be taken to mean that the mobilization of the periphery is being done exclusively or predominantly by the dominant party. On the contrary, as reported elsewhere,[16] the Labour, Socialist, Praja Socialist, and Communist parties are more or less exclusively periphery-oriented and largely periphery-based. But, being minor parties in the local political system, they have no high political office to offer to those whom they mobilize from the periphery. For the same reason, again, in popular elections, they have to bank upon the 'social acceptability' and superior resources of their higher status activists.

The distributions of the six party groups in the second row of Table XI are a rough indicator of leadership displacement within the parties. We observe that, compared to the other parties, the Labour, Communist, and Jana Sangh party units have smaller proportions of 'displaced' leaders. This is suggestive of the existence of a greater degree of oligarchic professionalism within these latter party units. In the Jana Sangh this professionalism is provided by a religious elite, viz. the Brahmins, although, of late, it is making a deliberate effort to recruit non-Brahmin notables into its top leadership positions. The oligarchic professionalism within the Labour and Communist party units is provided by their trade union specialists.

CONCLUSION

The formation of a national democratic political community in Baroda started as the movement of a people who were subject to a native ruler under the paramountcy of a foreign government. Historically, it had several strands to it: an anti-British movement; a movement for responsible government from the native ruler; a social reform movement meant to bridge the centre-periphery gulf in the social system that had kept the Harijans and women under suppression; a movement for economic equality advocated by the Congress Socialists (who eventually formed the Socialist/Praja Socialist Party) and by the Communists; and a religious-nationalistic movement, organized by the Rashtriya Swayam Sevak Sangh, the Arya Samaj, and the Hindu Mahasabha. In the post-independence period the formation of the politically active stratum and the larger political community has been shaped by some additional developments, namely, the formation of the Jana Sangh, which took up the cause of Hindu revivalist nationalism;

linguistic provincialism that came to the fore during the Mahagujarat movement, which served as a spur to oppositional politics; a conservative, *laissez-faire* ideology advocated by the Swatantra Party; and an enhanced ideologization of politics attendant upon and following the Congress split.

These several pathways of entry do indeed serve to keep the politically active stratum open. Almost all sections of the society can find a convenient or congenial entry route into the political stratum. The availability of several competitive agencies of political mobilization and recruitment contributes to the expansion of the politically active stratum. This is good in so far as it helps to bridge the centre-periphery gulf in the society. After all, it is through such bridging that a society approximates the democratic goal of political equality.

In a genuine sense, then, a society progresses towards the democratic goal in proportion to the expansion of its political stratum. But if in the process the political cleavages within the political stratum become too intense, the very viability of the system comes to be threatened; it either disrupts or gets caught up in a condition of *immobilisme*. If, for instance, those who enter the politically active stratum have been socialized and mobilized for *Weltanschauung* politics, their integration with, and tolerance of, the other partisan groups will be difficult to achieve. In Baroda, as probably elsewhere in India, it would appear that the objectives for which the different sets of party activists are being socialized and mobilized are not all compatible with one another. Some of these objectives are: secular nationalism, religious nationalism, 'the inviolability of fundamental rights', democratic socialism, and communism. These 'divisive ideologies', although functional to the mobilization of the periphery, tend to lend an inchoate character and a disintegrative potential to the larger political community that is being formed in the process. Hence it would seem that mechanisms and practices to moderate the intensity of political cleavages and, relatedly, to enhance the legitimacy of governmental structures are at least as important for the institutionalization of a democratic political system as are the means of expanding the political stratum.[17]

NOTES

3. INDIVIDUALS AND THE DIALECTIC: A MARXIST VIEW OF POLITICAL BIOGRAPHIES

1. See K. W. J. Post and G. D. Jenkins, *The Price of Liberty: Personality and Politics in Colonial Nigeria* (Cambridge, 1973).

2. Author's Preface to the first edition, *Capital*, I, translated by Samuel Moore and Edward Aveling (London, 1946), p. xix.

3. See Marx, *The Eighteenth Brumaire of Louis Bonaparte*, and *The Class Struggles in France*, and Engels, *The Housing Question* and Prefatory Note to *The Peasant War in Germany*.

4. I refer to 'The Role of the Individual in History'. I have had access only to a French edition in writing this paper, so all quotations are my translations, here then G. V. Plekhanov, *Les questions fondamentales du Marxisme* (Paris, 1947), p. 258.

5. 'The Problem of the Capitalist State', *New Left Review*, 58, November–December 1969, p. 70. Emphasis in the original.

6. W. H. Morris-Jones, 'Political Recruitment and Political Development' in Colin Leys (ed.), *Politics and Change in Developing Countries* (Cambridge, 1969), p. 121ff.

7. Plekhanov, loc. cit.

8. Reference should be made to relevant pioneering work in the Caribbean context, A. W. Singham's *The Hero and the Crowd in a Colonial Polity* (New Haven, 1969), which in my opinion, however, fails to pay enough attention to the perspectives of 'the crowd'.

9. Morris-Jones, op. cit., p. 116.

10. It is an interesting comment upon some of the conceptual problems of this seminar that a number of reviewers of the Adelabu biography have claimed that he was never other than of middle rank, and therefore undeserving of such lengthy treatment.

11. This still leaves open a great range of differences, structural and otherwise, between British African and West Indian colonies. At least let it be said that the Colonial Office certainly considered the experience of, for example, Sierra Leone and Northern Rhodesia to be relevant to Jamaica in the late 1930s.

12. Jamaica did not attain full internal self-government until 1959, and its constitutional development is complicated by its participation in the abortive West Indian Federation in the period 1958–61. I regard the period 1952–55 as decisive because it marked the consolidation of North American interest in the island with the beginning of bauxite mining in 1952 (within a few years Jamaica was the world's biggest producer), the purge of the Marxists from the trade union movement and Manley's People's National Party, and the electoral victory of the latter which made Jamaica a two-party system.

13. A. A. Adelabu to C. M. Booth, 30 September 1950, Adelabu Papers.

14. G. St. J. Orde Browne to Secretary of State, 9 December 1938, CO 137/830, file 68989. For a preliminary analysis, which my book will supersede, see my 'The Politics of Protest in Jamaica, 1938: Some problems of analysis and conceptualisation', *Social and Economic Studies*, 18, 4, 1969.

15. From December 1938 onwards the Jamaican Marxists were in sporadic contact with the British Communist Party.

16. 'The Case for a Militant Nigerian Nationalism', typescript, Adelabu Papers, p. 5. Emphasis in the original.

4. POLITICAL CENTRALIZATION AND LOCAL POLITICS IN GHANA
[This article is drawn from material collected during a field-trip (financed by the SSRC) to Ashanti, 1969–70.]

1. Cf. B. Barry, *Sociologists, Economists and Democracy* (London, 1970), p. 14. But see also Wright-Mills' strictures on 'psychologism' as a denial of social structure in C. Wright-Mills, *The Sociological Imagination* (New York, 1959), p. 67.

2. Marx-Engels, *The German Ideology* (London, 1965), pp. 36 and 38.

2a. See A. Zolberg, 'The Structure of Political Conflict in the New States of Tropical Africa', *American Political Science Review*, 62, 1 (1968), pp. 70–87, for the anti-institutional view-point.

3. E.g. NLC members General Afrifa, and the Inspector-General of Police, Yakubu, were both actively involved in the affairs of Mampong and Dagomba, respectively. See M. Staniland, *The Lions of Dagbon* (Cambridge, 1975).

4. Chief of the *oman*—in colonial parlance, 'paramount chief'. See R. Crook, 'Colonial Rule and Political Culture in Modern Ashanti', *Journal of Commonwealth Political Studies*, xi, 1 (1973), pp. 3–27, for general background.

5. It should be noted here that 'communal' refers to a total community in the social and geographic sense, not the partial religious community implied by the term when it is used to analyse politics in Asian societies. For Ashanti during the period in question, the communities whose interests were being taken up by local political leaders should not be thought of as being purely geographically defined; particular villages were 'nodal points' for more widespread social and economic networks, some of them in a satellite relationship. Cf. J. Dunn and A. F. Robertson, *Dependence and Opportunity: Political Change in Ahafo* (Cambridge, 1973), pp. 10–41, 223–4, where the term 'politics of communal aggrandisement' is used to describe a similar, although not identical, phenomenon.

6. W. H. Morris-Jones, 'Political Recruitment and Political Development' in C. Leys (ed.), *Politics and Change in Developing Countries* (Cambridge, 1969), p. 118.

7. Interview, 19 September 1969.

8. OUC to CCA and Offinsohene, October 1943. 'Clubs and Associations File' in Offinso District Office (ODO).

9. The CPP was formed in 1949. See D. Austin, *Politics in Ghana, 1946–60* (London, 1964), Chapter 1, for the general period.

10. See D. Apter, *Ghana in Transition* (New York, 1966), originally published as *Gold Coast in Transition* in 1955, pp. 165–7, who uses the phrase to describe the young primary-school leavers of the 1940s and early 1950s, and characterizes them as a social group 'whose roots with rural areas were not dissolved but whose urban affiliations made possible quick and effective organization [for the nationalist cause]'. Later categorizations, such as 'subelite' (P. C. Lloyd, *Africa in Social Change* [Harmondsworth, 1967], p. 153), have focused more on the occupational and social status characteristics of groups who were important in the nationalist movements of this period—e.g. clerk, teacher, small trader—characteristics which were often but not necessarily associated with the possession of a Standard VII certificate. See also R. J. A. R. Rathbone, *Education and Politics in Ghana* (Gutersloh, West Germany, 1968), for a detailed critique of the Standard VII boy theory.

11. Interview, 18 September 1969. See also Austin, op. cit., p. 77. The term is a contemptuous one, used by the Ghanaian elite to describe penniless, often un-employed, urban migrants; it was extended, perhaps unjustly, to encompass Nkrumah's followers from the subelite, and then adopted as defiant self-identification by local CPP militants.

12. Offinso and Ejisu were the leading states in the 1901 Yaa Asantewaa War, or 'rebellion'. (F. Myatt, *The Golden Stool*, London, 1966, p. 157.)

13. This was the system introduced during the Second World War under which a government marketing board bought the whole cocoa crop, through licensed buyers, at a fixed price. After the war the price continued to be fixed well below the world price, a fact of which the farmers were not unaware. They had hoped that the CPP would reform the system but were disappointed when the Cocoa Marketing Board was not abolished in favour of 'producer's control', and the price policy was continued as a means of extracting capital from the farmers.

14. See Apter, op. cit., pp. 241–51. The new local government was intended to replace the old Native Authorities with a modern, democratic system. Two-thirds of the council were elected, one-third nominated by the 'traditional authority', and it was expected that the councils would provide local political bases for CPP dominance, while destroying the power of the colonial Native Authority chieftaincy. But there was considerable ambivalence in the reform, which left local powers over land and the judiciary split between the chieftaincy and the new local authority.

15. Offinso Local Council—Minutes of 1st meeting, 27 May 1952, in ODO.

16. See *Ashanti Pioneer*, 15 September 1952; interviews with Duncan-Williams, Wiafe Akenten, and other ex-CPP leaders; State Council and Local Council files in ODO.

17. Interviews, 17 August 1970 and 20 July 1970, Duncan-Williams and Kwabena Nsiah.

18. Enquiry of Offinso Local Council into illegal arbitration court; report sent to GA, 3 March 1954. Offinso State Council file, ODO.

19. See Austin, op. cit., Chapter 5.

20. See D. Austin, 'Opposition in Ghana 1947–67', *Government and Opposition*, July/October 1967, pp. 568–83, and R. J. A. R. Rathbone, 'Opposition in Ghana: the National Liberation Movement', in *Opposition in the New African States* (University of London Institute of Commonwealth Studies *Collected Seminar Papers No. 4*, 1969). The NLM was based in Ashanti, although it attracted the support of similar local elites in the southern cocoa areas of the country, and other opposition groups, particularly the older 'constitutional' nationalists who had been displaced by the CPP. Its main political proposals were for a federal constitution and another election to test national support for itself and its programme. In the event, the NLM won seats only in Ashanti. The federal proposals were supported to some extent by other 'regional' parties in the North and Trans-Volta-Togo-land.

21. The Brongs were traditional subjects of the Ashanti. Between 1950 and 1954 a Brong 'secession' movement gained the support of the CPP. Offinso and the bordering Brong states had long memories of ancient rivalries, and were still in dispute over land claims.

22. 'Commander of the advance guard', military title of sub-chief.

23. See Austin, op. cit., pp. 274–5.

24. The CPP eventually became an anti-farmer, or rather 'anti-kulak', govern-ment: see especially its policies for total state control of all buying, as well as marketing, of cocoa.

25. The Chiefs (Recognition) Act 1959. See Ghana National Assembly Debates, vol. 14, cols. 307–11.

26. This section is based on CPP files in ODO, and Ashanti CPP Regional Steering Committee minutes.

27. Interview, 17 August 1970. This was, in fact, inaccurate. There had been Ghanaian Government Agents in Offinso in 1957–59 (Government Agent was the new title for District Commissioner, 1951–59).

28. Kumasi North Local Council, file DC/KN63, DC to Chairman of LC, 7 December 1959.

29. The Farmers Council was a state buying organization, the Trading Corporation a CPP-controlled whosesale and retail import-export business.

30. He did, however, 'repay' by giving them a separate Court.

31. In 1961 an official 'Order of Merit' was ordered to be drawn up.

32. Bureaucratization of the party did not, however, involve the adoption of pure meritocratic standards of recruitment. A party seminar in 1962, for instance, attacked the application of civil service machinery 'to the letter', since it caused 'ill-feeling' amongst party activists (see note 26, DC/KN 14). Party loyalty and political ability remained the overriding criteria for appointment.

33. D. Apter, 'Ghana' in J. Coleman and C. Rosberg (eds.), *Political Parties and National Integration in Tropical Africa* (Berkeley & Los Angeles, 1964), p. 312.

34. Although this analysis is based on Ashanti material, it is considered that the pattern revealed here may be equally useful in looking at other areas of Ghana, especially the Colony area in the south and Eweland; also, in a rather different form, the north.

5. THE ELIGIBLE AND THE ELECT

1. See Erving Goffman, *Asylums* (New York, 1961), p. 125, and the entire section, 'The Moral Career of the Mental Patient'. See also Erving Goffman, *Stigma* (Harmondsworth, 1968), esp. pp. 80–92.

2. For a particularly poignant report on this, see Samuel G. Ikoku, *Le Ghana de Nkrumah* (Paris, 1971).

3. B. F. Kusi and B. K. Senkyire (see Dramatis Personae, pp. 62–5).

4. Sociologists have recently become very much clearer as to the limited political insight provided by cohort studies. See particularly Anthony Giddens, 'Elites in the British Class Structure', *Sociological Review*, Vol. xx, 3 (August 1972), pp. 345–72, and more extensively in his important *The Class Structure of the Advanced Societies* (London, 1973). I do not, of course, wish to suggest that important political information cannot sometimes be provided by sensitively conducted cohort analyses: For an excellent sample, see R. W. Johnson, 'The British Political Elite, 1955–1972', *Archives Européennes de Sociologie*, xiv (1973), pp. 35–77.

5. Cf. Hegel's letter to Niethammer, written on the day the French occupied Jena, partially (and more accurately) translated in Walter Kaufman, *Hegel: Reinterpretation, Texts and Commentary* (London, 1965), p. 316.

6. David Hume, 'Of the Independency of Parliament', in *Essays, Moral, Political and Literary by David Hume* (London, 1904), p. 42.

7. W. H. Morris-Jones, 'Political Recruitment and Political Development', in Colin Leys (ed.), *Politics and Change in Developing Countries* (Cambridge, 1969), p. 118.

8. Morris-Jones, op. cit., p. 113, etc.

9. Hence Richard Crook's decision in his contribution to the present volume to compare the careers of two men, one of whom became a career chief and the

other a career politician. There are no traditional offices in Ahafo with the political status of the paramountcy of Offinso, discussed by Crook. Plausible candidates for modern political office in Ahafo would not be likely to find the rewards of an Ahafo chieftaincy much of an incentive.

10. See Judith Brown's contribution to the present volume.

11. The distinction is drawn here between those who held major office as a representative of a modern political party in the constituency, along with those who aspired actively to do so—MPs and candidates for nomination as MPs—and other political actors who did not hold or aspire actively to hold such positions.

12. This has not proved to hold good elsewhere in Ghana, either in the case of northern chiefs (J. A. Braimah, S. D. Dombo[?], and the Tolon Na), or of retired police officers (Madjitey)—let alone of those who aspired to unite these two roles. It is likely not to hold good in the future in the case of retired army officers.

13. It does not seem likely that it would be appealing for anyone in Ahafo to campaign for modern political office as an investment in improving his chances in competing for a traditional office. (Cf. J. H. Cobbina's NAL candidacy in Kumasi in the unsuccessful quest to become Asantehene.)

14. This would not be true in a situation such as the Tanzania elections of 1965, when the party itself could not lose but where it permitted genuine competition between individuals.

15. I have discussed this election at length in a chapter published in Dennis Austin & Robin Luckham (eds.), *Politicians and Soldiers in Ghana* (London, 1975).

16. Cf. Jean Rouch's conception of super-tribe, 'Migrations au Ghana (Gold Coast), enquête 1953–55', *Journal de la Société des Africanistes*, xxvi, 1 & 2, pp. 33–164.

17. Similar solidarities appear to have been created in Offinso too: see Crook's contribution to the present volume.

18. Former UP seats in the Volta region, former CPP seats in the Akan areas, possibly also the two Nzima seats.

19. Goffman, *Asylums*, pp. 199–200. (In Goffman's parlance, secondary adjustments = 'working the system'; primary adjustments = being the system.)

20. See R. Crook, unpublished seminar paper, Institute of Commonwealth Studies, Oxford, summer 1973.

21. Joan Vincent, *African Elite: the Big Men of a Small Town* (New York, 1971).

22. Walter L. Barrows, "Comparative Grassroots Politics in Africa', *World Politics*, xxvi, 2 (January 1974), pp. 283–97.

23. See, e.g., Gavin Williams, 'Political Consciousness among the Ibadan Poor', in E. de Kadt & G. Williams (eds.), *Sociology and Development* (London, 1974).

24. Goffman, *Asylums*, p. 135.

25. This is, of course, a pragmatic, not a philosophical argument. A good brief rebuttal of it from a philosophical point of view by a sociologist is the title essay in W. G. Runciman, *Sociology in its Place* (Cambridge, 1970). Pragmatic rebuttals of any force would not be easy to find.

26. There are strong reasons (clearly Marxist in ancestry) for looking at the leadership of revolutionary movements in these terms. See, e.g., Barrington Moore, *Social Origins of Dictatorship and Democracy* (Boston, 1966), and John Dunn, *Modern Revolutions* (Cambridge, 1972).

27. Thomas Hobbes, *Behemoth*, edited by Ferdinand Tonnies, 2nd edition (London, 1969), p. 59.

6. SEIZING HALF A LOAF

1. I am grateful for the suggestions made by Kirsten Alnaes, Shem Bukombi, and members of the Seminar on Comparative Politics at the Institute of Commonwealth Studies, and for the research support provided by the Department of Political Science and Public Administration, Makerere University in Uganda. None of them can be held responsible for any errors included here.

2. 'Political Recruitment and Political Development', in Colin Leys (ed.), *Politics and Change in Developing Countries* (Cambridge, 1969), p. 118.

3. There is controversy over whether Benedicto Kiwanuka (Prime Minister and head of the DP) promised while campaigning in Toro that he would create a separate district for the Amba and Konzo. The Konzo and Amba voted DP in large numbers, partly in the belief that they had his promise. Kiwanuka later claimed he had agreed only to look into the matter.

4. '. . . an arena is a pattern of encounters.' Harold Lasswell and Abraham Kaplan, *Power and Society* (New Haven, 1950), p. 80. The task for the researcher is to find the boundaries by examining which encounters between specified actors predominate in a particular situation.

5. See the *Report of the Commission of Inquiry into the Recent Disturbances amongst the Baamba and Bakonjo People of Toro* (the Ssembeguya Report) (Entebbe, 1962), and Martin R. Doornbos, 'Kumanyana and Rwenzururu: Two Responses to Ethnic Inequality', in Robert I. Rotberg and Ali A. Mazrui (eds.), *Protest and Power in Black Africa* (New York, 1970), pp. 1109–30.

6. Prior to independence the government could create a district by administrative fiat. Afterwards, the concurrence of two thirds of the members of the National Assembly and two thirds of the members of the assembly in each district affected by the change was required to alter district boundaries. Since a separate district was inconceivable to the leaders of the Toro government, a constitutional solution was out of the question. The spread of an organized secession movement was not a surprising response under the circumstances.

7. See Stacey's account in *Summons to Ruwenzori* (London, 1965).

8. By 1970, four years after Mukirane's death, the government had declined in area controlled and in supporters still loyal. At this point the national government returned administration in these areas to the Toro government. While President Amin has made efforts to lure the dissidents out of the mountains, including the creation of a Rwenzori and Semuliki Districts as part of his general reorganization of Ugandan administration, there remains a Rwenzururu government collecting taxes, making occasional attacks, and issuing public statements.

7. THE POLITICIAN AS AGITATOR IN EASTERN UGANDA

1. C. Meillassoux, 'A class analysis of the bureaucratic process in Mali', *Journal of Development Studies*, vi (1970), pp. 97–110.

2. This paper largely depends on fieldwork in eastern Uganda between July and December 1965, though I have also made use of data collected while teaching extra-mural courses in Bukedi between 1962 and 1964 and (more intensively) during university vacations between 1967 and 1970. My greatest local debts are to Israeli Kabazi, Erika Higenyi, Japhat Madungha, and James Kivunike. Archival materials cited in this paper (not always directly) come from the repository adjoining the District Commissioner's office at Mbale, many of them from unsorted files of local petitions.

3. D. Rothchild and M. Rogin, 'Uganda' in Gwendolen W. Carter (ed.), *National Unity and Regionalism in Eight African States* (Ithaca NY, 1966), pp. 379–384.

4. Ibid., p. 382.

5. I owe this phrase to Professor B. A. Ogot.

6. See further my unpublished University of London PhD thesis, 'Politics in Bukedi 1900–1939' (1967), passim.

7. M. Twaddle, ' "Tribalism" in eastern Uganda' in P. H. Gulliver (ed.), *Tradition and Transition in East Africa* (London, 1969), pp. 193–208.

8. D. Marshall, *Annual Report on the Eastern Province, 1960* (Entebbe, 1961), p. 1.

9. Uganda Protectorate, *Report of the Commission of Enquiry into Disturbances in the Eastern Province* (Entebbe, 1960).

10. Ibid., pp. 55–7.

11. Cf. A. W. Southall, 'The trouble with Bukedi', *Uganda Argus*, 1 February 1960; F. G. Burke, *Local Government and Politics in Uganda* (Syracuse, 1964), pp. 178–222.

12. Japhat Madungha initiated me into Nyole sociology. For an extended account for outsiders we must await the work of Michael and Susan White, who did anthropological fieldwork in Bunyole county in 1969–70.

13. E. M. K. Mutenga, 'Other people's influence on Abanyuli', *Makerere College Magazine*, iii, 2 (May 1941), p. 69.

14. This was the comment of an early Mill Hill Father. Still the best short account of Kakungulu's career is H. B. Thomas, 'Capax Imperii—the story of Semei Kakunguru', *Uganda Journal*, ii (1939), pp. 125–36.

15. DC Bugwere to PC Eastern Province, 2 March 1925; Mbale Archives 5/1440/46.

16. *Native Administration* (Entebbe, 1939).

17. Cf. especially his memorandum which was circulated to all DCs, 'Native administration in the eastern province. Past, present and future policies' (Jinja, 1941).

18. 'Record of a meeting between the provincial commissioner and certain petitioners from Bunyuli', 20 April 1951, and 'Draft circular', undated copy, unsorted files, Mbale Archives.

19. DC Mbale to PC Jinja, 26 November 1943; unsorted files, Mbale Archives.

20. 'Report of the 6 chiefs who were sent out by the DC', encl. DC Mbale to PC Jinja, 24 February 1944; copy loc. cit.

21. 'Extracts from evidence given before the commission appointed to enquire into the agitation in Bunyuli', DC Mbale to PC Jinja, 19 June 1944; telegram to governor, 8 November 1944, by Musa Kasakya; Kasakya to Colonial Secretary, 16 November 1944; 'Copy of a note by HE the Governor of a meeting held on 14 March 1945 in which His Excellency granted an interview to certain Banyuli petitioners'; all copies in unsorted files at Mbale.

22. Tororo CID to DC Mbale, 3 March 1936, loc. cit.; 'The life history of Erika Higenyi' (in Lunyole), trans. J. Madungha, undated; DC Mbale to PC Eastern Province, 8 December 1949, copy in personal file on Nasanaeri Hamala, Mbale Archives.

23. DC Mbale to PC Jinja, 27 March and 31 March 1951; copies in unsorted files at Mbale.

24. See note 18.

25. Cf. D. A. Low, *Political Parties in Uganda* (London, 1926), passim.

26. Max Weber, 'Politics as a vocation', citing the translation in H. H. Gerth and C. Wright Mills (eds.), *From Max Weber* (London, 1948), p. 125.

27. *Uganda Empya*, 15 October 1953.

28. *Politicians and Policies: an essay on politics in Acholi, Uganda, 1962–65* (Nairobi, 1967).

29. Burke, op. cit., p. 217.

30. See further W. H. Morris-Jones, 'Political recruitment and political development' in C. Leys (ed.), *Politics and Change in Developing Countries* (Cambridge, 1969), p. 120.

8. KRISTO DAS PAL

1. In defining a political system, I subscribe to the theory outlined by David Easton in *A System Analysis of Political Life* (New York, 1965).

2. In nineteenth-century usage, this term refers to a European resident in India.

3. An example of how *dalapatis* are ranked in relation to other *samajiks* (members) within a *dal* is given in N. N. Laha, Suvarnavanik: *Katha O Kirti* (Calcutta, 1940–42), Vol. III, pp. 153–91.

4. For a more comprehensive discussion of this indigenous political system, see S. N. Mukherjee, 'Class, Caste, and Politics in Calcutta, 1815–38' in Edmund Leach and S. N. Mukherjee (ed.), *Elites in South Asia* (Cambridge, 1970), pp. 33–78.

5. Some other Hindus who fit this description are Ram Gopal Ghose, Digambar Mitra, Rajendra Lal Mitra, Haris Chandra Mukherjee, and Mahendra Lal Sircar.

6. Nagendra Nath Ghose, *Kristo Das Pal: a Study* (Calcutta, 1887), p. 6.

7. *Hindoo Patriot*, 28 July 1884.

8. As quoted in Ghose, op. cit., p. 68.

9. Ibid., p. 6.

10. *Papers Relating to the Hindu Metropolitan College with which is Incorporated Seal's Free College* (Calcutta, 1857).

11. Ghose, op. cit., p. 6.

12. K. D. Pal to S. C. Mukherjee, 5 April 1870, letter No. 46, in *Bengal Past and Present*, IX (July–December 1914), pp. 143–4.

13. Although the official documents relating to this incident have yet to be located, Pal's efficiency in his later career suggests that he, like Surendra Nath Banerjea some years later, was a victim of an unfair judgement.

14. This conclusion is based on a collective biography which I am working on at the moment.

15. Ghose, op. cit., p. 12.

16. Ibid., p. 9.

17. *Bengalee*, 26 July 1884.

18. See, for example, Miss Sujata Ghosh, 'The British Indian Association (1851–1900)', *Bengal Past and Present*, lxxvii (July–December 1958), pp. 99–119.

19. *Hindoo Patriot*, 21 March 1870. For comments on Pal's support of the salt tax see *Bengalee*, 20 March 1869.

20. *Hindoo Patriot*, 14 February 1876. For criticism of Pal's stand on this issue, see *Amrita Bazar Patrika*, 19 November 1875, 3 February 1876, 1 March 1876.

21. *Brahmo Public Opinion*, 11 September 1879.

22. *Bengalee*, 24 November 1883, 15 December 1883.

23. A settlement enacted by the British in Bengal in 1793, which declared *zamindars* to be the proprietors of the land in return for a fixed share of the revenues from each estate.

24. See, for example, *Englishman*, 19 July 1864; *National Paper*, 11 August 1869; and *Bengalee*, 29 April 1882.

25. See, for instance, Ram Chandra Palit (ed.), *Speeches and Minutes of the Hon'ble Kristo Das Pal* (Calcutta, 1882).

26. *Englishman*, 19 July 1864.

27. Temple to Northbrook, 25 December 1874, Temple Collection, F 86/2.

28. See, for instance, policy as outlined in Bethune to Dalhousie, 23 September 1848, Dalhousie Papers, GD 45/6/144, and Wood to Canning, 26 July 1860, Wood Collection, IOLB 3, p. 260.

29. As quoted in Ghose, op. cit., p. 35.

30. Temple to Northbrook, 17 February 1875, Temple Collection, F86/2.

31. *Englishman*, loc. cit.

32. *Bengalee*, 2 September 1882.

33. Ghose, op. cit., p. 15.

34. For an analysis of the reasons for the formation of these associations, see *Sadharini*, 14 November 1875.

35. Ghose, loc. cit.

9. PATHWAYS TO POLITICAL ADVANCEMENT: PROBLEMS OF CHOICE FOR TALUQDAR POLITICIANS IN LATE BRITISH INDIA

1. Details are taken from *List of Taluqdars in Oudh up to November 1935* (Lucknow, 1935), which was a BIA publication. Additional information from N. H. Siddiqui, *Landlords of Agra and Avadh* (Lucknow, 1950).

2. There may be some connection between Khattri activity in the general political sphere and this Khattri *taluqdar* activity, but l have no clear information on this. For some indications of the importance of Khattris in the municipal politics of the Oudh city of Faizabad from the 1890s onwards, see Harold Gould's studies 'Traditionalism and Modernism in UP: Faizabad constituency', in M. Weiner and R. Kothari (eds.), *Indian Voting Behaviour* (Calcutta, 1965), and 'Religion and Politics in a UP constituency', in D. E. Smith (ed.), *South Asian Politics and Religion* (Princeton, 1966).

3. P. R. Brass, *Factional Politics in an Indian State. The Congress Party in Uttar Pradesh* (Berkeley and Los Angeles, 1965), chapter iv.

4. See the Raja of Muhmudabad's article, 'Some memories', in C. H. Philips and M. D. Wainwright (eds.), *The Partition of India. Polities and Perspectives 1935–1947* (London, 1968). Pipur was the chairman of the 'Committee appointed to inquire into Muslim grievances in Congress Provinces' which produced the 'Pirpur Report' for the Muslim League in 1938.

5. Interview with Jagannath Baksh Singh, Lucknow, 17 March 1962. For details of the NAP, see Reeves, 'Landlords and party politics in UP, 1934–37', in D. A. Low (ed.), *Soundings in Modern South Asian History* (London, 1968), pp. 261–91.

6. Interview, 17 March 1962.

7. Siddiqui, op. cit., p. 371.

8. 'The villager's life', *Landholders Journal* (Calcutta), vol. iv (November 1935), pp. 116–17.

9. Statement in *Pioneer*, 26 March 1946, p. 3; *National Herald*, 27 March 1946, p. 3.

10. Interview with Guru Narain Seth, Lucknow, 17 March 1962.

10. THE SHASTRIS OF KASHI AND LAHORE

[I am grateful to Dr T. Raychaudhuri, Dr P. D. Reeves, and the participants in the Comparative Politics seminar at the Institute of Commonwealth Studies, London, for comments on an earlier draft.]

1. Sri Prakasa, *Bharat Ratna Bhagavan Das* (Meerut, 1970), pp. 78–9.

2. Satya Narain Tripathi on 'National Education', *Aj*, 1–2 March 1929. See also Banarsidas Chaturvedi Papers (National Archives of India, New Delhi), General

Correspondence, 1053, Acharya Gidwani's speech at the third convocation of the KV.

3. UP Educ. (Confid.) Dept. 127/1930 (Secretariat Record Room, Lucknow), 'Comment on the Activities of the Banaras Hindu University', 14 June 1930.

4. All India Congress Committee Papers (Nehru Memorial Museum, New Delhi) G2/1931, Pt I, 'Report on Civil Disobedience', by General Secs, AICC, October 1931, p. 57a.

5. UP GAD 241/1930 (Secretariat Record Room, Lucknow), Jagdish Prasad, Chief Secy., UP, 'Note' of 27 May 1930, and comment on it by Dy. Commissioner, Rae Bareli.

6. D. R. Mankekar, *Lal Bahadur Shastri* (New Delhi, 1973), p. 39; J. N. S. Yadav, *Lal Bahadur Shastri* (Delhi, 1971); and incidental references in LSM records found in the P. D. Tandon papers (National Archives of India).

7. Tandon Papers, File 52, No 231, 'Servants of the People Society, Lahore', brief report of work done during 1930–34.

8. UP Police Dept. File 1504/1934 (Secretariat Record Room, Lucknow) 'Note on Subversive Movements and Organisations (other than Terrorist) in India . . .', Director, Intelligence Bureau, Govt. of India, September 1933.

9. Loc. cit.

10. Hailey Collection (India Office Library, London), vol. 51, letter to D. A. Low, 10 January 1961.

11. Sri Prakasa Papers (Nehru Memorial Museum, New Delhi), File 'From G. B. Lambert', Lambert—Sri Prakasa, 12 December 1928.

12. Even in the late 1930s and the 1940s, when nomination for elections to the provincial legislature and appointment to ministerial or parliamentary-secretarial posts became important, success in the Congress was an essential pre-requisite for anyone whose wealth could not buy a Congress 'ticket'.

13. The biographical details used in this paper have been collated from a variety of newspaper reports, 'Who's Who's, biographies, and interviews.

14. Interview, Raja Ram, Lucknow, 23 November 1972.

15. 'When asked by my father of what I was accused', Mazzini recalled about an early arrest and imprisonment, '[the Governor of Genoa] replied that the time had not yet arrived for answering that question, but that I was a young man of talent, very fond of solitary walks by night, and habitually silent as to the subject of my meditations, *and that the government was not fond of young men of talent, the subject of whose musings was unknown to it.*' Kedourie comments: 'There was no efficacious means of controlling the musings of such young men, for they were not the fruit of a conspiracy. They were inherent in the nature of things; they emanated from the very spirit of the age.' Elie Kedourie, *Nationalism* (3rd edition, London, 1966), p. 105.

16. It did not have to be the LSM, of course. It could have been a nationalist newspaper or a national educational institution.

17. Tandon Papers, File 35, s.n. 1338, Algu Rai—Tandon, November 1931.

18. For some details, see my Oxford University DPhil thesis, 'The Indian National Congress and Political Mobilisation in the United Provinces, 1926–1934'.

19. Yet it is significant that Gautam who, like Lal Bahadur, worked among the *kisans*, but who did not have the same close personal links with Tandon or Nehru, rose almost as rapidly as Lal Bahadur to a ministerial post at the centre and to front rank Congress leadership. He was helped in this, without a doubt, by his position in his home district of Aligarh. But in Allahabad itself he had pioneered the Central UP Kisan Sangh in 1931, and thereby attained prominence in the UP Congress before Lal Bahadur.

11. GANDHI'S MEN, 1917–22

1. Sir M. O'Dwyer to Chelmsford, 21 April 1919, National Archives of India, Home Pol., B, May 1919, nos. 148–78.

2. I take 'big man' in this context to mean not the landed magnate or urban notable whose networks of clients and followers depend on his social and economic position, but the western educated leader who chooses to operate primarily in the modern political arena and tends to have access to fewer of the resources which these other sorts of influential men can deploy.

3. J. Dwarkadas to A. Besant, 27 February 1919, Besant Papers. Sir P. S. Iyer declined to help lead Gandhi's Rowlatt *satyagraha* because of personal commitment to A. Besant. 'My long relation with her makes it my duty not to array myself against her in what she takes to be a faction opposed to her.' Iyer to Gandhi, 23 March 1919, Gandhi Papers, Sabarmati, SN no. 6465 (hereafter SN).

4. For evidence on Gandhi's lieutenants in Champaran, see M. K. Gandhi, *An Autobiography. The Story of My Experiments with Truth* (London, 1966), pp. 337–349; letter from local lawyers to Gandhi, 13 April 1917, *The Collected Works of Mahatma Gandhi*, vol. 13 (Delhi, 1964), p. 569; Gandhi's notes on Champaran situation, 14 May 1917, ibid., p. 391; undated letter from Bettiah Sub-divisional Officer to Commissioner, Tirhut Division, B. B. Misra (ed.), *Select Documents on Mahatma Gandhi's Movement in Champaran 1917–18* (Patna, 1963), pp. 339–43; Rajendra Prasad, *At the Feet of Mahatma Gandhi* (Bombay, 1961), p. 8.

5. Bombay Presidency Police, Secret Abstract of Intelligence of 1918, paras. 64 (a), 204, 315; Gandhi, *Autobiography*, pp. 363, 365.

6. Gandhi, *Autobiography*, p. 356.

7. Bombay Presidency Police, Secret Abstract of Intelligence of 1919, para. 826 (a).

8. Rajendra Prasad, *Mahatma Gandhi and Bihar. Some Reminiscences* (Bombay, 1949), p. 19; undated letter from Bettiah Sub-divisional Officer to Commissioner, Tirhut Division, Misra, op. cit., p. 339.

9. Quoted in K. L. Panjabi, *The Indomitable Sardar* (Bombay, 1964), p. 27.

10. Prasad, *Mahatma Gandhi and Bihar*, p. 19.

11. Instructions to volunteers, 17 April 1918, *The Collected Works of Mahatma Gandhi*, vol. 14 (Delhi, 1965), pp. 350–1.

12. *The Bombay Chronicle*, 18 November 1918.

13. See D. V. Tahmankar, *Sardar Patel* (London, 1970). Further evidence of the complementary initiatives in the process of lesser leaders' recruitment into Gandhi's constellation is in A. Bhatt's study of Surat district, 'Caste and Political Mobilisation in a Gujarat District', R. Kothari (ed.), *Caste in Indian Politics* (New Delhi, 1970), pp. 299–339.

14. Undated letter from Bettiah Sub-divisional Officer to Commissioner, Tirhut Division, Misra, op. cit., p. 339.

15. Prasad, *At the Feet of Mahatma Gandhi*, pp. 18–19. The title of this book is significant, and is very similar to other reminiscences of lesser leaders in Gandhi's circle; for example, Balvantsinha, *Under the Shelter of Bapu* (Ahmedabad, 1962). These indicate one strong strand in the relationship between Gandhi and his lieutenants, and the psychological gains of security and guidance which they gained from association with him. Jawaharlal Nehru was also attracted to theosophy and the SIS before joining Gandhi; he also expressed the excitement younger men found in Gandhi's new political techniques. See J. Nehru, *An Autobiography* (London, 1936), pp. 15, 30, 35.

16. J. M. Brown, *Gandhi's Rise to Power: Indian Politics 1915–1922* (Cambridge, 1972).

17. Gandhi, *Autobiography*, p. 366. B. G. Gokhale, 'Sardar Vallabhbhai Patel: the Party Organizer as Political Leader', R. L. Park and I. Tinker (eds.), *Leadership and Political Institutions in India* (Princeton, 1959), pp. 87–99.

18. Instructions for *satyagrahis*, 30 June 1919, *The Collected Works of Mahatma Gandhi*, vol. 15 (Delhi, 1965), p. 415; M. Desai, *The Story of Bardoli* (Ahmedabad, 1957 reprint), p. 38.

19. Governor of Bombay to Secretary of State for India, telegram received 26 November 1930, India Office Library, L/PJ/6/1998, P & J 6789, 1930.

20. M. Desai to J. Nehru, 7 April 1930, Nehru Memorial Museum & Library, J. Nehru Papers, part i, vol. xvii.

21. Fortnightly reports from Bihar and Orissa, 18 April and 1 July 1919, Home Pol., Deposit, July 1919, no. 46, and August 1919, no. 51; Hasan Imam to Gandhi, 25 May 1919, SN no. 6626.

22. For Gandhi's relationship with other politicians during his continental campaigns, particularly his dependence on middle-rankers in each locality, see R. Kumar (ed.), *Essays on Gandhian Politics. The Rowlatt Satyagraha of 1919* (Oxford, 1971); Brown, op. cit.

23. It is significant that in 1920 peasant delegates outnumbered educated, professional people at Bihar's political conference; while in Kaira the Patidars became the backbone of the local Congress.

24. Evidence of local organizers is available in police reports on civil disobedience, in provincial fortnightly reports, and in details of judgements delivered in courts for civil disobedience offences. For example, a letter from the Government of India (Home Department) to the Under-Secretary of State for India, 25 September 1930, enclosing a judgement against Kalidas Jeskaram Zaveri (one of Gandhi's Kaira middle-rankers) for instigating the public not to pay land revenue and for abetting the boycott of government servants, at a public meeting at Limbashi on 17 June 1930. IOL, L/PJ/6/1998, P & J 5858, 1930.

12. THE LESSER LEADER AMID POLITICAL TRANSFORMATION

1. *Census of India*, 1941, xxiii, 2 (Bangalore, 1942), p. 356.

2. These so-called dominant 'castes' were, and are, somewhat artificial social categories. They are used as terms in this discussion merely for convenience. The various levels of social organization within these categories have been discussed more fully in J. Manor, 'The Evolution of Political Arenas and Units of Social Organization: the Lingayats and Vokkaligas of Mysore' in M. N. Srinivas (ed.), *Aspects of Change in India* (forthcoming).

3. For an introduction to this problem, see W. H. Morris-Jones, 'India's Political Idioms' in C. H. Philips (ed.), *Politics and Society in India* (London, 1963), pp. 133–54.

4. For a study of this in Madras presidency, see C. J. Baker, 'Politics in South India, 1917–1930', University of Cambridge PhD thesis, 1972.

5. This section is based on interviews with T. P. Krishnappa, Tumkur, 11 October 1972; Gubbi Rajagopalachar, Bangalore, 21 October 1972; R. S. Aradhya, Bangalore, 7 October 1972; T. N. Kempahonniah, Tumkur, 10 October 1972; T. P. Brahmiah, Tumkur, 9 October 1972; M. Doraiswamy, Banglore, 9 September 1972; Anantharama Setty, Tumkur, 9 October 1972; and on the K. Rangaiengar papers, Gokhale Institute of Public Affairs, Bangalore.

6. This is a familiar name to many. As chief minister of Mysore in the 1960s, Nijalingappa became known as one of the king-makers of Indian politics. He was president of the Indian National Congress at the time of the great schism and, in the struggle which followed, he was arch-adversary of Indira Gandhi. He is now

in retirement. But before independence he was a very representative lesser leader in the party. This section is based on the following interviews, all at Bangalore: S. Nijalingappa, 24 August 1972; J. M. Imam, 31 October 1972; M. J. Imam, 21 July 1972 and 20 October 1972; V. S. Narayana Rao, 19 June 1972 and 13 September 1972; B. N. Gupta, 25 May 1972; R. S. Aradhya, 7 October 1972; T. Siddalingaiya, 20 November 1972; K. Guru Dutt, 27 July 1972; and Mulangi Govinda Reddy, 30 July 1972.

7. This section is based on the following interviews: Agaram Rangiah, Mysore, 5 June 1971; M. L. Nanjaraj Urs, Bangalore, 31 October 1972 and 5 December 1972; S. Rangaramiah, Mysore, 4 June 1971; B. P. Nagabhushana, Mysore, 4 July 1972; and Paramasivamurthy, Mysore, 9 July 1972.

8. Except where noted below, this section is based on interviews all in Bangalore, with the following: B. N. Gupta, 5 and 7 August 1971, 25 May 1972, and 15 June 1972; S. N. Gupta, 23 July 1971 and 20 September 1972; K. A. Venkataramaiya, 15 September 1972; and G. R. Ethirajulu Naidu, 25 November 1972.

9. B. N. Gupta to J. Nehru, 19 June 1942, with enclosure, 'History of *Janavani*', in Nehru papers, correspondence vol. xxx, Nehru Memorial Library, New Delhi.

10. File P-14/1936, AICC papers, Nehru Memorial Library, and *The Hindu*, 18 September 1936, pp. 12 & 17, 9 January 1937, p. 18, and 5 May 1937, p. 6.

11. *The Hindu*, 18 January 1937, p. 7, and 19 January 1937, p. 14.

12. *The Hindu*, 28 October 1937, p. 7.

13. Krishnappa's place in the district Congress office won him the admiration of people in the universe in which he moved—Tumkur town. Nijalingappa assumed the leadership of his district Congress because nationalism had grown sufficiently popular among his fellow-castemen and urbanites in the district to guarantee that the office would enhance his prestige there. Gupta could have made a better living from business than from politics (even at the height of their success, his papers made little profit), but he took up the latter because he knew that trade better and it offered him a chance to influence people's opinions and to find a place in the public eye. Even Channabasappa, who joined Congress because it enhanced his chances of capturing the district presidency (the only office of the day with any concrete patronage powers), had originally entered politics out of boredom with farming and a desire for the kudos which a seat on the board offered.

14. Interview with B. N. Gupta, 25 May 1972, at Bangalore.

13. KONDA LAKSHMAN BAPUJI

1. All quotations (except one) are either from interviews with Konda Lakshman Bapuji on numerous occasions between 1962 and 1972, or from the *Souvenir* published on the occasion of his Golden Jubilee, 27 September 1966.

2. Interview with B. Ramakrishna Rao, Hyderabad, 1962.

3. Communication from Dr Dagmar Bernstorff.

14. SOME LESSER LEADERS OF THE COMMUNIST MOVEMENT IN KERALA

1. Research was carried out in India from November 1971 to November 1972 and from April to September 1973, with the help of grants from the Central Research Fund of the University of London and the School of Oriental and African Studies. I would like to thank Cecil Rowling for comments and suggestions.

2. The information is mainly from interviews and such reference books as the *Who's Who in the Kerala Legislative Assembly*, published for each Assembly by the Assembly Secretariat in Trivandrum. I interviewed all but one of the six and

many of their political colleagues; to all of them I would like to express my thanks.

3. P. R. Nambiar, one of the leaders of the strike, made this point to me in an interview.

4. I am not certain of the exact number. Much higher figures were given me. This figure is simply from lists in the official Madras *Fort St George Gazette*, part I—B for 1 January 1940, pp. 21-2, 21 November 1939, p. 756, and 30 January 1940, p. 98. Of course, a far larger number of teachers took part in the strike.

5. There were various reasons for this. On the one hand, there was dedication to the revolutionary and nationalist ideal. During their time in Congress one group, for example, had vowed not to marry until India was free. On the other hand, workers of a banned political party, whose prospects seemed to be jail or even death, were not much sought after as prospective husbands. It was only when they left the underground that they were able to get married, sometimes into 'party families'. A significant number married across the boundaries of community, caste, or sect. Of the six subjects of this paper, four married after the age of thirty and one into a 'party family', across sectarian boundaries.

6. He was born in 1922.

7. Robert L. Hardgrave, Jr, 'The Kerala Communists: Contradictions of Power' in Paul R. Brass and Marcus F. Franda (eds.), *Radical Politics in South Asia* (Cambridge, Mass., 1973), p. 127.

8. Prakasam's father was born about 1877. He married twice. Prakasam himself was born in 1927.

9. There have, of course, been a larger number who have, especially recently, contributed to party funds as an attempted bribe or for insurance.

10. This is unusual. The division between Syrian and Latin Christians is generally considered strict, for it is not merely a sectarian difference but is also traced back to the castes from which conversions were made.

11. Of the 64 members of the top state party committees in 1956, at least 7 had been manual workers, including 4 from Alleppey. Naturally, they have been involved mainly in the trade unions, but, as Solomon's career shows, they have also played important parts in party work as well. S. Kumaran in CPI and the late Azhikkodan Raghavan in the CPI(M) were former workers who reached the very top of the party. For the other Communist strongholds in India, Marcus F. Franda writes of West Bengal: 'The leadership of the movement has been drawn from rich, influential and highly respected Bengali families . . . the Communists in West Bengal have not succeeded in bringing members of low status groups into leadership positions in the party' (*Radical Politics in West Bengal* [Cambridge, Mass., 1971], p. 6); while Mohan Ram writes of the 1946 period in the Andhra area (but the pattern does not seem to change): 'The CPI leadership was still essentially elitist, belonging to the middle and rich upper landlord upper castes' ('The Communist Movement in Andhra Pradesh' in Brass and Franda, op. cit., p. 290). Others have had a different view of the Communist Party in Kerala from the one expressed in this paper; R. Ramakrishnan Nair, for example, says: 'It is not, and it never was led by class-conscious workers or peasants. Its leadership remains with the same class of people who lead other political parties in the State, the middle class. The difference is only in degree.' ('The Communist Party in Kerala', in Iqbal Narain (ed.), *State Politics in India* (Meerut, 1967), p. 445).

12. Unfortunately, I did not interview M. K. Krishnan. I have based this account mainly on the chapter on him in Pavanam, *Parichayam. Keralathile Rashtriyane thakkalude Thulikachithrangal* (Kottayam, 1968), pp. 349-59. I would like to thank A. V. Jose for translating this for me.

13. In an interview.

14. At the risk of mixing my metaphors still further I would suggest that there is in fact a three-fold distinction: (1) 'catchment area' (e.g. just being a student, the group or population 'at risk'); (2) 'entry station' into public life (e.g. through being associated with some campaign or activity of the national movement); and (3) 'recruitment ground' into the party.

15. I have looked at the 'where?' rather than at the 'why?', at what can simply be observed rather than relying on speculation. It is, however, clear that people entered the national movement, for example, from a whole variety of motives.

16. See his *In the Cause of the People. Reminiscences* (New Delhi, 1973).

17. He has published a stream of writings since the early 'thirties. He sums up the history and politics of Kerala in *Kerala Yesterday, Today and Tomorrow* (Calcutta, 2nd edition, 1968).

18. He was also an effective agitator. He was probably the foremost leader of the party until his death in 1948 at the age of 42. See T. V. Krishnan, *Kerala's First Communist. Life of 'Sakhavu' Krishna Pillai* (New Delhi, 1971).

15. FIVE SINHALESE NATIONALIST POLITICIANS

1. The six major parties, in order of parliamentary strength in 1974, are: the Sri Lanka Freedom Party, Lanka Samasamaja Party, United National Party, Federal Party, Communist Party, Tamil Congress. The major communities, in order of size, are: Low Country Sinhalese, Kandyan Sinhalese, Ceylon Tamils, Indian Tamils, Ceylon Moors (or Muslims), Indian Moors, Burghers and Eurasians, Malays.

2. J. Jupp, 'Constitutional Developments in Ceylon since Independence', *Pacific Affairs* xli, no. 2 (Summer 1968), p. 169.

3. In 1956 a coalition between the Sri Lanka Freedom Party and several other groups, collectively known as the Mahajana Eksath Peramuna and led by S. W. R. D. Bandaranaike, won 40% of the vote and fifty-one seats out of ninety-five.

4. *Biographical Details:*

DAHANAYAKE, Dr Wijayananda: b. 1902, educated at St Thomas' College, Mt Lavinia, first employed as schoolteacher. Elected to Galle Municipal Council 1939, to State Council 1944, and to House of Representatives for Galle in 1947, holding it until now except for four months in 1960. Minister of Education 1956–59, Prime Minister 1959–60, Minister of Home Affairs 1965–70. Respectively member of Bolshevik Leninist Party, Lanka Samasamaja Party, Bhasha Peramuna, Sri Lanka Freedom Party, Lanka Prajathantrawadi Pakshaya, United National Party, and now an Independent MP.

GUNAWARDENA, Don Philip Rupasinghe: b. 1901, educated at Ananda, Trinity Kandy, Ceylon University College, and the universities of Wisconsin and Illinois. Lived in England 1928–32. Founder member of Lanka Samasamaja Party in 1935, elected for it to State Council in 1936. Unseated after detention in 1942. Elected for Avissawella in 1947, unseated in 1948 and re-elected 1956–70. Minister of Agriculture 1956–59, Minister of Industry and Fisheries 1965–70. Died in 1972. Respectively member of Lanka Samasamaja Party, Viplavakari LSSP, Mahajana Eksath Peramuna.

IRIYAGOLLE, Imiya Mudiyanselage Raphael Abhayawansa: b. 1907, educated at Ananda and Vidyodaya Oriental College. First employed as policeman but principally as a Sinhala journalist, teacher, and translator. Elected to the House of Representatives in 1947–60 and 1965–70. Parliamentary Secretary, Ministry of Home Affairs 1956–57, Minister of Education 1965–70. Died in 1971. Respectively an Independent, SLFP, Samajawadi Mahajana Peramuna, and United National Party.

RAJARATNE, Konara Mudiyanselage Podiappuhamy: b. 1927, educated in Badulla, Colombo, Bandarawela and Kotte, and at Ceylon University. Elected for Welimada in 1956 but unseated. Re-elected 1960, imprisoned 1961, re-elected 1962–65. Parliamentary Secretary 1956–57, a Senator 1969–72. Member of the SLFP and Jathika Vimukthi Peramuna.

SENANAYAKE, Richard Gothabaya: b. 1911, educated at Royal College, Colombo, and Cambridge. Elected to State Council in 1944 and to the House of Representatives for Dambadeniya 1947–1970. Died in 1971. Respectively a member of the United National Party, the SLFP and the Sinhala Mahajana Peramuna.

5. See Calvin B. Woodward, *The Growth of a Party System in Ceylon* (Providence, RI, 1969).

6. Since 1947 all prime ministers except Dahanayake have been related either to the Senanayakes or to the Bandaranaikes.

7. These include T. B. Tennakoon, D. G. H. Sirisena, and P. M. K. Tennakoon. Only three wage-paid workers have sat in parliament: M. S. Themis (MEP), a postal peon; D. G. William (LSSP), a bus driver; and R. Jesudason (Ceylon Workers Congress), an estate worker. The last two were nominated Senators.

8. The Senanayakes made their wealth through plumbago mining and plantations and were regarded as socially inferior to the Bandaranaikes (at least by the latter).

9. Ananda was known for the devotion of many of its teachers and principals to the nationalist cause. In 1960 Philip Gunawardena joined with the former Ananda principal L. H. Mettananda in launching a campaign between his MEP and Mettananda's Dharma Samajaya Pakshaya for a 'Buddhist government'.

10. See K. M. de Silva, 'The Reform and Nationalist Movements in the Early Twentieth Century' in K. M. de Silva (ed.), *History of Ceylon*, vol. 3 (Colombo, 1973), pp. 381–407.

11. For details of the forces supporting Bandaranaike in 1956, see I. D. S. Weerawardena, *Ceylon General Election 1956* (Colombo, 1960).

12. S. W. R. D. Bandaranaike, *Speeches and Writings* (Colombo, 1963). See especially 'Return Home' (pp. 81–6), and 'Why I Became a Buddhist' (pp. 287–290).

13. *Muhandiram* was one of several titles applied by the British to officially appointed headmen.

14. See K. M. de Silva, op. cit.

15. The population of Galle was only 65,000 in 1963, but this make it the third largest town after greater Colombo and Jaffna.

16. Sinhalese constitute 69·4% of the population. Buddhists made up 66% of the population and perhaps 60% of Sinhalese belong to the Goyigama caste. See F. Nyrop (ed.), *Area Handbook for Ceylon* (Washington, 1971), chapters 4, 5, and 11.

17. Because Dahanayake had been politically critical of Bandaranaike, some suspicion of complicity in the assassination initially attached to him. He was, however, completely exonerated by the official commission of enquiry established by Mrs Bandaranaike. See Sessional Paper III, 1965: *Report of the Bandaranaike Assassination Commission* (Colombo, 1965).

18. Arjuna (pseud.), *Philip Gunawardena Caritaya* (Colombo, 1969) (in Sinhala).

19. See, e.g., Sir Charles Jeffries, *OEG—Sir Oliver Goonetilleke* (London, 1969), or Lakshman Seneviratne, *Bandaranaike—a Biography* (Colombo, 1964) (in

Sinhala). Most other biographies are simply short propaganda or pictorial pamphlets.

20. See Bryce Ryan and Murray Strauss, 'The Integration of Sinhalese Society', *Research Studies of the State College of Washington* 22 (December 1954) and Murray Strauss, 'Childhood Experience and Emotional Security in the Context of Sinhalese Social Organization', *Social Forces* 33, 2 (December 1954).

21. Olcott eventually lost patience with the Sinhalese nationalist interpretation put on the Buddhist revival by Anagarika Dharmapala (born David Hewavitarane and taking the religious title Anagarika in 1886; a co-founder with Olcott of the Buddhist Theosophical Society schools). See K. M. de Silva, 'The Government and Religion' and 'Nineteenth Century Origins of Nationalism in Ceylon' in K. M. de Silva (ed), op. cit.

22. See R. N. Kearney et al., 'The 1915 Riots in Ceylon—a Symposium', *Journal of Asian Studies* xxix, 2 (February 1970).

23. The almost universal belief in astrology, the intervention of the gods and the power of magic make it particularly difficult to apply western concepts of 'normal behaviour'. All election dates and political events are fixed by astrologers. What in western societies would be regarded as 'bad luck' is generally believed in Ceylon to be evidence of magical intervention by personal enemies, giving rise to 'paranoic' political attitudes at times of crisis.

24. A. F. Davies, *Private Politics* (Melbourne, 1966), in which he attempts a psychologically based study of five Australian politicians.

25. D. B. Dhanapala, *Among those Present* (Colombo, 1962), p. 106.

26. Ibid.

27. Iriyagolle, though nominally a Buddhist, was also a disciple of the Hindu reformer Krishnamurthy, a fact made known by his political opponents. His criticism of the clergy was that it needed self-purification.

16. ROLES AND CAREERS OF MIDDLE RANK POLITICIANS: SOME CASES FROM EAST BENGAL

1. *Report of the Electoral Reforms Commission, 1955* (Karachi, 1955).

2. G. W. Choudhury, *Constitutional Development in Pakistan* (London, 2nd edition, 1969), p. 247.

3. *The Times*, 26 April 1956.

4. Richard A. Wheeler, *Politics in Pakistan* (Cornell, 1970), pp. 214–15.

5. After the end of the Mujib regime on 15 August 1975, when Mujib and his family were killed in a military coup, the changed political situation provided a new opportunity for Zahiruddin, when he was appointed the country's first ambassador to Pakistan; this may mark a new stage in his political career.

6. *Morning News* (Dacca).

7. G. W. Choudhury, 'Democracy on Trial in East Pakistan', *International Journal* (Autumn, 1958).

8. M. Rashiduzzaman, 'The National Awami Party of Pakistan: leftist politics in crisis', *Pacific Affairs* (Fall, 1970).

9. G. W. Choudhury, 'Bangladesh Today', *South Atlantic Quarterly* (Summer, 1974).

10. Ghulam Azam, though still an exile in London, may also soon expect a change in his political fortunes as his Islamic party and rightist groups are gaining new support in the post-Mujib era, particularly as a result of the increasing tensions of the relationship between India and Bangladesh, and the consequent revival of Islamic forces.

17. THE FORMATION OF THE POLITICALLY ACTIVE STRATUM

[The research on which this paper is based was supported by a grant from the Indian Council of Social Science Research. Some of the findings reported here were presented in a seminar at the Institute of Commonwealth Studies, University of London.]

1. Sidney Verba and Norman H. Nie have generalized such findings under 'the standard socio-economic model of participation'. Cf. Verba and Nie, *Participation in America* (New York, 1972), pp. 13–14 *et passim*. The social bases of party recruitment in Baroda City, the locale of the present study, are analysed in Thomas Pantham, 'The Social Bases of Party Recruitment', *Journal of Commonwealth and Comparative Politics*, xiii, 2 (1975).

2. This point is well argued and developed in W. H. Morris-Jones, 'Political Recruitment and Political Development' in Colin Leys (ed.), *Politics and Change in Developing Countries* (Cambridge, 1969); and Kenneth Prewitt, *The Recruitment of Political Leaders* (Indianapolis, 1970).

3. This figure is exclusive of the populations of two suburban complexes, namely, Fertilizernagar (population = 5,000) and Jawaharnagar (population = 6,000).

4. The university and the business elite of Baroda form the foci of two recent studies, viz. Susanne H. Rudolph and Lloyd I. Rudolph, 'Parochialism and Cosmopolitanism in University Government: the Environments of Baroda University' in Rudolph and Rudolph (eds), *Education and Politics in India* (Delhi, 1972); and Howard L. Erdman, *Political Attitudes of Indian Industry: A Case Study of the Baroda Business Elite* (London, 1971).

5. See R. L. Handa, *History of Freedom Struggle in Princely States* (New Delhi, 1968), p. 89 *et passim*.

6. See D. N. Pathak, M. G. Parekh and K. D. Desai, *Three General Elections in Gujarat: Development of a Decade, 1952–1962* (Ahmedabad, 1966); and R. W. Stern, *The Process of Opposition in India* (Chicago, 1970).

7. He had supported Mrs Indira Gandhi at the time of the 1969 Congress split, and was made a permanent invitee of the Congress-R. But on his return from the Congress-R meeting in Delhi, the Congress-O bosses in Gujarat (and Baroda) persuaded him to recant, which he did; he remained in the Congress-O till the eve of the 1972 elections, when, in the wake of the 'mass exodus' from the Congress-O into the Congress-R, he resigned from the former to support the latter. But, as he could not get immediate readmission into the Congress-R (whose government, incidentally, had in the meantime 'de-recognized' the princes), he sat as an Independent in the Lok Sabha. As he did not belong to any political party up until the data analysis stage of our study, he has not been included among our 310 respondents. At the time of writing (November 1974), he has been admitted into the Congress-R.

8. The National Labour Party was formed on the eve of the 1972 election by the Majoor Mahajan, a Gujarat-level federation of trade unions, which broke away from the Indian National Trade Union Congress in the wake of its close cooperation with the Congress-R. In the 1972 election the Labour Party had electoral understandings with the Congress-O.

9. In our tabular analysis, we have combined the activists of the two communist parties into one group. We also interviewed 7 activists of the Socialist Party, but because of the smallness of their number, they have not been included in this analysis. It may, however, be noted that many members of the erstwhile Praja Socialist and Samyukta Socialist parties (whose merger in 1971 brought the Socialist Party into being) joined the Congress-R.

10. Some notable 'omissions' from our study population have been mentioned in footnotes 7 and 9 above.

11. For a perceptive analysis of these 'legacies', see W. H. Morris-Jones, *The Government and Politics of India* (London, 3rd edition, 1971), chapter 1.

12. That political development is facilitated by a proper sequence of changes is persuasively argued in Eric E. Nordlinger, 'Political Development: Time Sequences and Rates of Change', *World Politics*, xx, 3 (April 1968).

13. For perceptive analyses of the implications of this relationship see Rajni Kothari, 'India: Oppositions in a Consensual Polity' in R. A. Dahl (ed.), *Regimes and Oppositions* (New Haven, 1973), and R. Kothari, *Politics in India* (Delhi, 1970), chapter 5.

14. The behaviour of the different parties during the 1969 Hindu–Muslim communal riots in Gujarat is analysed in Ghanshyam Shah, 'Communal Riots in Gujarat: Report of a Preliminary Investigation', *Economic and Political Weekly*, v, 3–5 (Annual Number, January 1970).

15. See Thomas Pantham, 'The Social Bases of Party Recruitment'.

16. Ibid.

17. Some such 'mechanisms and practices' are dealt with in Thomas Pantham, *Political Parties and Democratic Consensus* (New Delhi, forthcoming), especially chapter 8.

INDEX